If I Only Had a Brain

DENNIS GLOBUS

Copyright © 2014 Dennis Globus

All rights reserved.

ISBN: 1497441218
ISBN-13: 978-1497441217

Somebody Out There Likes This Book

Dennis Globus happens to have a style that I'm particularly fond of, with an easy to read, well-structured, fascinating story that can be enjoyed purely on that level alone—but upon reflection, actually has connections and parallels throughout which give it depth. It's like he knows he's smart, but is comfortable with how smart he is not to have to prove it, but it's clearly there. In his book *If I Only Had a Brain*, Dennis exposed me to, among other things, sticky floors in porn theaters, acid trips, and syphilis. He has managed to write about

almost every topic or image I have spent years trying to repress or forget. If he were one of my kids, I would so punish him for doing this. Instead, I'll just blame him for having the nerve to write a book so unique, well-crafted, and hilarious that I found it almost impossible to put down.
—Emily Colas, author of *Just Checking*

This is Dedicated to the Ones I Love

For Jamie, who is the source of all
things good in my life

and …

For Ken, who is on every page of this book.

CONTENTS

Preface	i
Out of Diapers, Into the Labor Pool	1
The Cotton Candy Machine	7
Dirty Laundry	51
If I Only Had a Brain	71
The Secret Life of Duct Tape	97
Bachelor No. 3	151
Sybil Servant	173
Mashed	295
O, Christmas Tree	319
The Magic Kingdom	339
Reading Group Guide	371
Thank You	379

Preface

One winter morning, not too long ago, my wife Jamie and I decided to lash the skis to the top of the Subaru and head on up to Stevens Pass, a little ski area about 90 minutes from Seattle. Not too far outside of Woodinville, we lost radio reception and discovered I'd forgotten to take along the iPod I'd set by the front door. Oh, well, we figured—we'll play a memory game instead. After considerable thought, Jamie came up with this: I had to name every job I ever had, in chronological order, no matter how brief the employment.

Interesting idea. I knew there were a lot of hirings in my past, but I hadn't thought about most of them in years. By the time I was done counting, I'd recalled over 30 separate jobs—beginning when I was five years old when I worked on a golf course in Las Vegas (see *Out of Diapers*) and ending with my writing a wine column for a newspaper.

Jamie was shocked by the sheer number of things I'd done in my life, and stunned when I described some of the details (see *The Secret Life of Duct Tape*). She found many of my descriptions so funny I think she may have accidentally peed a little.

After we got to the ski area, we were riding up the ski lift to take our first run of the day, and she said something that startled me: *Why don't you write a book.* Wow, I thought. Write a book? That has the possibility to be enormous. Life-changing, even. I was stunned. Steamrolled. And by way of responding to her, to show her how I truly felt about the enormity of her offer, I did what any sane person would do who's been given the opportunity to write a book: I thought about pushing her off the chair lift.

You'd think a book about my own life—one in which I only need to reach back into my memory for material—would come flooding out of me in torrents. You're saying to yourself, *This freaking book should have taken you two, three weeks to write, tops.* Sadly, that wasn't the case. Since this was my first book, and since I'm a person who's plagued by self-doubt, I spent a year kvetching and agonizing and finished a total of about 100 pages. That's less than a third of a page a day, which is pathetic by anyone's standards. It was at that point that Jamie put a boot firmly up my ass and "requested" that I make better use of the opportunity she's giving me. And in the next few months, I knocked out about 300 pages. Never let it be said that I can't be persuaded.

When I finished the first draft, I realized I didn't have a title, and I wondered if I should submit it to publishers that way, then remind them of the untitled Beatles white album. Thinking it's a bit presumptuous for a first-time author to compare himself to the Beatles, Jamie convinced me to reconsider. So my first thought was to call it *Odd Jobs*. A brilliant title, I thought, until I walked into a book store one day and saw a copy of something called *Odd Jobs* lying on the 30%-off table. A writer friend of mine suggested *Working Stiff*, an obvious allusion to my employment in a porn theater. Thinking that title was a little too on the mark, I went back to the drawing board and came up with *The Clock Punches Back*. I liked it but most of my friends thought the titled sucked, so I tried *The Secret Life of Duct Tape* on for size. No, too many people thought it was an allusion to Home Depot.

It was at that point that Jamie reread the manuscript, probably for the eighth or ninth time, and suggested that I borrow one of my chapter titles: *If I Only Had a Brain*, a title she believed perfectly captures the lack of expertise and self-awareness I brought to each of my jobs.

I often wonder if other authors struggled as much as I did with the naming of their books. Was the story about the white whale originally called *Fish on Friday*? Did Melville have a eureka moment and come up with *Row vs. Wade*? Was he drying off at the mirror when he noticed a rash, and he ran down his little street screaming, "I've got it ... I've got it! It shall be called *Moby Dick*!"?

Considering the highly unusual jobs I've had (wrapping towels around naked actresses, singing for Judy Garland, tossing rowdy patrons out of a porn theater, auditioning for *The Dating Game* while on LSD), you'd be right (and by *you*, I mean Oprah) to wonder if all of this stuff really happened to me. The best way to respond to that, without the use of firearms, is like this: as you might have guessed, I didn't go through life with an iPad to take notes on. I just bumbled along like everyone else, never for a minute thinking I was going to write a book one day. Keep in mind that many of the incidents and conversations that I recount here happened a long time ago. So if the book isn't a hundred percent accurate, at least I've written it the way I *wanted* to remember events. I recreated real conversations as best I could and, yeah, in doing so, I'm sure I invented some dialog. I may have even unintentionally shifted a few events in time, place, and circumstances.

Most authors include a little blurb about how they changed the names of their characters to protect the innocent. In my case, the people I like got to keep their names. They'll enjoy downloading it from the iBookstore, casually opening it to their name, and acting like big-shots. Come to think of it, I should probably get some new friends. What a cluster of egocentrics!

Some people's names got changed simply because I couldn't remember their real ones. As for the people in the book who come off looking something less than stellar (and possibly litigious), they typically got renamed. While it's my ethical responsibility to inoculate myself and my wife from legal exposure, I'm just pissed off enough at certain people to erect only the thinnest of veneers to disguise them. If they read this book, they'll recognize themselves. But they'll have a damned hard time proving it in court.
— *Dennis Globus*

Out of Diapers, Into the Labor Pool

This has been a year of firsts for me. On the plus side, it's the first time I've learned how fun it is to smooch girls, my little neighbor Eva-May being willing to lead me on this thrilling path to discovery.

I've given this a lot of thought, and it's not the kissing that's so interesting—it's the fact that girls exist at all, and I'm finally old enough to recognize one when I see it. Until now, I thought girls were just boys whose idea of a rollicking good time is playing with unicorn figurines.

One thing I was shocked to discover while spelunking with Eva-May is that she doesn't have those little dangly things between her legs which, she insists, is what makes her a girl and me a boy. Apparently, it has nothing whatsoever to do with unicorns. It's the dangly things. Who knew?

On the minus side, I'm learning that those dangly things can be the source of extraordinary and incapacitating pain.

I have plenty of time to consider this phenomenon, because for the last ... well, who knows how long, I've been in a meditative state that began with a lightning bolt to my zipper, a bright white flash, the sensation of my body keeling over like a redwood, a short dream that included Howdy Doody chasing my naked grandmother through Disneyland while thrusting an ear-wax-removal bulb at her, all followed up by an intense pain in my crotch.

I'm clawing at the ground, panic-stricken by my inability to take in air. Gasping now, coughing up phlegm, feeling as if someone is holding my head under water. Heart thumping, head pounding, and after several moments of this, I'm able to take in a tiny bit of air, then a little more and, after a couple of minutes, a little more.

As I open my eyes, I wake up to see a circle of about twenty boys around me, mocking smiles on their dirty little faces, and I remember where I am: on a golf-course driving range.

"What happened?" I hear a big boy say.

"Didn't you see it, stupid?" a bigger boy says. "That guy over there on the tee—well, he was there a minute ago—he shanked one clear across the driving range that skipped off the one-fifty marker and drilled this little punk right in the nuts. Funniest thing I ever saw!"

"And the guy didn't even yell fore," another kid says, and all the boys screech with laughter.

"Here," a serious little boy in overalls says, handing me a ball as I get to one knee.

"What's this for?" I say, barely able to talk.

"It's the ball that hit you."

What's he thinking? That I'm going to put it in a trophy case?

"Hey, there he is!" one of the boys says, pointing at a man in the parking lot hastily dropping his clubs into the trunk of a new turquoise and white Chevy Bel Air.

"Let's get him!" another boy says, and they each snatch up a bucket of balls and stampede toward the car. The man, wide-eyed, flings open the car door, guns the engine, and peels out of the lot as a hundred white, dimpled missiles barely come up short. When one of them thumps off the right rear fender, the car suddenly screeches to a stop and the man leaps out and races toward the kids who scatter like cockroaches.

I'm finally able to drag myself to my feet, the air slowly returning to my lungs, a throbbing ache in my groin. This, of course, is all my mother's fault. Why on earth would she think that shagging balls on a driving range is an appropriate thing for a five-year-old to do? Why, at this point in my life, do I need to have a job at all? What's going on here? Is she trying to pay me back for having spoiled me? Is this some misguided attempt to instill in me some fiscal responsibility? Does she want me out of her hair for a few hours on the weekend? Is she simply tired of me and finds this to be an effective way to get me killed? Is she a lunatic, or what?

I don't want to be here, and not because it's dangerous and not because I'm in pain and not because I cried in front of the big boys and have snot running down my face. No, I don't want to be here because it's a job. Yeah, maybe it was fun picking up balls on the first day, and I felt like a grown-up, but now I think working stinks. I really thought I wanted a job. Turns out I just wanted money.

It's not just the job that's awful; it's what it symbolizes: it means I've crossed a threshold, from a life of whining to get what I want ... to a descent into the burning fires of daily toil where I'll suffer stupefying boredom, suffocating schedules, and sadistic ridicule for the rest of my life. And I don't want to be like my dad! I've been to his office, and I was stunned by the dreariness; it looks like Hell with fluorescent lighting.

The scary thing is that I don't really know what work is, except for picking up balls on a driving range. So how will I know to avoid other work that comes along? For starters, if it has the word *work* in its name, it's to be avoided at all costs. Housework? Yardwork? Homework? Not a chance.

The primary lesson I've learned from my brief foray into the labor pool is this: work hurts. And I'll never try it again.

The Cotton Candy Machine

"... and then we visited my grandma in Bakersfield and she gave me a Raggedy Ann doll. But I don't like to visit my grandma because her mouth smells bad and—"

"Thank you, Lucy," the teacher says and scans her attendance book as the girl sits down. "Okay, Bobby Corrigan ... are you ready to tell us what you did over the Christmas holiday?"

Bobby stands up and immediately starts pulling on his penis through his pants.

"Would you please put your hands in your pockets, Bobby?"

Bobby shrugs his shoulders, then slides his hands into the pockets of his jeans. "We took a train to

Reno and ..." and one of Bobby's hands creeps out of his pocket and begins to pull on his penis again.

"Hand back in your pocket, Bobby."

I don't know any of these odd-looking jug-eared kids, and if history holds form, I won't be around them for very long. I'm sorry to say that at six years old, I'm already developing into something of a cynic and a pessimist. That's what happens when you're in the first grade and you've already lived in five different houses.

"... and a Howdy Doody puppet and some new underpants because I accidentally poop," Bobby says, and all the kids laugh. But I don't find him particularly funny. I sit right behind him and have an unobstructed view of his habit of picking his nose and carefully placing the boogers behind his ears—presumably for future enjoyment.

This is my third grammar school in a little over a year and the one thing school has taught me is not to make friends with kids I'll just be saying goodbye to in the not-too-distant future. I'm six, and we've already moved from Los Angeles where I was born, to Las Vegas, back to Los Angeles, up to Hayward in Northern California, and back to Las Vegas. You'd think my dad was a migrant farm worker, but he rents linen to hotels and restaurants. It's an absolute mystery to me why we've moved around so much, but from what my mom tells me, it has something to do with my dad changing jobs. It's never been clear if he's extremely ambitious or just incompetent, although he never struck me as a go-getter.

"… we stayed in Las Vegas and went to a different hotel every day," a girl says. "My daddy likes to stand outside the back door and wait for the showgirls to walk out. He says I'm his little lucky charm."

"Thank you, Molly," the teacher says. "Let's see … Susie Elliott. Please tell us what you did over the holiday."

Susie clears her throat and wipes her hands on the front of a crisp, white shirt. "We went to Lake Mead and—"

"Please stand up, Susie."

Susie glares at the teacher for several moments and finally slides out of her seat. "My mommy says it's not nice to interrupt."

"I'm sorry, Susie, but that doesn't apply to teachers. Please continue."

"We went to Lake Mead and my dad took his speedboat and my mom waterskied and then my brother tried it and his shorts fell down and I saw his weeny and …"

My god, is this going to go on forever? What did we ever do to deserve having to stand up in class and spout inanities while the rest of the kids gawk? What pressure. My mom says that's why my oldest brother Jim stutters so much, because even though he's fourteen he's still so nervous when he has to stand up in class and recite things. Maybe that's why he hardly ever talks, even at home. And when he does it's as brief as possible. He uses an alternate vocabulary, having long ago learned which words he's likely to trip over, replacing them with words he's more comfortable with. I think F-sounds are the ones that really clobber him. I remember once he tried to say *fifty* and got so frustrated he ended up saying half a hundred. He doesn't even try to say fifty anymore.

"Kathy Galvin ... it's your turn. Tell us what you did."

Oh man, she's already up to the G's. I don't have a firm grasp on how this alphabetical order thing works, but I know that when we reach the G's, I'll be facing the firing squad soon. My mom says that my other brother Ken probably doesn't get nervous when he has to recite things in his classes. Even though he's only eleven, he already knows he's going to be an actor, she says, and reciting things is good preparation for his future career. Maybe that's why he never shuts up at home. Maybe it's all just rehearsal. Maybe—"

"... an Easy-Bake Oven. My dad says we're going to bake Jews," Kathy says cheerily.

The teacher seems to lose her balance for a moment and puts her hand on her desk to steady herself. After several moments, she composes herself, then runs her finger down a page in the attendance book until finding what she's looking for. "Class, I want you to meet ..."

Uh, oh.

"... Dennis Globus. He's brand-new to our school and I want you all to make him feel welcome here."

She's looking at me. Please, don't do it. This is my first day and you can't possibly—

"Does your family call you Denny?"

I shake my head.

"Do they ever call you Dennis the Menace?"

Great. Another classful of kids tainted. Thanks a lot, lady. I'll be hearing that one for as long as I'm at this school. I wonder if anyone in her family ever calls her the Village Idiot, but I decide to just shake my head again.

"Well, we don't know anything about you; so it'll be fun to hear how your family celebrated the holiday, won't it, class?" and they respond with a low moan which I take to indicate a distinct lack of enthusiasm.

The entire class is staring at me and I know I'm supposed to say something right now, but my ears are ringing so loudly I'm surprised we're not having a fire drill.

"Dennis?"

"Yes?" I manage to say.

"Why don't you stand up and tell us about your holiday."

I look around the class and see a bunch of suspicious faces I don't know. This is excruciating. Only Bobby in front of me is smiling as his hand disappears behind his left ear.

As if I'm watching a movie, I see my brother Ken standing up in his class. He's eager to get started telling the kids all about his Christmas vacation. I can't hear what he's saying, but I see the kids reacting to him, laughing along with the teacher. They're leaning forward now, thrilled to absorb every word, and Ken's making big gestures with his hands, pantomiming a golf swing and looking down the fairway while shading his eyes with a hand, and all the kids laugh again. The teacher is wiping a tear from her cheek, she's laughing so hard, and she's giving Ken an extra amount of time because the kids like hearing him so much. He finishes his story by drying his face with an imaginary towel, and this once again brings the class to a frothing boil of laughter.

As if some unseen hands are guiding me, I rise to my feet. I feel both a sense of terror and my hand moving toward my penis, but I'm able to stop it in time and jam it into my pocket. Now what? What should I tell these people? How much do they want to know? Is telling them what toys I got really the smartest thing to do? Precisely what revelations will help me serve out my time here in peace until I tunnel under the south wall and wind up in another school?

* * *

Some families have a picnic on the weekend. Others, I'm told, engage in a spirited game of softball. Or an invigorating hike. My family prefers to torture itself.

How else to explain the fact that every Saturday, at precisely nine in the morning, my dad shoehorns the family—all five of us—into our '53 Buick, starts the car with a carefree grin, and proceeds to drive across the street to the Las Vegas Municipal Golf Course where we experience a day of frustration, aimless wandering, and non-stop bickering?

I hate to say this, but golf is shaping up to be just like fishing, our most recent family-togetherness hobby, which we likely would still be doing if it weren't for the fact that my brother Ken accidentally dropped the outboard motor into the lake and flung a brand-new rod and reel into the water when his foot slipped while he was casting.

Poor Dad. I'm sure he thought fishing would be one of those seminal events that would define us as a family that could relax in a boat for hours on end, dangling our lines in the water, telling funny stories, and eating baloney sandwiches. Instead, what it turned out to be was three boys with perpetually tangled lines that took my dad twenty minutes to sort out each time. I'd cast my line, watch the sinker hit the water and dive to the bottom. Then when I'd glance down at the remaining line on my reel, it never failed to look like a plate of spaghetti. After the third or fourth time, my dad would go positively apoplectic, I'd start crying, and my mother would tell my dad to calm down, which would only turn his rage inward.

With regard to his fantasies of how fishing might draw us closer as a family, he was right about one thing: we ate a lot of sandwiches.

And now golf, a game that provides only marginally more entertainment than fishing, but with the added components of self-loathing and utter despair. I just don't get it. Why my dad—a guy with all the patience of a bottle rocket—imagines that golf will do for the family what fishing couldn't, I can only guess.

Is he just being optimistic? Can he possibly be thinking that golf—a sport where people walk independently of each other for several hundred yards on every hole, then meet briefly on the green—will bring us together? Is he somehow able to block out the miserable time he had last week when Ken slipped on the foot bridge and dumped his entire golf bag into the pond? Does he forget from week to week that he has a toxic combination of no patience, a shocking temper, an inability to hit a golf ball within thirty degrees of where he hopes it will go, and three sons who insist on doing things differently from the way he'd do them, which he finds maddening.

I'm only six years old, but already I have the feeling we're not using our free time well. It dawns on me that a hobby where my dad doesn't have to teach us anything or fix our mistakes would give us a better opportunity for success. Maybe we should consider free reading, independent puppetry, or listening to the radio. We might be able to pull off one of those without bloodshed.

As that thought occurs to me, my older brother Jim steps up to the first tee, takes a deep breath and a perfectly arced back-swing, then bludgeons the ball. The rest of us stand slack-jawed as the ball screams down the center of the fairway about ten feet off the ground, improbably rises like a jet fighter, reaches the crest of its momentum, then gently plops onto the green and stops about eight feet from the pin, some two-hundred-eighty yards from the tee, which is not bad for a fourteen-year-old. Jim is already striding down the fairway, having grabbed his bag and put his club away before the ball even landed.

Interesting to me is that Jim walks down the center of the fairway, as if it's simply inconceivable that Ken or my dad could possibly hit him with their tee shots. As if to prove the point, Ken steps up to the tee. He digs his feet into the ground, then engages in about twenty seconds of nervous tics in which he'll hunch his shoulders several times, repeatedly draw the club face away from the ball only to set it back down, waggle his hands, then stare at the ball for several seconds as if asking its forgiveness for what he's about to do.

"Hit the goddamn ball already!" my father says.

"Hal, watch your language," my mother says.

"Ken, I swear, if you don't knock off all that crap and just hit the ball, I'm sending you home."

In all the Saturdays we've played golf, and I think it's going on eight months, my dad still hasn't learned that, once interrupted, Ken has to begin his routine all over again, Ed Norton to my father's Ralph Kramden. In order to control his temper (although I'm not sure if it's directed at Ken or my mother—I'm just glad it's not me), my father has to turn away from his annoying middle son and take several violent practice swings while he mutters something unintelligible and sighs loudly. By this time, Ken is very anxious about having ticked my dad off, which extends Ken's compulsive pre-shot routine by about fifteen seconds, pissing my dad off even more. Finally, Ken, who I believe is starting to hyperventilate, takes a huge cut at the ball, whiffs, and watches his driver fly into the woods about thirty yards up on the left-hand side of the fairway, his hands still curled around the shaft of a non-existent club. I find this extraordinarily funny and screech with laughter until my father shoots me The Look.

"Dammit, Ken …"

"Sorry, Dad."

"You are sorry. That was the sorriest shot I've ever seen."

"For christ sakes, Hal, he's eleven years old!" my mother says, exasperated at having to again remind my dad to lower his expectations.

My father glares at Ken who can't look him in the eye and instead picks up his golf bag and heaves it over his shoulder. Finally, my dad steps up to his ball, sneers at it, jerks his hands back, then lunges at the ball. Instead of the thwack sound that Jim's club head made when striking the ball, all I can hear from my dad's shot is *pffffft*. We stare down the fairway, but there's no sign of the ball. What we do see is an enormous piece of turf and mud landing about fifteen yards in front of my father. I look at the ground where his tee stood only moments before and see what looks like a furrow in a plowed bean field, a welcome mat-sized piece of terra firma clinging to the face of his three iron. Something tells me his club and the ball didn't achieve optimum contact, but then that's what happens when you dig a foot-long trench behind your ball. I look up in the sky and see the ball just beginning its downward trajectory.

"Man oh man, Dad," I say, "that thing's up there with the Sputnik!"

After several seconds, it lands about forty yards down the fairway, bounces straight up in the air, then finds a spot it likes about two inches behind a sprinkler head.

"Wow," Ken says, "that was a real elephant's ass, dad."

"Huh? What?" my dad says, stunned. "What do you mean?"

"You know ... high and stinky."

Jim, of course, has seen none of this, having already drilled his putt and trotted to the second tee. He missed our parents arguing about the rules of golf when my mom called my dad a cheater for moving his ball from behind the sprinkler head and my dad calmly reminded her that she's never played a round of golf in her life or read the rule book, but she just knew he was cheating and it escalated from there. Jim missed Ken trying to hit his ball from behind an out-of-bounds stake, snapping the head clean off his three-wood. He also missed Ken's sick stomach that resulted in an acute case of flatulence which seemed to be most pronounced during my father's back-swing—with predictable results. Jim missed me whining, then crying, about not being allowed to play golf and my father finally giving in and promising to get me some clubs next week. Poor Jim.

* * *

I want to eat the rest of my mashed potatoes, but I need something left to cover up the string beans I've been bulldozing through the gravy on my plate for the past fifteen minutes, and I can't bear to leave any meat loaf. Jim, as usual, is reading a photography manual at the table. He seems to get obsessed with things, and photography suits him perfectly. Like golf, it's something he can pursue entirely alone, and he spends hours in his darkroom every evening. Ken, on the other hand, has spent the entire dinner talking about this and that—what he did in school, how he wants to take up the drums, what it will be like when he's a famous actor. I've noticed that on those rare occasions when he eats over at a friend's house, there is virtually no discussion around our dinner table, so Ken manages to fill the huge gaps thoroughly, if not compellingly.

My father seems particularly chipper tonight, laughing often at the jokes and stories Ken tells. In general, I don't understand much of what Ken has to say, but I've come to recognize that something is quite funny when milk spews out of my mother's nostrils. It's not a frequent occurrence, but it happens often enough so that she's learned to grab her glass the moment Ken fills his mouth with food.

The dinner's officially over when my mother tells Jim and Ken to clear the table and do the dishes. She lights up a cigarette and leans back in her chair, takes a big drag, and blows the smoke up toward the light fixture that hangs over the dining room table. My dad, who would normally do the same thing, leaves the room.

"Are you feeling all right, Hal?" my mother says, but he's already gone.

After a few moments, he returns with three golf clubs and hands them to me. "Here," he says, "I had the guy in the pro shop cut down a few ladies' clubs. You can start playing golf now."

I leap up out of my chair, not believing my ears. "Wow!"

Jim rushes into the dining room from the kitchen. "Hey, how come this little twerp gets clubs? I had to buy my own."

My mother stamps out her cigarette and puts both hands on top of the table. "Hal, it's four weeks before his birthday! Couldn't you have waited?"

Ken dashes into the room, water dripping on the floor from a dish he's drying. "Oh boy, Den. Now I can teach you how to play golf!"

I'm elated, hopping up and down and giggling. Ken takes one of the clubs, draws it back, and pulverizes the cookie jar on a shelf, the pieces crashing to the floor.

"Dammit, Ken! my mother says. "Put that club down." She storms out of the room, but I barely notice, I'm so ecstatic. Jim turns on his heals and goes back to the kitchen where he makes a ruckus with the pots and pans.

"Where's the golf bag, Dad?" Ken says.

"There isn't one."

"No golf bag?" I say, the faintest trace of a whine in my voice.

"You can buy one yourself."

"I ... I can?"

"Sure. Just get a part-time job at the golf course. You'll have enough money for a golf bag in no time."

A job? I'm six years old. What's he thinking I'm going to do there? Serve drinks in the bar? Handle accounts receivables? Does he not remember my brief stint on the driving range? "What ... what kind of job?"

He's stumped and it's clear he hasn't thought this through. He lights a cigarette, his mind working through the problem. "You remember that shoe shine kit we gave you for your birthday?"

Yeah, I do. Weirdest present I ever got. I wondered at the time what the folks were trying to tell me with that gift, considering I don't own a pair of leather shoes. At the time I thought, What, am I supposed to go to the airport and earn some money? It just didn't make sense.

Of course, that wasn't the only present that left me scratching my head. They also gave me a machine that makes cotton candy. Ken and I were excited to try it and we couldn't wait to get it going. Step 1: set cotton candy machine on flat surface. The dining room table seemed flat. Step 2: pour a teaspoon of the sugar mixture in the hole in the center of the machine. In went the blue sugar. Step 3: plug machine into any 110-volt wall outlet. We didn't have a clue what a 110-volt wall outlet is, but the thing has a plug, so we just jammed it into the little holes in the wall where my mom plugs in her fondue thing. Step 4: using the cardboard tube from a roll of paper towels, move the tube in a circular motion around the inside of the machine to capture the cotton candy as it is spun from the special sugar mixture. Boy, this one really stumped us. We didn't have an empty roll of paper towels, and it looked like there was another week's worth of use out of the roll in the kitchen. Not to worry, he assured me, and unspooled the entire roll into the trash can. Perfect! That Ken's a genius. Step 5:

enjoy your cotton candy, and order a refill of the extra special mixture from us for only $1.19.

We stared at the machine for several seconds as the cup in the center of it spun and whirred. As we watched, strands of cotton candy started to appear from the holes in the cup. That's not all. The cup began flinging molten sugar, and several blobs of it hit my face causing me to instantly scream in pain and alarm. I was so terrified, I started running around the dining room table in circles until Ken finally tackled me.

"My face is on fire! I'm burning!" I said, screeching at the top of my lungs.

Ken crawled along the floor, like a soldier under barbed wire, liquefied sugar flying over his head and splattering against the walls, and jerked the machine's cord out of the socket. All at once the room grew quiet. What the hell are the folks trying to do? Blind me?

So, as it stands, I've gotten approximately seventeen seconds of use out of the two presents I received on my sixth birthday. And teeny welts on my face that took three weeks to heal.

Yeah. I remember the shoe shine kit," I say, increasing the whine in my voice.

"Just take it to the golf course on the weekends and offer to shine some shoes. You'll make lots of money."

"But I don't want to shine shoes," I say, sniffling.

"It's easy. Go get the kit," he says, bolting out of the room.

"I don't want to shine shoes," I say to Ken.

He shrugs his shoulders. "Too late now. You better go get the kit."

I stomp out of the dining room, make a show of loudly slamming my bedroom door behind me, and throw myself on the bed. I don't want to shine shoes. But why? Why don't I? I want a golf bag and working at the golf course sounds like fun. So what's the issue here? Is there something about shining shoes that's especially undesirable as a vocation? No, I've seen my dad do it, and it doesn't look too taxing. Is it the commitment to be at the golf course every weekend? No, that's not it. I'm there every day as it is, usually watching Jim spend a couple of hours on the driving range or chipping balls onto the practice green. Or is it that once I prove I'm old enough to work, I've let the genie out of the bottle?

Ken pokes his head into the bedroom. "Dad's waiting for you."

I take a deep breath and roll off the bed. The closet is filled with toys and I fling them behind me onto the floor until I see a wooden box in the far corner.

My dad is lighting another cigarette at the dining room table, and he brightens when he sees me carry the box into the room and set it on the table. I take a seat at the far end of the table, cross my arms over my chest, and use the scowl that generally proves ineffective but satisfying for my mother.

"Sit over here," he says, gesturing at a nearby chair.

With a big sigh, I move next to him.

He flips the metal latch on the box—something I'd never done—opens it, then peers inside. "Yeah, looks like everything you need." He pulls out a little circular brush with a handle, a flat can of shoe polish, a rag, and a large finishing brush. He opens the can of polish and spits several times in the lid. "Okay, you take this little brush and dip it into the spit."

Is he insane? This is disgusting.

"Then you rub it around in the polish until all the bristles are covered, then you start polishing the shoe," he says, using a circular motion to lay the polish all over a dress shoe.

I don't really want to learn how to do this, but there's something mesmerizing about the process. I'm not sure why, but it's fascinating that a battered and dull shoe can be covered in polish, wiped with a rag, buffed with a large brush, then emerge gleaming and twinkling.

"Think you can do that?" he says.

"I suppose," I say unenthusiastically.

My dad stabs his cigarette out, and his lips purse, a gesture I recognize as Step One from the How to Lose Your Patience pamphlet, and what I know from watching my dad deal with Ken is that there are only two steps. "If you want to play golf, you're gonna have to buy your own damn golf bag, 'cause you're not gonna use the clubs until you have a bag. Now, what's it going to be? "

"I guess I'll buy it," I say, resigned to my fate.

"Fine. Tomorrow's Saturday; take this kit to the golf course and stand outside the bar. When a man approaches the door, you stop him and ask if he wants his shoes shined while he's inside. Got it?"

The idea of talking to strangers is really unappealing, and my mind flashes to Bobby Corrigan pulling his penis in front of the class. "Yeah. I guess."

"One more thing, Dennis," he says gravely. "You're going to be on the golf course by yourself for the first time. I want you to be polite to everyone, don't make a pest of yourself, and don't tell anyone we're Jewish. Got it?"

"Yeah." I understand the first two parts; those are just the general rules that apply whenever I step out of the house. But that third one? I don't have any idea what he's talking about. "What's Jewish, Dad?"

He appears to give this a lot of thought. "Well, some people are Methodists, some are Catholics, and some people are … well, I can't think of any more. But we're Jewish." He stands up suddenly, knocking the large brush onto the floor, and bolts from the room.

* * *

It's Saturday and I arrive at the golf course early on a cool November morning. I open the door to the pro shop, the wooden box in my arms, and stand at the counter waiting for someone to wait on me, but no one shows up. I've been in the pro shop dozens of times with my dad, Ken or Jim, but it all feels different now that I'm about to be a consumer. There are several sets of clubs on display, enticingly fanned out to show the range of clubs each set offers: usually beginning with a three-iron and ending with a five-wood. Setting the wooden box on the glass counter next to a goldfish bowl filled with tees, I move to a table in the center on which are stacks of boxes containing new golf balls. I pull a golf glove from a display rack and try it on. It's ridiculously big on me and the ends of my fingers don't even protrude past the palm of the glove. As I look around the shop, I'm struck by the variety and colors of the shirts, windbreakers, slacks, and shoes. That's what I want to wear when I get bigger. And against the far wall, golf bags. All of them seem like huge leather monstrosities, but one in particular seems fairly suitable. It's made from white canvas, has a green canvas strap and, most importantly, costs three dollars. I don't have any concept of money except that anything whose price is shown as a single digit looks promising. I take the bag down from the hook, grab three clubs from a display, and slide them inside the bag. Hoisting it onto my shoulder, I'm struck by how light it feels—not at all like Jim's. I also notice how ridiculous the adult-length clubs look sticking out of the bag. To get a sense of how it might feel to carry the bag on a round of golf, I march around the store, occasionally stopping and sliding a club out. It's easy to imagine myself teeing a ball up and whistling it down the center of the fairway.

"Hi, Dennis," a man's voice behind me says. It's Jerry Belt, the club pro and the guy who gave my dad lessons. "You looking for something special?"

"I'm gonna buy this golf bag," I say, fondly picturing the day when I can make my first-ever purchase. I carefully put the clubs back in the display.

"I thought you'd be needing one with your new clubs. I put new grips on 'em that should fit your hands nicely. Do you like them."

Hey, this is fun. I'm having a conversation with an adult, and my dad's not here. "Holy cow! Yeah, they're great. I can't wait to use them!" I say, and picture Jerry and me strolling down a fairway together after clobbering our drives. In my imagination, he's complimenting me on my perfect swing and asks me to be the assistant club pro—in charge of teaching kids how to play golf.

"What's that in the box there?"

"It's a shoe shine kit. Wanna see inside?"

"You bet."

I flip the latch on the box and raise the lid. Jerry peers inside. "Whewie! Looks like you've got everything you need in there, including a peanut butter sandwich."

"And jelly! My mom made it for me. Wanna see it?"

"No, that's okay. You going to shine shoes here at the golf course?"

"My dad says I have to if I wanna buy a golf bag."

"Here, let me put that in the back of the shop for you," he says, taking the bag. "That way no one will buy it."

He takes a tag out from underneath the counter, writes *Sold to Dennis* on it, then attaches the tag's string to the bag's handle. "It'll be here when you're ready for it." He takes the bag and disappears into the back room of the shop. I hoist the box from the counter and make my way to the bar. There's a sign over it that I can't read, but my dad calls it The 19th Hole. I set the box on the ground beside the door and sit on top of it, my back against the stucco wall. After a few moments, the door opens and two men come through, shielding their eyes from the bright sun. My dad told me to talk to the guys going in to the bar, not the guys leaving it. I decide to follow his orders, so I don't approach the men.

Well, this is boring. I'm starting to get fidgety, and I discover that I can use my thumbnail to snap off the little peaks of textured stucco on the wall behind me. I'm startled by two men approaching the door and I leap off the box. They lean their clubs against the wall next to me, take a pair of street shoes out of their bags, and slip out of their golf shoes.

I know I'm supposed to say something to them, but I'm scared and ... darn it—there's that Bobby Corrigan image again! I'm sorry I ever saw him yanking his dork. I clear my throat and take a big gulp of air. "Shine your shoes, mister?" I say to the friendlier-looking of the two, a tall, skinny man in a lime green cardigan.

He looks down at the golf shoes in his hand, then at me, down at the wooden box, back to me, down at the box, over to his friend, down at the box, then back to me. "No way." And the two men disappear through the door into the darkened bar.

How about that. It never occurred to me that someone might say no. What I need to do is somehow get them to feel sorry for me, and when I see three men approach, I walk around in small circles, affecting the limp Grampa uses on *The Real McCoys* where he holds his fists next to his hips, takes a faltering step forward and pumps his fists downward in a shamelessly exaggerated display of stiffness or injury. I never believed for a second that he was really limping and I wish Pepino or Little Luke would run a tractor over him.

Three men stop at the door and stare at me. One of them seems particularly concerned. "Are you okay, son?"

"I'm limping," I say.

"I can see that. Did you just hurt yourself here at the golf course?"

"No, I always limp. Even when I was first born." Nice touch. Let them know I've been afflicted with a limp from the moment of birth. I see the men exchange glances and look down at my legs. I think this ruse is working. "Shine your shoes, mister?"

"Sure, son." He hands me a pair of black leather golf shoes and I set them on the ground next to the box. "How much do you charge?"

Huh. Now, there's something I hadn't considered. Why didn't my dad warn me about this? No matter—I'm on the spot and I've got to come up with something, so I pull a wild number out of the air, a number I think is high, but not so high that it might scare him away. "Ten cents?" I say, somewhere between a declaration and a plea.

"Hmmm," the man says thoughtfully. "Are you sure?"

Darn it. I got greedy. "How about a nickel?"

"I was thinking more along the lines of a quarter," he says.

Good god ... a quarter? "Wow!"

The three men chuckle and disappear into the bar. This is so exciting! I immediately flip open the box and pull all of the supplies out and set them on the ground. I open the can of polish, and spit several times into the lid, then go to work on the man's shoes.

When he comes out of the bar, I hold up the shoes for him and he seems genuinely pleased. I've spent the better part of a half hour buffing them with the finishing brush and, if I say so myself, they look really spiffy.

"Very nice job, son." He fumbles in his pocket for some change, finally handing me a quarter. "Honest pay for an honest day's work. Here's your quarter … and another dime as a tip."

"Wow! Thanks, mister." I'm elated and I can't believe my good luck. My dad was right: this is easy.

No sooner do I pocket the money than another guy approaches the bar. Man, at this rate, I might have enough money for my golf bag by the end of the day. "Shine your shoes, mister?"

He looks at me, then down at the box, and back at me. "How much?"

Well, if the first guy was willing to pay me so much, logic tells me I must be worth it. "A quarter."

"A quarter?" he says, chuckling. "When I was a kid, I used to shine shoes for a nickel."

I don't quite know what to make of this. Is he just making conversation or is he negotiating? I wish Ken were here. He'd know what to do. I'm waiting for the man to tell me it's okay for me to shine his shoes, but he's just staring down at me, grinning, and I'm starting to feel flustered. "We're Jewish," I finally say, for no apparent reason.

The smile vanishes from his face. "Well, no wonder you want so much money. Forget it." He walks past me and into the bar.

What on earth made me utter the one thing my dad warned me against saying? As I consider what kind of trouble I've just gotten myself into, four men, talking animatedly about their golf games, approach the door.

I look down at their feet and see which one has the dirtiest shoes, which belong to what I guess to be the oldest member of the foursome. He's thick and bald, built like a can of tuna, with glimmering blue eyes and arms that remind me of Popeye's. "Shine your shoes, mister?"

He looks from me to the box several times. "You're awfully young to be working at a golf course."

There's a long pause. It's an interesting observation, I suppose, but not one that requires any commentary on my part.

"You ever shine shoes before?" he asks.

"Yes, sir ... just a few minutes ago. I got a quarter and a dime," I say enthusiastically.

"I don't know ..."

"Go ahead, Art," a rail-thin man says. "Might as well get 'em shined up while we're having a beer."

"Well ... okay, kid," the man says. He undoes his laces and steps out of the shoes, then walks into the bar in his socks.

I take out my supplies, close the lid, and sit on the box. Interesting shoes. The upper part is black and the lower part is white which has several grass stains and mud on it. I wipe it off as best as I can and polish the uppers. When I'm done with that, I make a curious discovery: I have no white shoe polish—only black and brown. Well, that certainly presents a dilemma. What, I wonder, would my dad want me to do? I make a mental checklist of all the things he's ever said to Jim or Ken about working:

Important Business Observation Number 1: when you're hired to do a job, do it right. Well, what does do it right mean in this context? I can't do it right because I don't have any white shoe polish, which leads me to Important Business Observation Number 2: in the unlikely event that you're without all the necessary tools to complete the job effectively, improvise. Okay, now we're getting somewhere. I don't have all the tools. But, darn it, I'm not going to let that stop me.

When I finish, I exhale some breath onto the shoes and wipe it off for that extra bit of gleam. I'm proud of my work and pleased that I applied logic to a thorny problem. I set the shoes down next to me and proceed to snap off a few stucco peaks. Darn, that hurts when it gets stuck under my thumbnail.

The man comes out of the bar and looks down at me. "All done?" he says.

"They're shiny now," I say confidently.

"Wonderful. Where are they?"

He must have gotten snockered in the bar. They're right in front of him. I pick them up and hold them out to him.

"Wha ... these aren't mine?"

I don't know what to say. Of course they're his. He gave them to me and they're the only shoes I've worked on since he entered the bar. "They're polished now," I say.

"What the fuck, kid? I gave you a brand-new pair of black and white shoes, and you try to give me these black and brown sh ... hey ... wait a minute ... did you ...

I pick up the wooden box and consider Important Business Observation Number 3: When in the event that the job doesn't go as planned, run like hell.

* * *

I still don't know what everybody got so upset about. The guy gave me two-toned shoes, and that's what he got back. It hardly seemed necessary for Jerry Belt to stop by our house to tell my parents about it. They expressed shock and outrage that I could have been so irresponsible, but Jerry was kind enough to suggest that maybe I was a little young to shine shoes.

He had one other suggestion: that if I wanted to continue working at the golf course, I could shuttle things like soft drinks, bags of chips, weenies, and buns from the clubhouse supply room to the little snack stand that fortifies famished golfers at the turnaround point—near the tenth tee. That's what I'm doing this morning.

It's an easy job that requires me to do nothing more than to push a wheelbarrow-like cart along the various paths, all the while watching golfers in their colorful outfits hit their shots, swear, then pound their clubs into the ground as if they're pummeling gophers. There seems to be a lot more frustration in golf than there is pleasure, and I've yet to figure out if the game attracts ill-tempered people or simply makes them that way. In either case, I've seen hundreds of happy, hopeful people lace up their spiked shoes, only to turn into shrieking psychopaths minutes later. The number four hole—a three-par—seems to be a particular problem, and I can't even remember how many times I've seen a guy drive his third or fourth ball into the pond, then become so incensed that he snaps the club over his knee and throws the two pieces in the pond with his collection of balls. In fact, there are so many balls in that pond that some of the older kids wade in there after dark to collect them for sale to the pro shop where they were originally purchased. A golf course is a very circular economy.

    I knock on the door to the Snack Shack, and after a few seconds I hear some shuffling feet inside until Wendell finally opens the door. He's an old guy with a very wrinkled face who, I've been told, has been working in the shack for over thirty years, doling out a steady stream of hot dogs and beers every day. He's also blind, which I've always found fascinating because he's the first blind guy

I've ever seen. My father, who has no patience for slow service, seems to be very tolerant of Wendell as he putters around the inside of the shack, moving deliberately to fetch a bottle of Coke or a Snickers bar, feeling the coins for size that the men slap onto the counter, then slowly making change. Wendell asks each golfer how their game is going so far, and when they give him a gruff answer, he reminds them that the worst day on a golf course is better than their best day in an office.

As the door opens, he stares out past me, and he's surprised when he hears my voice coming from approximately two feet lower than where he's expecting it. "You must be Dennis," he says.

"Yes, sir."

"Oh heck, don't call me that. Makes me feel old. Everybody on this golf course calls me Wendell." He reaches out and lowers his hand until it touches my shoulder, and he pats it a few times. "You got some pogey-bait for me?"

"I ... I ... don't think so. I've got some Three Muskateers bars ... and some pop. But I don't think they gave me any pogey-bait," I say, rifling through the contents of the cart.

"Oh heck, that is pogey-bait. Least, that's what we used to call it in the Marines back in World War I. Course, back then it was just known as the Great

War, 'cause there weren't no World War II yet," he says, his eyes moving independently of each other.

"Are you blind, Wendell?"

"Sure am, sonny."

"We're Jewish." I say.

Wendell tilts his head back and guffaws. "Oh heck, that's the funniest thing I heard all week. You think being Jewish is some sort of affliction?"

"What's a ... fliction?"

"Some kinda illness or disease or injury."

"I don't know what it is."

"Well, don't you worry none. People being the way they are, I'm sure plenty of 'em will remind you what it is over the years. Anyway, let's get this pogey-bait in the shack. You bring it on up to me and I'll put it away." He turns and disappears through the doorway.

I begin carrying in the contents of the cart and setting them down on the counter. With each load I bring in, I see Wendell feeling the packages and putting the items away in their appropriate places. He moves slowly but self-confidently, and I'm fascinated by his ability to distinguish between the items I bring in. He puts the bottles of Seven-Up in one section of the boxy Coke cooler, the Coca Colas in another section, and the beers in yet another.

"How can you tell the Cokes from the Seven-Ups?" I say.

"Easy," he says, and pulls a bottle of each out of the cooler. "This is the Coke in my left hand; the Seven-Up in my right. "Close your eyes, sonny, and hold out your hand."

I do, and feel a bottle being placed into my hand.

"Now, feel the surface of that bottle."

"It's got bumps on it," I say, feeling the ridges in the pattern of the glass.

He takes the bottle from me, followed moments later by another one being placed in my hand.

I run my other hand along its surface. "It's smooth."

"That's how I do it," he says, holding up the two bottles for me to see. "I do the same thing with them candy bars and chips. I can tell which is which by the size or the smell of 'em."

A man with thinning white hair walks up to the counter and slaps a bill on it. "Hey, Wendell."

"Howdy, Paul. Schlitz, as usual?"

"Four of 'em … for some thirsty golfers."

"This a five or a ten?" Wendell says, taking the bill off the counter, and I wonder why he can't tell what kind of money it is by feeling or smelling it. He presses down a couple of keys on the cash register and a drawer pops open.

"It's a five, Wendell," the man says, then notices me by the back door. "Who's your little assistant?"

"That's Dennis. He's a right fine shoe-shiner from what I hear." Wendell lays a few bills and coins on the counter.

"Oh, yeah. I heard about him," the man says, popping the cap from his beer and scooping up his money.. "He blind, too?"

"We're Je—"

"Nope. He sees real fine. Got a good future here on the golf course."

"Well, time to hit a few in the pond," the man says. "Catch you later, Wendell."

"Take 'er easy, Paul."

I watch the man join three others at the tenth tee. He hands a bottle to each of them.

Wendell puts the last of the inventory, a box of Fritos, on a shelf. "You want a hot dog, Dennis?"

"Wow! You bet!"

Wendell grabs a pair of tongs and places a hot dog in a bun, and hands it to me. "Mustard, ketchup, and relish on the counter," he says. But I'm happy to eat it just the way it is. "Dennis, I got to take a savage piss. You be all right for a couple of minutes?"

"Yeff," I say through a mouthful of food.

"Okay, hold the fort," he says, and heads out through the door.

There's a little stool under the counter, and I slide it out and sit on it. I'm feeling so lucky because it's a beautiful day and I've got a hot dog and a job, and I can't imagine what else I'll ever need in the world. In fact, I could do this—

I'm startled when a man raps his knuckles on the counter. "Anyone home?" he says. He's much younger than the first man and has a haircut that looks like the pictures of Elvis Presley I've seen on the TV, with his hair combed back and long sideburns.

"I'm not home. I'm here," I say.

"Where's the old guy who's usually here?"

"He's taking a savage piss."

"Yeah. Well, I'll take a pack of Lucky Strikes," the man says.

"What are those?"

"They're cigarettes. In a white pack with a circle on it. The old guy keeps them up here," he says, leaning in over the counter and pointing up at a shelf full of cigarette packs above the opening. I slide the stool over, climb on top of it and sort through the packs until I find a white one with a circle on it. I put the pack of cigarettes on the counter, and the man hands me a bill. I stare at it, not sure what I'm supposed to do next.

"Hey, kid. You're supposed to give me change."

"Change?"

"Yeah, it's that green stuff in the cash register."

"Oh." I remember that Wendell pressed some keys on the cash register. I try it and the drawer pops open and I stare at all the money inside.

"Just give me a few of those bills on the left there," the man says.

I pull out three bills. "These?"

"Perfect," the man says, taking the bills from me and walking away.

* * *

I had no idea, when I walked into the pro shop and saw Wendell sitting in a chair while two policemen stood over him, that he was being accused of stealing money from the Snack Shack. No idea at all until Jerry Belt made another visit to my house and had a second chat with my parents who expressed some more shock and outrage. From my bedroom, I could hear Jerry trying to calm them down. And when I was sternly called into the living room, I told them I didn't see Wendell steal any money. Jerry asked me if Wendell left the shack while I was in there, and I told him about the savage piss and the guy who looked like Elvis and looking through the cigarettes to find the white pack with the circle on it. I even told him—proudly—that the guy gave me a bill and I opened the cash register and the guy told me which bills to give him back. I made change!

    I was told to go back to my room and wait, which I did, and I could hear Jerry tell my folks that this was all a big misunderstanding and he'll get Wendell out of jail and give him his job back.

* * *

    "Two-eighty-five ... two-ninety-five ... and a quarter makes three-twenty," Ken says, on his knees beside my bed, pushing the coins around on the blue bedspread. "How much does it cost?"

    "Three dollars," I say. "Do I have enough?"

    "Yeah, more than enough. Let's go buy a golf bag."

    "Yippee!" I say, and clap my hands. I scoop up the coins and shove them in my pocket, and Ken and I head to the front door.

    "Where are you two going?" my mom says.

    "We're gonna buy my golf bag!" I say, excited.

"Really?" she says, although it doesn't sound exactly like what I've come to know as a question. "Be back before dinner."

"Okay, Mom," I say, and we shoot through the front door, across the street, through the gate, past the tenth green (the one Jim chips balls onto from our front lawn), and up the gravel road to the pro shop.

Jerry comes out of the office when he hears the door open, and smiles. "What can I do you for, boys?"

"I want my golf bag!" I say, and begin pulling fistfuls of coins out of my pockets and dropping them on the counter.

Jerry fetches the little white canvas bag from the office, and looks at the pile of coins. "How much we got here?"

"Three-twenty," Ken says.

Jerry slides two dimes back at me. "Your change, sir," he says, and I feel all tingly that I've just made a grown-up purchase and Jerry called me sir and gave me change.

"Yippee! Thanks, Jerry!" I make a beeline for the door and Ken rushes to keep up with me as we head back home. I sling the bag over my shoulder and imagine how it'll feel with my clubs in it. I can see myself standing at the tee, sliding a club out, laying my bag down, and crushing my ball down the fairway. Ken will congratulate me, and we'll have a big-boy conversation and laugh and eat hot dogs at the Snack Shack.

I can't wait to get home, and Ken has to run to keep up with me. We cross the street to our front lawn and I see the front door open and my mom step out.

"Lookit!" I say, holding up the bag. I'm wild with excitement and out of breath from running. "I bought a golf bag." I run up to my mother to show her the bag, but she has her arms folded across her chest and doesn't seem interested in it.

"Did you spend all your money on this thing?" she says.

"Yes. Except for these." I pull two dimes out of my pocket.

"Now, how are you going to buy Christmas presents for everyone?" She turns around, goes into the house, and shuts the front door behind her.

I'm speechless. And I'm vaguely aware that my mouth is open. And I'm feeling something I've never experienced before.

"Wow!" Ken says. "She's really trying to make you feel guilty."

So that's what this feeling is. And if I'm understanding her correctly, I've apparently hurt people by buying a golf bag.

"Wow!" Ken says again.

I run into the house and throw my bedroom door shut behind me and sit on the edge of my bed, the canvas golf bag lying across my lap. My clubs are leaning against the wall in the corner by my closet. As I stare at the clubs, I know this is the moment I've been waiting for. About a hundred times I've pictured those clubs in the bag, just waiting for me to sling them over my shoulder, walk across the street to the golf course, and play a round of golf.

The clubs seem to be calling to me, but I'm reluctant to answer them, and for several minutes I just watch them, the persimmon head of the driver buffed to a gleam. I slowly get up and take the clubs in my hand. The metal shafts are cool, I think to myself, as I slide them into the golf bag. The closet door opens quietly, and I prop the bag up in the far corner. Behind the cotton candy machine.

Dirty Laundry

Cats were a great idea in the prototype phase. But somewhere in the execution stage, the product got totally bungled. Think of it. What started out as a hugely vicious saber-toothed tiger evolved to the common house cat. It was nature's idea to begin with a fourteen-foot-long carnivore and, through natural selection, reduce it down into the handy portable package we know today. The problem is, there was a bug in the design for the revision. The outer container was correctly scaled down, but the inner workings were left in their primitively aggressive state. And cats remain the monstrous, single-minded killing machines they've always been.

As far as I can see, anyone who owns a cat is asking for the worst that nature has to offer since cats seem to take some sort of incomprehensible pleasure in ignoring you just when you need affection, pestering you just when you need solitude, and raking their claws across your arm just when you've decided to wear short sleeves.

If you can forget about their unparalleled narcissism and lethal unpredictability, you're left with an animal whose sole purpose in life is to drag eviscerated squirrels through the kitty door.

No, give me a dog any day ... an animal whose greatest pleasure in life is a few simple moments of contact per day with a person it forever regards as a god. Which is why my mother marches me into a Tucson, Arizona, animal shelter, past all the cages that contain adorable and loving puppies, straight to an area that houses hissing, psychotic cats. My mother insists that I can choose one to my liking, not that such an animal exists in the cat section. After scanning the offerings, I decide on the one that appears the least homicidal, a deduction I make upon observing a single sleeping cat. It's an orange tabby, and it's the only one that doesn't give me the sensation that it will lock its fangs in a death grip on my jugular vein.

With some reluctance, and several manipulatively longing and useless glances at the dog cages, I point to the tabby. "That one ... I guess."

"Are you kidding?" my mother says. "It's too skinny. He's probably got distemper. Let's take this one over here," she says, pointing to an obese gray ball of fur. "Now, that's healthy!"

The gray one it is.

On the way home in the car, I'm given a list of my responsibilities regarding caring for the cat, none of which I plan to undertake. In a transparent effort to get me interested in the beast, my mother instructs me to name it. I raise the lid on the cardboard box and stare inside. The animal appears to be completely out of proportion.

"Fat Head," I say importantly, as if planting a flag atop a newly discovered mountain peak.

I fully expect my mother to reject the name out of hand, but there's something in it she apparently finds appealing, and I see her mouth working in silence to pronounce the animal's new name.

I spend the next six months completely ignoring the cat, who forms what I can only describe as a truce—as opposed to an attachment—with my mother. She is surprisingly tolerant of Fat Head and shows him a level of affection I wouldn't have thought her capable of. But the affection is delivered on her terms, when she is most willing to give it, and not necessarily when the cat seems to need it.

Now that I think about it, my mother couldn't possibly have imagined that an eleven-year-old boy in Tucson would get much enjoyment out of a cat. It's not the kind of animal you take over to a friend's house for a swim in the pool. It sure doesn't give me a big, wet, sloppy greeting when I come home from school. And I can't take him with me on walks through the great cactus deserts. What a boy needs is an animal he can romp with, and cats are mostly rompless. Instead, I get indifference from my pet. He is my mother's cat.

* * *

At the beginning of summer vacation, I observe an amazing ritual taking place in the back yard. In the early morning, before the summer sun in Tucson can incinerate every living thing in its path, Fat Head lays on top of a four-foot-high brick wall that surrounds our yard. He stretches out, eyes closed, resting his chin on the back of his paws. He is completely at peace, even as the blue jays begin squawking in our plum tree. One of the jays, presumably the boldest among them, hops out of the tree and begins flying a thirty-foot circle around the cat, screeching at him the entire time. Fat Head appears not to care in the least.

This is a rite I see repeated each morning for thirty days, complete with provocative shrieking, all details remaining the same except that the blue jay, feeling a little more emboldened every day, reduces the size of the circle. After a few weeks of this, the circle has tightened to a three-foot radius, by which time the jay slaps the cat with its wings and pecks at his head as it flies by. And in all this time, Fat Head has not so much as opened his eyes to wonder about the assault—until one day he jerks a paw into the air, grabs the jay by the throat, reels him in, and consumes him on the wall in full view of all the other jays who are now insane with rage and fear.

It takes only a few days for the jays to forget the event, and send the next boldest among them out of the tree to begin the fly-by all over again. The process of bravery, hubris, and death is repeated like clockwork.

Within that amazing thirty-day cycle is life's most valuable lesson, as interpreted by me: survival doesn't go to the biggest or the strongest; it goes to the most adaptable. All of my compliant behavior has gotten me nowhere. From this point on, I'm going to stop being a submissive little puke and change into a person who takes control over everything around him. Just like Fat Head. Just like my mother.

From this day forward, I am no longer a banana slug. I am a dragon.

* * *

I am now a person who sneers at obstacles, ignores all advice, and follows the paths in life I choose for myself. If my mother will just let me do those three things, I know I will control my own destiny. The dragon doesn't fear her anger. The dragon coughs up fireballs at those it deems nuisances. Yes, I'm letting the dragon out of its cave ... starting right now.

We're sitting around the kitchen table eating dinner, the only sounds being those of two adults and three boys inhaling what was only twenty minutes ago a rather large roast beef.

"Would you guys go do the dishes?" my mother says to my two brothers. "We want to have a talk with Dennis."

"Uh, oh," Ken says, laughing at my predicament, whatever it is.

The three of us—my mother, my father, and me—watch as Jim and Ken clear the table, taking the dishes into the kitchen. We wait until we hear the sounds of running water and clattering plates.

My mother looks at me sternly. "Your father wants to have a talk with you," she finally says, words that force my two-pound allotment of beef to make a sudden U-turn.

My father looks at her quizzically. "I do?"

My mother is clearly annoyed. This is apparently something they've talked about. She glares at him until he either caves in or remembers the topic.

"Oh, right," he says, clearing his throat excessively. "Your mother thinks it's time we had a little talk about … well, you know."

I don't know. I don't have a clue what he's referring to.

"About the birds and bees," my mother says.

Ah, sex. The topic—one that is much thought about but never discussed in our house, except by me and Ken who has several bizarre theories on the subject, almost none of which are based on actual experience. Sex—something I lately became aware of ever since I discovered that magazine in the garage in my dad's junk drawer, which I at first mistake for a car repair manual, but none of the pictured tools looks familiar. Yes, sex—a concept I'm able, on an intellectual level, to apply to the girls at school who are growing breasts and taking special "health" classes that none of the boys are allowed to attend, which makes us hyperventilate with curiosity. Sex—it is, I am told by my friends, why our penises have recently gotten hard and pretty much stayed that way as if bronzed. Although what to do with them next mostly escapes us. Sex—it is the reason why my father's face is beet red at this moment, and why he appears to be communing with the boomerang pattern on our formica tabletop. It is a difficult subject, and he cannot make eye contact with ... the dragon.

"Tell him, Hal," my mother says.

My dad swallows hard. "Would you," he says to my mother without looking up at her, "mind if we do this in private?"

She does, since in her absence she can no longer control the subject's pace or content. My father and I watch as she grabs her pack of cigarettes, slowly gets up from the table, and leaves the room. The moment she's gone, he lights a Salem, takes a huge inhale, and expels the smoke slowly through his nostrils. About forty-five seconds have elapsed since my mother left.

"Dad?"

"Yes?"

"You wanted to say ...?"

"Yes. I think it's time I talked to you about sex," he says, tapping his lighter on the edge of the ashtray.

"Sure, Dad ... what do you want to know about it?" I say, trying to help him relax. Ken and Jim giggle in the kitchen.

"What?" He's confused.

"What about sex, Dad?" The dragon is gathering strength.

He is now staring into the light fixture that hovers above the table, probably contemplating jamming a wet finger into a light socket as a reasonable way out of this situation. But he gathers himself. "At your age," he begins slowly, "you probably think a woman's naked body is very beautiful."

Yeah! No shit. But I'm not sure if he's expecting an answer, so I say nothing.

"Well," he continues, "just picture her sitting on the toilet." And with that, he leaves the room and heads down the hall.

I'm stunned. And I sense that there are just a few details missing from the explanation.

* * *

It's becoming more obvious that my mother regards our family as a tree full of noisy blue jays.

And the beauty in the way she controls us is that we rarely suspect we're being eaten until it's too late.

Sure, she can be obvious, wanting things just so—merely because it pleases her sense of order or simply because there is pleasure to be had in the act of dominating.

For example, every spring and summer in Tucson is a time—the only time—when the family actually participates in a group event. We sit in the back yard and listen to Dodger games on a little Sears Silvertone transistor radio my mom places on a folding, metal TV tray next to her pack of Winstons. She begins each broadcast with a cigarette in one hand, and with the other she tunes the radio until there's nothing but static, then centers the dial on the station—exactly where she started.

At the sound of Vin Sculley's voice—a sound almost as beautiful as the last school bell before summer vacation—I am instantly transported to a seat along the third-base line at Dodger Stadium, a Dodger Dog in one hand, a Pepsi in the other, a frozen malt between my knees.

"Why is it that none of us can turn the radio on, Mom?" Ken says.

This is my father's cue to don shining armor. "Because," he says, "your mother knows exactly where the station is."

"We're not stupid, Dad," Ken adds, not altogether wisely. "I manage to tune the radio in my car. Don't you think I can handle this cheap-shit little radio?"

My dad snaps. "Don't swear in front of your mother!"

This is the system my mother and father have erected for the family. She's possessive and controlling, and it's my father's job to explain why it's all for our own good ... that what she's really being is selfless and diligent.

But that's the small stuff, the issues where we know at the time we're being controlled. When she's really needy, she's able to both control and neutralize at the same time. Like when she gets sick or depressed, which is fairly often. It's at these times when my dad has to fetch things for her, when the boys can't listen to music, when her every whim must be catered to. She'll blame her illnesses on us, pin her recovery on our willingness to serve her, and then tell us we're failing to make her feel better. We are simultaneously managed and defeated.

My mother has turned controlling into abstract art. We all know there's some theme or message swirling among the dark colors, but it's beyond any of us to interpret it.

God, she makes it look like fun! The dragon can at least appreciate that.

The dragon wakes from its slumber, stretches its wings, and yawns when my mom instructs my dad to ask me to clean the garage. Sure, I could push around a few boxes. Maybe organize the Christmas decorations. But that's not how I do things now. The dragon takes them beyond expectations.

The look on my dad's face when I take off his blindfold says it all. He's noticing that every one of the sixty or so paint cans, jars of screws and nails, and boxes of faucet washers has a hand-written hang tag taped to it, explaining in detail the name of the contents and what they're used for. I've taped a tag to a small jar that says BOLTS. THEY GET SCREWED IN TO NUTS. Pure genius.

He's seeing the new pegboard above his workbench. And he's appreciating the fact that all his tools are individually hanging from the pegboard against a hand-drawn outline so he can quickly figure out where to put away his tools. You just hang the hack saw on the two hooks against the outline of the hack saw. It's a brilliant and inspired system.

I am reading his expression, which seems to say, *You, young dragon, have learned the lessons of life well. You have attained far greater powers than I, and have used them for the betterment of mankind. I can only bow to your wisdom, your intelligence, and your kindness.*

Or something like that.

If only my mother had the same appreciation for my efforts. You'd think, having seen this model of order in the garage, she would be motivated to duplicate the results with her little kitchen tools. But she gets upset when I hang up all her spatulas, ladles, garlic presses, and turkey basters against an outline of the tool drawn on the kitchen wall. Let me get this straight—you can organize the garage but you can't organize the kitchen. The dragon is disoriented.

My mom, perhaps sensing my growing power, is determined to eliminate the competition, and suggests that I spend the summer working at my dad's laundry.

I've never much cared for where my dad works. Renting towels, sheets, and napkins to motels, restaurants, and mortuaries isn't my idea of intellectual stimulation. Still, after an intense negotiating period, I agree to work for him. While he doesn't come right out and say it, my guess is that he perceives my increasing potency, and probably wants me to evaluate the plant's operations and develop a productivity model that could be in place by the end of the summer. How else to explain the fact that he puts me to work in the soiled linen room, the grubbiest, foulest place in the entire plant. I reason that it's the point of entry for my dad's inventory, and the place where inefficiencies are likely to be the most obvious. This is the area where the drivers drop off huge bags of soiled towels and sheets.

It is my immediate job to empty the bags, then sort all the stuff into big piles. All the king-size sheets go onto pile A, the queens on pile B, the bath towels on C, the wash cloths on D, etc. Of course, the only way to know if a sheet is a king or a queen is to compare it to your arm span. So I have to spread the sheets out in front of my nose, which is not a very pleasant thing to do when the sheets have spent the previous night at motels or mortuaries. Man, some of the stuff smells bad! And there are stains even FBI criminologists couldn't identify.

Since the job doesn't require any actual thought in order to assure its completion, I turn my attention to the other workers. My evaluation of the plant's productivity will begin with them. Fernando, Maria, and Esteban have all worked at the plant for over thirty years, but they don't look particularly appreciative that they are being given a steady wage. One dollar and thirty-five cents per hour is nothing to sneeze at. Not that their benefits would have covered them if the sneezing had turned into a real illness.

Flexing my newly discovered muscles, I try to make conversation about them doing their jobs better, but they mostly ignore me. Then I remember a show I saw on TV about some scientists who played rock music at earsplitting levels in order to increase the anxiety level in captive rhesus monkeys. Since the monkeys reacted to the din by moving around in an agitated state, I speculate that Fernando, Maria, and Esteban might exhibit some increased workflow.

The next day I bring in my record player from home and give my subjects a loud helping of *Leader of the Pack* for eight straight hours. In all this time, I play only this one song so my research subjects can develop a sense of security about their work environment.

The day after that, Maria calls in sick. And Esteban develops a mysterious bleeding from the ears, and has to leave early. I know he's a very religious man, so I'm thinking his affliction is some sort of weird stigmata offshoot.

It is just me and Fernando, who graciously offers me a taste of his lunch. He has a big burrito kind of thing. I start to take it from him, but he says, "No, no ... I geev." And he shoves it at my face. It is a huge mouthful of food, and Fernando watches as I chew it as best I can, then swallow it. No sooner has the food reached my throat than I am stricken by the most intense pain I've ever experienced. I immediately lose my breath, and my body pours sweat by the buckets full.

"You sock dirk, señor Music Man?" Fernando says, grinning.

"Sock Dirk?" I say. "I don't know Dirk. Did he do something wrong?"

Fernando stands up and unzips his fly. "You sock dirk?"

* * *

My dad transfers me to another area of the plant before I have to sock Dirk. While I haven't completed my investigation of the soiled linen room, I decide that moving to a different location might give me an opportunity to get an overview of different departments before revisiting them for a longer stay.

My next assignment is the linen press. The press machine is the industrial equivalent of a steam iron, only instead of holding it in your hand and passing it over an article of clothing, you feed a bed sheet between two huge pinch rollers, each of which weighs about a thousand pounds. Some kind of internal goings on heats the sheet and applies steam. Then the perfectly pressed sheet is spit out the back, to be quickly folded by Vladis, a recent arrival from Lithuania.

Vladis must have seen me eyeing the press machine, because he smiles and pantomimes unzipping his fly (apparently, he's worked with Dirk, too), then pulling something long out of the fly, and feeding it into the press. Finally he squeezes his two hands together in the shape of a flattened pancake and laughs uproariously.

"What are you trying to tell me?" I ask him.

"Yes," he answers.

"'What are you trying to tell me' is not a yes or no question."

Now, I may be only eleven years old, but I'm not so young that I can't recognize the danger in working around machinery like this, a topic I am only too willing to discuss with my father when he comes to check up on me.

"Dad, has anyone ever been hurt operating this machine?"

"Hmmm." My father appears to give it great thought. He looks up at the ceiling, like he's searching for an answer there. "Yeah, I think a guy got his hand caught in this press ... about fifteen, maybe sixteen, years ago, something like that."

"Did anyone ever catch his penis in the machine?"

"His penis? What makes you ask a question like that?"

"I don't know. It just seems like there's a real possibility a guy could accidentally get it caught in the machine."

My dad nods and thinks about this for a second, obviously impressed with my logic. "I would imagine that as long as you keep it in your pants you stand very little chance of losing it in the machine."

The dragon is displeased. It's thinking like this that gets people hurt. That afternoon I make a call to a local TV station to discuss the safety of my dad's machines. They mention they will send a reporter over to have a look. Pretty responsive, I'd say.

* * *

I spend the rest of the summer working at various jobs around the plant by day, then pounding away on my productivity report by night. Finally, on September the third, I type out two sets of the eighteen-page report, then attach spiral-bound and embossed covers. One of the sets I mail to Mr. Gunderman, my dad's boss. He's going to be very impressed with my findings.

The other report I hand to my dad as we sit down to dinner.

"What's this?" he says.

"It's my report."

"Something for school?"

"You're going to like this, Dad. I analyzed the productivity of your entire plant with—"

"You did?"

"—with a specific breakdown on each department. There's some heinous waste going on in there, you know."

My dad quickly flips through the report. "This thing's eighteen pages long," he says.

"Well, with the table of contents, source attributes and dedications, it's up to twenty-one pages. But it's okay, Dad. It's my gift to you."

I study my dad's face as he randomly opens the report to various places and reads short passages.

"You realize," he finally says, "that this report consistently blames me as the plant's largest barrier to increased productivity."

"I wouldn't call it blame, Dad. Anybody who reads this would see that it mentions you as the person with the greatest opportunity to turn things around."

My dad closes the cover on the report, slowly gets up, and walks out of the room.

I think the report really inspires my father to better himself, because after a few more days, he stops going to the plant, and starts looking for other work full time. It just may be that this report has lit a fire under my dad, showing him what he is really capable of, giving him a glimpse of a world beyond a linen rental plant.

Until he finds just the right thing, he's working as a night manager at Pedersen's Groceries. I stop in on his first night to say hi and to look the place over. Mr. Pedersen will be getting a complete report early next week.

If I Only Had a Brain

Turns out it really is possible for a fourteen-year-old boy to sustain a boner for an entire semester.

I've got Miss Lefkowitz to thank for that. Everything about my eighth-grade typing teacher creates in me an almost volcanic sexual energy: her platinum hair, shellacked high in what might be called a beehive if about half the bees hadn't knocked off early for the day; her paint-by-numbers makeup, in loving homage to the Yardley look; the aroma of patchouli oil I see her slender finger slowly apply to her throat; the denim skirts she wears about fourteen inches above her knees; her white vinyl go-go boots with little silver taps on the soles; and the way she stands in front of my desk, bending over at the waist to inspect my typing upside down. I am positively idiotic with lust.

Not that she doesn't share my feelings. Sometimes I'll be in the middle of a typing exercise, and glance up to see her looking at me. It's at times like these when I know exactly what she's thinking: *You, young Mr. Globus, see right through me in a way and to a degree no man even my own age is capable of. And I intend to reward you for your insight with sexual delicacies the likes of which haven't been written about in three thousand years of erotic literature.*

Or something like that.

In the middle of that precise thought, two unforgettably awful things happen. The first is that a student walks into class and hands Miss Lefkowitz a note, which she opens, reads with a grave expression, until finally she looks up at me. I am instantly terrified by the possibilities. The second is that she asks me to stand up and go to Mr. MacNamara's office. I am in no condition to stand. And, if history is any indication, I won't be for quite a while. Still, she asks me to accompany the messenger to the principal's office. I gather up my books, holding them conspicuously at waist level, and walk toward the door. As I exit, I know that my departure is tearing her heart out, because she's looking in her grade book, unable even to make eye contact with me. I plunge out the door.

"What did you do?" the student messenger says, the hint of a smirk on his acne-ravaged face.

"I got a hard-on," I say, wrongly assuming he's referring to my strategically placed books.

"Jesus, they're sending you to Mr. MacNamara for that? There isn't a guy in school who's safe."

I don't have a clue what he's talking about, nor do I, at this particular moment, care to engage him in conversation. I'm too busy tilting every ounce of my intellectual capacity toward coming up with a defense. Which is somewhat difficult to do when you're not quite sure which infraction you've been busted for.

"Ah, Mr. Globus," Mr. MacNamara says as I enter his office. "Again we meet."

"I'm sorry, sir."

"Really? What exactly are you sorry for?"

Silly man. I know a trick question when I hear one, and I'm not about to fling myself on my knees and offer up contrition for an infraction he doesn't even know about. But I'm vaguely aware that my boner, like all other pleasant thoughts, has receded to a point where I suspect it is no longer accessible. I take a deep breath.

"I'm sorry that I'm here again, Mr. MacNamara."

"Do you have any idea why I called you to my office today?"

Again, the question. Another variation on the inadvertent-confession gambit. He's pushing another pawn up the board. I ruminate on the potential strategic advantage of his move as he sits benignly at his desk. He smiles. Time passes. He's good at this.

It's time to make a move. "Is it that bra thing with Marlene Geller?" Queen's knight to rook three.

"No, but I'll look into that one later." Check.

I forlornly watch him scribble something on a pad of paper.

"Does this," he says, producing what appears to be a silver cigarette lighter, "look familiar?"

It does. "No, sir." I slide a piece back to protect my king.

"Really? What do you suppose I'm doing with it?"

"Sir, I appreciate the offer, but I really don't think smoking is allowed on campus." Bold move.

A slight, almost indiscernible, smile appears, illuminating little creases around his eyes and mouth. I get the feeling he perceives no threat from my move.

"We found a student smoking in the boy's room this morning, Mr. Globus."

"You really should install exhaust fans in there, sir."

"What I really should do is expel you."

Ouch. Captured knight.

"Sir, it wasn't me you caught smoking!" I say with just the right amount of outrage.

"No, but oddly enough, the student was caught with this cigarette lighter on him," he says, flicking open the lighter's hinged top.

My stomach is turning and little white stars are beginning to flash in front of my eyes.

"He says that you sold him the lighter, Mr. Globus."

I'm doomed, and I consider knocking over my king. But... is that an opening I see? "No, I remember selling him something. But I don't think it was a lighter."

"Then what did you sell him?"

Oh, jeez, I really botched that one. I'm making this way too easy. "I don't remember, Mr. MacNamara. It might have been some Pixie Stix."

"I don't think so."

He turns the lighter over in his hand and holds it up. Even from this distance I can see two initials engraved in the silver.

"Who's J.G.?" he says. Captured queen.

"No idea, sir."

"You sure?"

"Absolutely."

"Here's what I'm thinking, Mr. Globus: that you took this lighter from someone you know." Check.

"Because of the initials? What about Jackie Gleason, John Garfield, and Jimmy Gurante?"

"Who?"

Christ, I'm flailing. "Sir, there are a lot of J.G.'s in the world."

"I suppose there are," he says, his eyes betraying a sudden lack of confidence in his argument. "Suppose we call your mother—Jeanette Globus—or your brother—Jim Globus—and ask them which of the world's J.G.'s this lighter belongs to." Checkmate.

Nothing—not the stomach flu, a two-week-old burrito, or the time my friend and I consumed a six-pack of beer—makes me more sick than what happens next.

Mr. MacNamara picks up the phone and starts dialing.

* * *

Of all the people I've met in life, no one is more predictable than my mother. Whether I bring home a D in geometry, spill a milk shake down our car's dashboard speaker or break one of her antique beer steins from the Old Country, wherever that is, you can set your watch to her behavior pattern. The first hour will consist of outright indifference, where I am simply invisible to her. After that, some chemical in her brain starts to surge, and she transitions into passive aggression. She'll actually spend this period cleaning the house, even humming along to Della Reese or Andy Williams or the soundtrack from Man of La Mancha as she vacuums every room but mine. I'll hear her singing Moon River or Dulcinea over the sound of the upright vacuum, which she'll use to bludgeon like a battering ram the outside of my bedroom door. What she's telling me is this: *I am daughter of Hoover, and goddess of all things clean and powerful. I will use this sucking instrument to extract the evil you continue to bring into my house. And then I will flay you open so that the jackals can eat your putrid intestines.*

Or something like that.

And then she'll spend the next two hours alternately reaming, interrogating, and threatening me. If there's one thing I've learned (although good behavior apparently isn't it) from years of doing battle with her, it's that you can't possibly make any headway with a person who is both manipulative and in a rage. In an argument, no territory is safe or out of bounds, no matter how hurtful. No past discretion is forgotten. And certainly not forgiven. Always, the raving will wind up in a dominion that's enormously comfortable for her: how she is affected by my behavior and what people think of her as a mother. Which is precisely where she's taking it right now.

Then she throws me a huge, bending curve-ball that catches me looking: she instructs my brother Ken to drive to Sears to buy me a guitar.

Man, that one totally came out of left field. In the entire universe of responses, I'd have never predicted this particular one. She tells me that I have too much time on my hands, and that learning to play a musical instrument will fill that time and give me a chance to be more like Ken, whose status as an aspiring movie star reflects well on her.

If my mother lives to be a hundred, this may truly be my only chance to string these particular words together: my mom is right. At least, in the sense that the guitar does take up my free time, which I have plenty of since she grounded me for a year over the cigarette lighter thing. And I find that I have ... well, not exactly a desire to learn, but I seem to have something of an aptitude. Ken shows me how to form chords with my left hand, how to strum with my right. He corrects and belittles like a Soviet ballet teacher. He has me listen to Peter, Paul & Mary albums. He buys their song book, and we learn to play schmaltzy numbers like *If I Had a Hammer* and *Lemon Tree*. He sings the melodies and I handle the high harmonies, and I discover for the first time that I'm actually pretty good at something.

Despite the fact that I'm fourteen and Ken is nineteen, my mother takes every conceivable opportunity to have us play our guitars and sing for dinner guests, as if we're precious little children. I am horribly shy and reluctant to perform, but refusing Ken and my mom is not an option. As we take our guitars out of their cases and begin tuning up, I always see panic in the eyes of our guests. Ken's incessant babbling and my continuous brooding have done nothing to convince them that we will provide even a shred of entertainment. They immediately dread having to sit through The Longest Show on Earth, sure that they'll be called upon to express their most profoundly insincere amazement that my mother could produce two such outstanding prodigies.

But we surprise them. We're actually pretty good. Charming even. We've worked up an act that includes three rousing songs, a little rehearsed patter, some rudimentary comedy stolen from the Smothers Brothers. My mother grins as if she's hearing all of it for the first time, cuing the audience to laugh. She makes requests. Interrupts at will. Competes with us by frequently pulling everyone's attention toward herself. She wages an internal battle, alternately pushing us forward so that she can bask in the envy of her guests, then yanking them away from us when she feels competitive. And when she does let us play, she anxiously shifts her focus from her sons to her guests, gauging their reaction as if it holds the key to our future.

Strangely enough, it does. Because one of our guests (a friend of my oldest brother Jim) is a real Hollywood insider with "big, big connections." Somehow, despite the family's performance of Dysfunction On Parade, Russ Bernhardt, Hollywood Publicist, declares that we have talent and that he'd like to represent us.

Ken and I screech and whoop it up. Russ puts his hands in praying position and makes little satisfied clapping motions. My mother smiles, then looks pained. My father lights a cigarette. Jim leaves the room.

I'm trying not to work myself into a lather about our big break by reminding myself to maintain a little perspective about Russ. Sure, we've all heard about small-time Hollywood talent scouts and agents who have clients like Tom and His Amazing Singing Clams or the midget who can fart the entire 1812 Overture. Russ's specialty is ancient has-beens, representing Hollywood actresses who are about 30 years past their prime, a prime that consisted of a few lines in a forgettable Depression-era film. His most successful client is Fifi d'Orsay. And his entire stable of actresses looks like a collection of Nora Desmond understudies. But whatever perspective I'm attempting to maintain is quickly evaporating, because we're now professional entertainers.

* * *

Ken and I are forty-five minutes early to the meeting we've set up with Russ, and we sit in our booth in the Hamburger Hamlet in Beverly Hills drinking Cokes and talking about our fortunes. Ken instructs me to let him do the talking, which I'm only too happy to do. Russ arrives thirty-five minutes late, then spends the next seventeen minutes schmoozing his way through the restaurant. It's a fascinating scene because Russ apparently knows every near-death actor and pretty-boy in Hollywood. It's clear that Russ isn't a mediocrity to them. He represents some sort of hope that he can connect them with a life they have never known, but through whose knot-hole fence they have seen what stardom looks like. Sadly, not only is Russ incapable of making any of these people famous, he's unable even to make himself relevant in anything but the fringes of the entertainment industry.

Who cares? Ken and I are absolutely wide-eyed as Russ begins his proposition while at the same time consuming a hamburger with barbecue sauce. As he explains the details, tiny pieces of bun, meat and lettuce are launched our way. He explains that a clothing boutique on La Cienega Boulevard has contacted him for some publicity concerning their grand opening in two weeks. The name of the boutique: The Yellow Brick Road. Would we be interested in singing a song at the opening with a number of important Hollywood people in attendance?

We would.

Would we be interested in singing a song from *The Wizard of Oz*?

We would.

Would we be interested in dressing up as the Scarecrow and the Tin Woodsman?

Uh, we would.

Would we be interested in singing the song directly to a movie star?

Gulp.

Russ, obviously pleased with both his presentation and our reaction to it, dabs at the corners of his mouth with a paper napkin. Then he performs an after-meal ritual I've never seen: he removes his upper dentures and sucks the extraneous food bits from between the teeth. Ken has to look away, but I find the spectacle riotously funny.

The next two weeks are spent getting hold of the sheet music for our song, learning it, and being fitted for costumes. All of this takes place at Russ's West Hollywood apartment, where he introduces us to Monty Pine, a long-out-of-work way-off-Broadway musical performer who is to be the Cowardly Lion to my Scarecrow and Ken's Tin Woodsman. Monty has an enormous overbite, a profound speech impediment that forces him to take a long running start at the letter L, and a jet black wig that looks as if it were purchased from a mail-order taxidermist with a static electricity problem. But I must say, he attacks his role with a verve and energy I admire. This despite the fact that he pronounces the name of his character The Cowardyee Yion.

Russ has decided that renting our costumes is too costly, and he puts one of his ninety-year-old clients to work. The Lion's pelt comes from three huge stuffed animals Russ has bought for his little niece's Christmas presents. She'll understand, he assures us. Ken's Tin Woodsman outfit consists of a short vinyl rain jacket spray-painted silver. I simply wear a straw hat and a jacket with hay sticking out of it. It's my first costume, and I'm too excited to notice how cheesy it looks.

* * *

I haven't slept for a second the night before the performance and, in the morning, I get out of bed ready to vomit, I'm so nervous. Ken wakes up absolutely buoyant, and makes himself a breakfast consisting of six poached eggs, a pound of bacon, and half a loaf of toasted Wonder Bread. I can't watch him eat. Instead, I find an onion matzoh in the cupboard and take it to my room and slowly eat it on the bed. Since Ken doesn't reseal packages, it's completely stale.

I spend most of the day in my room reading *On Her Majesty's Secret Service,* trying to take my mind off this misery. I can't, and find that I have to reread virtually every paragraph. In four hours, I've consumed a total of twelve pages. As the minute-hand pinwheels around the clock, I become more paralyzed with anxiety, and consider bolting through the front door and never coming back. At two in the afternoon, Ken bursts into my room and insists we rehearse. I'm too sick, and I ask him if I can be replaced for tonight's show. He lifts me off the bed by my trachea, as if I'm a piece of Samsonite luggage, then plays the opening chords of our song on his guitar, and I find that singing my verse actually calms me down. I'm relieved to discover that I still remember the words, and after a run-through, I'm feeling more confident. We just may pull this off after all.

At five o'clock, Ken decides we'll go to the performance in our costumes. He spends the next hour applying silver makeup to his face and hands, immediately breaking out in a knobby rash. He applies a little white makeup to my face in the belief that a scarecrow should have a pale, wan look about him. I don't need makeup for that.

Finally, it's time, and we arrive at The Yellow Brick Road a few minutes before seven. I'm immediately struck by what a wonderful job they've done with the place. The boutique itself is nothing but a tiny shack, but the entire front courtyard—about a hundred-forty by eighty feet—is painted in perspective to look like Munchkinland with the road leading to Oz (the boutique) in the distance. I get goose bumps.

Monty shows up a few minutes later. He refuses to talk to anyone, so immersed is he in preparing for his role. He stands facing a wall painted to look like a forest, repeatedly muttering, "I'm a yion ... I'm a yion."

At seven-thirty, the press starts arriving. Photographers take pictures of each other. Caterers slip food to photographers. Bartenders become everyone's best friend.

Ken has an idiotic grin pasted on his face that makes him look like a mental patient. I've learned over the years that this is the look Ken affects to assure everyone how relaxed and confident he is, but in his outfit I think he looks more like the killer from *Psycho* after inadvertently getting tangled in the shower curtain.

As people begin to show up, I notice something interesting about Hollywood events: people arrive at them in reverse order of their importance. The press first, the eager beavers next, then the has-beens, the starlets, and finally the famous people.

My brother Jim, a freelance photographer who was also hired by Russ, is busily snapping pictures of starlets who are too poor to afford limos. It's fun watching them shimmy out of old Plymouths and

Volkswagens. Virtually all of them are blonds, festooned from head to toe with costume jewelry, and bedecked in black gowns with plunging necklines. I've never seen anything like this before.

Russ can only flit from place to place in the nervous belief that sliding a stuffed egg or a glass of champagne three millimeters to the left actually accomplishes something. He has arranged this whole affair, and I see how frightened he is that some tiny detail may have been overlooked.

Watching him is making me terrified again, and I want to suggest to Ken that we rehearse, to calm our nerves. But Ken, having found a way to simultaneously calm and arouse his nerves, is schmoozing a young starlet. He has her cornered where the farmland of Kansas meets the jungle outside of the Emerald City, and has his hand on the starlet's rear end, smearing silver makeup on her.

Since no one chooses to talk to me, except to tell me what a cute little scarecrow I am, I make my way to the buffet table to fix myself a turkey sandwich. I instantly drip mustard on my shirt, and try to cover it up with some straw from my jacket. As I turn around to walk away, I fall flat on my face, flinging the sandwich across the courtyard, when I trip over what I at first believe to be a child in a tuxedo, then discover to my utter horror that it's one of the Munchkins from the original film. In fact, it's the Mayor of Munchkinland. As I try to pull him to his feet, he yanks his arm away from me and glowers.

"Why don't you watch where you're going, fuckhead," he says, very un-Munchkinlike.

I'm now panicked and humiliated. Everyone is gawking in amazement at the sight of a fourteen-year-old dressed as a bale of hay being yelled at by an old man half his height. I try to apologize, but I can only stammer. I'd like to tell the Mayor that he has a squashed but still-lit cigar stuck to the front of his tuxedo jacket, but I'm unable.

Fortunately, everyone becomes distracted as the evening's one and only limo arrives. Russ bulls his way through the huge crowd that forms around the car, and attempts to open the door, but finds it locked. He taps on the window. "Would you open the..." he says in a stage whisper, but there's no response from inside the vehicle. He grins at the crowd, the smile disappearing as he turns back to the limo. A hand searches the car's window ledge for the locking mechanism, but can't seem to find it. "Yes, that's it," Russ says. "Just lift the..." The other passenger reaches across and lifts up the lock. Russ is enormously relieved, and he swings open the door with a practiced flourish. I can't see who's emerging from the vehicle, but from the sheer number of flashbulbs popping and general hubbub arising, it's clearly someone important. Monty moves up next to me and puts a trembling hand on my elbow.

"Oh, my god... I knew she'd come. It's Judy Gahryand!" he says, and bursts into great rasping sobs.

"Buck up, Lion," I say. "We're on in a few minutes."

I offer him a napkin from the buffet table, and he accepts it, not without some embarrassment and sniffles. He blows his nose prodigiously, then smiles at me.

"Yes. Buck up. I'm a yion!" And he growls at me and giggles.

The sea of people around the limo parts, and there's Judy Garland being escorted through the crowd, an elderly man on one arm, Russ on the other. Just like in the movies, photographers in cheap suits kneel and take flash pictures of her while the gathered throng screams out things like, "We love you, Judy!", to which she smiles and nods her head like royalty. As she gets closer to me, she seems to be walking with some difficulty. I take it to be a physical handicap, until Russ leads her up to me, and I smell the liquor emanating from her. Monty throws himself onto one knee and begins kissing her hand and bawling like a baby.

"Rise, Lion," she says. "Have you no more courage than that?"

But Monty is inconsolable and begins to yowl. Judy looks up at Russ who shrugs, then turns her to me.

"And you must be the Scarecrow," she says, beaming.

My throat feels like I've swallowed an anvil. "Eep!" I say stupidly.

"Well, you're certainly a cute little one," she says, then grins at the elderly man who's propping her up by one arm. "Honey, can we take him home and give him to Lorna?"

I don't know who Lorna is, but I'm relieved that everyone laughs uproariously.

"Poor Scarecrow," she says. "They coulda given you a little more stuffing right there," she says, pointing at my crotch.

Eerie silence. I feel myself blushing through the white makeup. Ken shows up just in time to be introduced.

"Ah, Tin Woodsman. Have you found your heart?" Judy says.

As the multitude laughs on cue again, it occurs to me that Ken has been groping that starlet all evening. So, while he may not have found a heart, he was certainly in the right vicinity.

"Ken's a fine little actor," Russ offers bravely.

"Really," Judy says. And there's a long, awkward pause while everyone tries to figure out what to make of that.

Russ, clearly uncomfortable, leads her away, and the crowd reassembles around a tearful reunion between Judy and the Mayor of Munchkinland, who has by this time removed the lit cigar. Judy leans over to give him a hug, staggers, and almost falls on top of him. Russ and the elderly gentleman, both stricken with horror, untangle her from the Mayor.

"Get your guitar," Russ hisses at Ken.

"Miss Garland," Russ offers, a magician using misdirection to divert everyone's attention, "it's time for our special surprise."

I am instantly nauseous, knowing that I am an integral part of the three-piece surprise. Ken, with great difficulty, tries to put the guitar strap around his shoulders, but it catches on the silver funnel he's wearing as a hat, which clangs to the ground and rolls about five feet away. As he rushes to pick up the funnel, it dawns on me that he has never practiced the song in costume, and the guitar is held out away from him at an awkward angle. He looks petrified by this realization, and the absurdity of his predicament is the only thing that relaxes me. He makes an excessive show of tuning up, something he should have done earlier, but is doing now in order to stall for more time. Finally, with the audience members shuffling their feet impatiently, he nods at me and plays a few shaky introductory chords. I clear my throat and begin…

I could while away the hours,

Funny, but I hadn't noticed Judy's hat earlier. It's hard to figure out how to describe it, except to say that it's black with a red feather and looks like something Robin Hood would wear to a funeral.

conferrin' with the flowers,

Christ, I never expected there to be so many flashbulbs. I'm blind. And I feel like an asshole, making a big show of pantomiming sniffing a flower, like Russ instructed me to. He thinks it's adorable.

consultin' with the rain.

We never could figure out how to pantomime consulting with the rain. I suggested pouring water out of an imaginary watering can and talking to it, but Russ thought I looked too much like a street person mumbling to his shopping cart.

And my head I'd be scratchin'

At this point, I make a huge Danny Kaye-like gesture of scratching my head, as if lost in the kind of deep, mysterious thought that can only happen in the movies.

while my thoughts are busy hatchin',

I'm gaining confidence. Judy, who has probably heard this song at least a thousand times, generously pretends that this is simply the most delightful performance she's ever been privileged to witness.

if I only had a braaaain.

By this time, I'm so comfortable in the song that I give the word brain a little extra flourish, and slide the note up and down, kind of the way Neil

Diamond does when he wants to let everyone know how choked up he's feeling about things.

My verse is over, and a part of me is sad to have it end, given what a prominent part of my life it's been for two weeks. In all, I thought it was a reasonably good performance. It started a little tentatively, but I think I grew into it, capturing the essence that is the Scarecrow, somehow articulating the frustration that comes from being mentally challenged. Ken begins his verse...

When a man's an empty kettle,

Now that my part's finished, I feel no need to pay attention any more, so I start looking at babes, and reflect on Show Biz Lesson #1: performing is actually less frightening than imagining yourself performing. And while considering this epiphany, I hardly even notice the little dance Monty has worked up during his "If I onyee had the nerve" verse. He takes little mincing steps to demonstrate the lion's timidity, then wheels around melodramatically as if someone's sneaking up on him with a machete. Monty's acting his heart out, his overbite belting out the lyrics, and Judy looks confused by the performance.

The song ends, and Judy turns on her heels and heads toward the bar, her elderly gentleman and Russ running alongside to steady her. Our part of the evening is done, and the three of us stare at each other. We all feel like kids after the last present has been opened on Christmas morning. Monty looks particularly sad.

"This has been fabuyuss exposure for us," he says, sniffling. "Don't be surprised if your phone is ringing off the hook."

Ken takes off his guitar, the back of it covered with silver paint. His costume has a guitar-shaped mark on it. "I can't wait to get out of this costume and makeup," he says.

"I packed a change of clothes for us," I say. "It's in the car."

"Do you need some help?" Monty says, hopefully.

"No thanks. I've got it," Ken says. "Anyway, I have to keep my costume on for the rest of the evening. Donna wants me to wear it to her house," indicating the blond with the silver hand prints affixed to her nether regions.

"Good luck finding a heart," I offer. And I watch as the Tin Woodsman, my ride home, takes his starlet by the hand and disappears down the yellow brick road.

The Secret Life of Duct Tape

The chamber of commerce would have you believe that Los Angeles offers three-hundred-sixty-five days per year of crystalline sunshine. But I know the real truth: each day is oppressively hot, a condition made even more cheerless by smog so dense I can't even see the Hollywood sign on a hill no more than two miles away.

I'd be grateful for today's weather being about ten degrees cooler if it weren't for the fact that we're getting about eight inches of rain in a single hour, fat drops slapping against surface-of-the-sun asphalt.

It seems as if the idea of rain never once occurred to the city planners, who apparently forget that the storm water collects into shallow pools, quickly expands into ankle-high ponds as the rain continues, until finally it overwhelms the curbs, swamping the front lawns and cactus gardens of the surrounding houses.

Did it not dawn on anyone to install storm drains—or at least remove the shopping carts, discarded mattresses, and dead prostitutes from the few that actually exist?

Of course, it's easy to be grumpy in the middle of a rain storm when you're driving a 1958 VW Beetle without working windshield wipers and a leak through the dashboard that results in about a pint per minute of rain water being hosed into my right shoe. I'd move my foot to drier territory, but I occasionally like to use the accelerator. Not that it's doing me any good right now, since my tires are hydroplaning across the pavement, the concept of traction being the last thing on their little bald minds. And when the car isn't actually skidding, the rising water is causing it to float down the street for terrifying stretches of twenty feet at a time, until a single tire manages to get a momentary fingernail grip on the pavement. It's simply a miracle that I haven't bludgeoned one of the dozen or so similarly stricken cars I find abandoned in the middle of the street by their fleeing owners.

I've lost all sense of direction now: first, because my car is lazily spinning as the water carries it along, like a big blue turd circling the drain; second, because I can't see a thing through the windshield and can only intermittently make out objects through the passenger-side window; and third, because the rising water has obliterated the road and the sidewalk, creating one vast dirty lake.

I'm completely disoriented, unable to discern the direction in which I'm traveling, and I consider bolting from the car when I feel a sudden lurch as the tires catch on something. There's a mailbox out the side window and a street sign. I must have rammed the curb and stuck there, all in all not a bad place to be.

It looks like I'll be sitting here for awhile, so I might as well get comfortable. Which means emptying my shoe of about a cup of water, popping in an Alice Cooper eight-track, and lighting up the little pipe I keep in the glove compartment. I settle back in my seat and take a huge hit of pot as the car quickly fills up with smoke. I consider opening a window, but a quick risk/benefit analysis of incoming rain versus exiting pot smoke changes my mind.

I jump at the sound of a knock on the passenger window, and for a brief moment I consider that it might be the police—although why they'd regard my car glued to the curb as worthy of investigation (when at least six others float merrily down the street) mostly escapes me.

I'm contemplating what to do about the knocking when the door opens and a young woman, dripping wet, flops into the passenger seat.

"Hi," she says.

"Hi," I say, and for several seconds, we blink at each other as if we're the last two remaining people on Earth at the end of a *Twilight Zone* episode. "Is there ... something I can do for you."

"No," she says matter-of-factly.

I stare at her for several moments while she readjusts the rear-view mirror to check her mascara. It is, apparently, just the way she likes it, and she then examines her teeth, finding them numerous and shiny. Everything else being in order, she finishes primping by pulling back the hood on her sweatshirt and foofing up her curly hair.

Something about her hair fascinates me, and I finally decide it's the color—somewhere between red and brown, as if the follicles stubbornly refuse to fully commit either way. Whatever, I find her wet ringlets enormously sexy which, being a man, makes me fantasize about her pubic hair which I can imagine using as floss which makes me remember that I have a dental appointment in the morning, and I just know my hygienist Miriam, a disturbingly smelly older woman with concentration-camp tattoos on the inside of her left arm, is going to find a textbook case of gingivitis and punish me for all the horrors she experienced in Treblinka.

But I'll deal with Miriam tomorrow. Right now I've got a gorgeous yet oddly enigmatic young woman sitting next to me in the car which inspires me to reflect on the bewildering nature of things. One minute you're leading a perfectly normal life, floating down the street in your car—the next minute a woman hops into it and doesn't feel particularly obligated to explain, apologize, or otherwise engage you in conversation.

"Is there something I can do for you?" I wait for a response, but she's staring out the passenger window, communing with the mailbox on the street corner. "A ride maybe?" I add meekly.

She snaps her head around, her lips pursed. "Look, this isn't what it looks like."

"It ... it doesn't look like anything. I just thought—"

"Well, don't bother thinking about it. I just want to get out of the rain. I'm not a hooker, you know."

"Too bad. We'd probably have a lot more to talk about."

"Is that the only way you can relate to women?" she says, looking for all the world as if her eyes are about to hemorrhage. "Yeah, you look like one of those guys who has to buy it."

"Come on, that's not—"

"Fuck you, asshole! This is 1970, and we don't have to get on our knees for you or anyone else," she says, removing a tube of mascara from her purse.

I'm vaguely aware that she's continuing to yell at me, her voice becoming more strident with each new thought, her hand clutching the mascara wand which she repeatedly thrusts at me to emphasize her outrage. But all I can hear is blah blah blah, punctuated periodically by a profanity, which she uses creatively and seems to have an endless supply of. Through some act of supreme self-preservation, I find myself disassociating from her.

Lalalalalala ... In 1814 I took a little trip, along with Colonel Jackson down the mighty Mississip. We took a little bacon and we took a little beans, and we met the bloody British near—

" ... I don't know where you get off treating me like a fucking whore, but—"

Drysdale into the two-and-two windup ... Robinson leaning out over the plate ... caught him looking with a fastball, strike three!

"... turned down better looking guys than you—"

The storm starts when the drops start dropping. When the drops stop dropping the storm starts stopping.

"... your goddam nose is too big and your ears—"

Maybe I'll pick up a book this afternoon. But which one? A friend recently recommended *Catcher in the Rye*, but I don't like sports books. Maybe I'll get—

" ... don't just jump in any guy's car, you know. I thought you had brains, but now I think—"

To be or not to be. That is the question. Whether 'tis nobler in the mind to suffer the slings and arrows of outrageous fortune or ... or what? For god's sake, outrageous fortune or what? I must know. I've got to finish this thing, otherwise I need something else to drown out this—

" ... tried a different color of lipstick this morning and—"

I was alone, I took a ride, I didn't know what I would find therrrrrrrre! Another road where maybe I—

Huh? Lipstick?

Apparently, and without one shred of participation from me, the young woman has exhausted her anger, and she's now bubbling over with cheeriness as if the previous reaming never happened. "So, I was on my way to work and my car stalled, so I thought I'd walk. Bad idea. Too much rain. Anyway, I saw you sitting in your car and thought you wouldn't mind too much if I joined you."

"I guess that's okay." She'd hate me for thinking this, but she's nice-looking, even sopping wet and hyperventilating with anger.

"No problem," she says, sniffing the air. "Man, did you burn a load of compost in here, or what?"

"No, just a hit off my pipe. Want some?" I say, reaching toward the glove compartment.

"Never touch the stuff. The body's a temple, you know. And I'm a rabbi's daughter."

"You're kidding."

"Nope. In fact, I'm studying to be a rabbi myself."

Whether it's the result of the pot, the absurdity of being trapped in a car or the fact that this lunatic will someday be a rabbi, or some combination of the three, I'm not entirely sure, I start giggling.

She stares at me for several moments, and I get the sense she's searching my face for an explanation, and finds nothing but dimwittedness. "There's something about my becoming a rabbi you find amusing?"

Uh, oh. I've offended her again. "Well, I, uh ..."

"What, you think I should spend my life bringing pound cake to B'nai B'rith meetings?"

"No, sorry. I just pictured you as a rabbi. You know, they're always kind of serious and bearded and everything."

"Any chance you can start the car and turn on the heat? These shmatas I'm wearing are soaked."

"It looks like the water is receding a little," I say. "Want me to drive you to work?"

"That would be great," she says, letting me wriggle off the hook. "Head toward Santa Monica and Crescent Heights."

I pull the car away from the curb and turn north on Fairfax.

"Some reason you don't use the windshield wipers?" she says.

"Yeah, they don't work."

"And the heater?"

"Ditto."

"What's a nice Jewish boy like you doing driving around in this piece of dreck?"

I'm momentarily tongue-tied. Being recognized as a Jew always seems to startle me, a reaction I suppose I've inherited from my parents who seem to regard our ethnicity as a closely guarded secret. "I don't put much stock in possessions," I finally say, hoping to impress her with a little trendy socialism. "You know, there's no point in allowing myself to be defined by my car."

"Unemployed, huh?"

"Yes."

"And you're, what … seventeen, eighteen?"

"Nineteen," I say, slightly insulted.

"And you're, what, pre-law at UCLA? "Pre-med at USC?"

"I'm not pre-anything. I'm a cinema major at City College."

"Cinema, huh? I just wrote a screenplay for a rock opera that's set in a delicatessen."

"What's it called?"

"*Schmeer!* But that's just a working title." She smiles at me for the first time, and we're content to listen to Alice Cooper shriek *Under My Wheels* for a few minutes, until finally she opens the glove compartment. "You got anything to nosh on? I'm starving."

"Sorry. No."

"That's okay. I'll get something at the theater."

That perks me up. "Theater? You an actress?"

"Candy girl."

"I'm not following you."

"My father owns a couple of theaters, and I work at one of them. I sell candy."

"I thought your father's a rabbi."

"He is. But he dabbles in entertainment on the side. My name is Rachel," she says, extending the hand she's been wiping on her jeans.

"I'm Dennis," I say, shaking it.

"You looking for a job, Dennis?"

"As a rabbi in training, in your rock opera, or at your dad's theater?"

"He's looking for a projectionist."

I make a left onto Santa Monica. The rain, emulating her mood, has lightened. People are leaping off curbs, over shrinking pools of water, rushing through traffic, and hopping into previously abandoned cars. "Aren't projectionists in some kind of union?"

"I guess the guys at the big theaters are. But you'd be working at a small place," she says, taking a business card out of her purse and handing it to me. "Why don't you go see him after you drop me off?"

"Today?" I say, looking down at my cut-off jeans and squishy shoe.

"Pah! He's a very easy guy to get along with."

I see two small theaters side by side. "This it?" I say, pulling over to the curb. The marquee on the smaller of the two theaters says, in giant blue neon script: QUICKIE THEATER, and under that, in large black plastic letters, REAR WINDOW. A Hitchcock film. Nice. Working in a little art house like this will give me a chance to watch some of the old classics I'm required to see in cinema class.

"Yeah, this is it, but pull around to the back."

I drive past the theaters and make a right at the first street, and another right into the alley, then nose the car into a space marked Theater Personnel Only. Rachel hops out of the car.

"Aren't you going to shut the engine off and go see my dad?" she says through the open door.

I'm completely unprepared for this and the idea of a man of the cloth interviewing me for a job unnerves me. "Well ... I probably should go—"

"Jesus, don't be such a nebbish, Dennis," she says, kisses the air at me, and disappears through a door in the back of the theater.

The door closes behind her and I feel stunned. What's a rabbi likely to ask me during the interview? Will he want to know if I have any theater experience? What'll I say if he asks which temple I attend? Will my cinema classes be a plus? Will he be put off that I don't know how to operate a projector? God, I wish I had time to think about this.

*   *   *

As I stand outside a door that's illuminated from twenty feet away by a bare bulb hanging from the ceiling, I squint at the business card. There's not much information on it. It says Mr. K on one line and Chutzpah Theater Corporation on the next. He's not exactly verbose. I knock on the door and wait several moments, but there's no response, so I decide to open it. It's a little room filled with large bags of popcorn and boxes of candy bars. I try the next door and find a small bathroom. Behind a third door is a box of marquee letters on an Oriental rug. As I start to close the door, I hear a man's voice say, "Hello?"

I poke my head in, but see no one. "Yes. I'm looking for the rabbi."

A short, thin man with graying hair appears in front of me. "You'll find a rabbi at the synagogue down the street," he says with a heavy Eastern European accent and a kind of sing-song delivery to his speech.

"I'm sorry, I'm not here to worship. I'm here for a job interview," I say, suddenly self-conscious of my bare legs.

"Oh, come in," he says, clapping me on the shoulder and shutting the door behind me. "I'm the rabbi. Here," he says, pointing to a chair in front of a large wooden desk, "plant your tuchas right there."

"Thank you, sir." I'm relieved he's not at all like I expected him to be. He's wearing a polo shirt and jeans over a pair of Keds.

He sits at the desk, picks up a soft drink cup, and sucks at the straw while appraising me out of the corner of his eye. "I'm Rabbi Kaszynski, but while you're in this building I must ask that you refer to me only as Mister K."

"Mister K. Yes."

"I like to be called Rabbi when I'm in my synagogue, and Mister K when I'm in the theaters. I never mix my *milchich* with my *fleishich*, to borrow an old Yiddishism. You look like you understand what I'm talking about."

There it is again. Still, I have to laugh at his metaphor. He never puts dairy products on the same plate with meat, because that's just not kosher. Neither, apparently, is mixing his rabbinical identity with his theater persona.

"I think I get the gist, Rabbi." I see his eyebrows shoot up. "Oops, I'm sorry … Mister K."

"You'll get used to it. Now," he says, taking another sip, "who recommended you for a job here?"

"Your daughter, sir."

"Ah, Ruchala. A blessing on my house. She's a terrrrrrific girl," he says, drawing out the r's and placing them far back in his throat so that he sounds as if he's gargling.

For several moments there's a slightly uncomfortable silence, which he finally breaks by slurping the remains of the soft drink through the straw.

I'm groping for conversation. "She said she's studying to be a rabbi ... like you."

"Pah!" he says, waving a hand dismissively. "She's a young girl. She's studying a lot of things."

Another awkward moment. "So ... Rachel said you're looking for a projectionist."

"I am," the rabbi says, pulling a small box of candy from a desk drawer. He offers it to me. "Raisinettes?"

"No, thank you."

"Yes, our last projectionist got a little frisky with some of the customers ... the putz." He opens the box, pours a small handful of Raisinettes into his palm, slaps them into his mouth, then chews thoughtfully.

"Do you want me to tell you about my job history?"

He shakes his head. "No, that's not important."

"Well, I'm a cinema major," I say hopefully.

"Nice, but not relevant."

"Then I'm stumped. What do you want to know about me?"

"Only two things: can I count on you to show up at work every morning?"

"Absolutely, Mister K."

"Well, that's terrrrrific," he says, a huge grin on his face.

"And the second thing?"

The grin disappears as he leans forward in his chair. "I want you to leave my daughter alone."

"Alone?"

"She's a little ... fermischt right now."

"Sir, don't take this the wrong way, but I have no interest in your daughter."

"Good," he says, and looks slightly hurt.

"Anyway," I say, changing the subject, "I'm looking forward to seeing the Hitchcock movie you're playing."

"Hitchcock?"

"You know ... *Rear Window*?"

"Schmuck! It's a fagala movie."

"But isn't *Rear Window* a Hitchcock film?"

"I suppose it is. But this one's about a rear window of another kind."

"I'm not foll—" Oh, sweet Jesus.

"You seem startled. Do you have a problem with that?" he says.

"Well, I—"

"I mean, if you are philosophically opposed to homosexuality or if you're struggling with your own preferences, maybe this wouldn't be the best place for you to work."

Christ, what nineteen-year-old guy isn't sitting around wondering if he's homosexual or not? I'm pretty sure I'm not. At least when I fantasize about sex, men aren't included in the picture. But what exactly would it mean if I take this job? That I'm gay? More likely, it means I'm desperate for money. Would a straight guy work in a gay porno theater, knowing that all the customers will think he's gay? Would I ever even see the customers? I mean, I'll be a projectionist, in a booth somewhere far removed from the customers. No one's going to see me. Still … gay porn. Will I become gay if I watch that stuff? Can you catch it like a viral infection?

"You should know," he says, "these movies are really terrrrrible."

Damn. Just when I'm sure he's about to say terrrrrific again, he surprises me. "Okay," I begin slowly. "I guess I'll take the job."

"Good. You seem like a nice enough fellow." He gobbles another handful of Raisinettes. "You a fagala, son?"

I'm not entirely sure how I should answer this. Does he want me to be a fagala? On one hand, being gay would seem to suggest that I'd leave his daughter alone. On the other hand, it might imply that I wouldn't leave his customers alone. "No, sir," I say.

"Then bring a good book to read, because you sure won't want to watch the movies."

* * *

It's nine-thirty on Monday morning and I'm a half hour early for my first day on the job. Mister K instructed me to be here at this time, explaining that it would take approximately thirty minutes to learn what I need to know to begin my career as a theater projectionist. That's not much time to grasp the intricacies of a new job, and it has me a little worried. I try to peer through the glass door of the theater, but it's covered with butcher's paper, so I'm left to examine the single poster near the entrance. It shows a guy completely naked except for a red starburst strategically printed over his genitalia. The white printing on the burst says *All Male Action: As Rough as it Cums*. Nice. Subtle. Behind him is a second man, wearing only black leather cowboy chaps and one of those goofy motorcycle hats that Marlon Brando sported in the *The Wild One*. His outfit strikes me as ridiculous, being a mixture of genres, but I still feel a sense of excitement starting my first day on the job.

"You Dennis?" a voice behind me says.

I turn to see a man in his fifties, about five-two and rail thin, with a neatly trimmed mustache and a graying crew cut cropped so short I can see his scalp through the hair.

"Yes. That's me." I extend my hand.

"Sorry, I don't touch anybody's dick skinners. Nothing personal."

"No problem. I guess shaking hands is an archaic form of—"

"Okay, cut the shit, kid," he says, and takes a menacing step toward me. "I don't give a rat's ass what you think about the history of hand shaking. For all I know, you're just another Jew fag Mister K hired to keep an eye on the Americans. I don't know you and you don't know me. Let's just keep it that way. Capeesh?"

I get the feeling this is a soliloquy he's wanted to deliver for a long time, and I've somehow provided him with an audience. What a doofus this guy is, but I have to admit, he scares the crap out of me. We've been chatting for—what?—twenty seconds, and already he's refused to shake hands with me, asserted that Jews are homosexuals and that we're part of some vast conspiracy aimed at keeping gentiles—the real Americans—in their place. Part of me is offended by this raving simpleton and part is vastly amused by his imitation of the Third Cop on *Dragnet*.

He moves in very close to my face, emanating an intoxicating mixture of coffee, onions, and Hai Karate.

"Something you want to say, kid?"

Tempting. So tempting. But it's my first day on the job. There's plenty of time to rat him out to Mister K later on. "You've given this a lot of thought."

"Fuckin'-A right I have." He grins, which I take to mean he's telling me he's slightly unbalanced and that I'd better watch my step. He needn't worry.

Mercifully, he takes a step back, but keeps his eyes locked on mine, as if I'm suddenly going to produce a weapon. He slowly reaches into his back pocket and extracts a leather wallet, which he flips open to reveal a card of some sort in a clear plastic window. I guess I'm supposed to look at it and, at this point, I don't want to freak him out, so I focus on the card. It's an identification that says Federal Bureau of Investigation on it.

"You have any further questions, dickless?" He snaps the wallet shut.

I know I'm supposed to say something at this point, but I'm totally intimidated by this guy and I'm afraid anything I say will result in him producing a sap and beating me senseless with it.

"Yeah, I didn't think so," he says, chuckling. After several excruciating moments of him sneering at me, he turns on his heels, unlocks the front door of the theater, and disappears inside. It's all I can do to snap out of my stupor and follow him.

It's pitch black inside, pretty much the last place I want to be with this psychopath. I can hear him walking away from me, then up a couple of wooden steps, and the lights fade up. Now I can see that I'm in a little corridor that constitutes the lobby of the theater. There's a small counter to my left, with about twenty dusty boxes of candy in a glass case. The guy is in what looks to be a five by five plywood box, elevated two feet off the ground by cinder blocks. "Candy?" he says.

"No, thanks."

"Yeah, I don't blame you. This shit looks pretty uninviting. We can go about two weeks without selling a single box of it. We move a lot in the theater next door though."

He's being oddly chatty for a guy who's likely completely deranged. "You work in that theater, too?" I say bravely.

Hi smiles. "I work in that theater only. This theater is for peter puffers," he says, looking down at me from his perch in the box. "You got a boyfriend, sugar?"

"I'm straight."

"Then what are you doing working at this fag house?"

How to answer him without him wanting to punch me in the face? "It's a living."

He finds this strangely funny and makes a sound that approximates laughing, a sound his face doesn't look comfortable producing. "Well, there's a lot of turn-over here. You may end up at the other theater yet."

"I can't wait," I say, chuckling. Yep, we're just two guys sharing a laugh in a gay porn theater.

"You got that right," he says.

"So, what time do the box office person and the candy girl get here?"

"Buddy, you're it."

"I'm sorry?"

"You're the entire staff at this theater. There's no cashier and there's no candy girl. Everything is done from this wooden box, and you'd need Vaseline to fit another person into it."

God, as bad as this indoctrination process is, actually working here is going to be even worse. I'm going to be working a twelve-hour shift alone. No wonder Mister K said to bring a book. "How do I get lunch or take a whiz?"

"There's no bathrooms in this theater, for obvious reasons. So if your delicate little bladder won't hold out, just run in to the theater next door and use the john there." He takes a movie out of a film can and slides it onto a spindle on the projector, the same kind the bored audio/visual guys rolled into my junior high classes, with a little Bell & Howell plaque riveted to the heavy black case. "Okay, this is so simple, even a dipshit like you can understand it. Just wind the film through like this." He grabs the end of the film and threads it through the projector, feeding it into an empty reel. "Got it?"

"Got it." I don't really get it, but I'm not going to tell him that. "Is there a schedule I'm supposed to follow?"

"Yeah, a very strict schedule. You start the film when Homo Number One walks through the front door and pays his five bucks. When the theater's empty, the projector's off. No sense running the movie when no one's here to appreciate it. When you're ready to launch, just press this button on the cassette player to turn on the background music. The movies don't have their own sound track." He presses the button and a song blares through a speaker.

Maria! I've just met a girl named Maria.

As he listens to the music, his eyes begin to roll back in his head, his right hand comes up and begins conducting the music in what I believe to be three-quarter tempo.

"That's a little incongruous, isn't it?" I say, shouting over the music.

"What is?" he says, dropping his hand.

"*Maria.*"

"Haven't had any complaints yet. Anyway," he says, checking his watch, "I've got to go open the other theater. Any questions?"

"Seems simple enough."

"Fuckin'-A right." He climbs down from the box and heads for the door, remembers something, and turns around. "Only three things to remember: number one, if you need anything, I'll be right next door; number two, don't steal any money. I don't want the head Jew to come down on my ass; and number three, you can't let the customers have sex in the theater."

"Sex? In the theater?" I say, hoping I don't look too horrified.

"What, are you stupid? What do you think guys come to this place for? Because they're on the Academy Awards nominating committee? They're here to meet other fudge packers, but we can't let them act out the movies from their seats. If they get outta hand, just kick their asses out and tell them to go find a motel."

Man, it never occurred to me that I'd have to be the bouncer, too. "What if they don't want to leave?"

A look comes across his face that isn't so much a smile as it is a placeholder for one. "Oh, they will. Most of these guys are married businessmen, and the last thing they want is to create a scene."

"You mean, having sex in a theater isn't creating a scene?"

"Getting arrested is creating a scene. Apparently, getting a blowjob in public isn't. Toodles!" he says, and disappears through the door.

What in god's name am I doing here ... where men come to watch awful movies with other men

… where I'll have to confront them and possibly throw them out … in a place where I'm by myself? And I forgot my book!

This could turn out to be more boring and tedious than one of those street-construction jobs where a guy stands around all day holding a sign that says Slow. I didn't think anything could be worse than that. But here I am.

Screw it. It pays a buck-twenty-five an hour, and I'm here. And I'm going to make the best of this.

I walk into the seating area of the theater and I'm shocked by how small it is. There are four rows of seats, with three seats in each row. Jeez, a total of twelve seats. This isn't exactly Grauman's Chinese.

Well, not much to see here, so I go into the projection booth and look around. There's an office chair on casters, which glide noisily over the plywood flooring. I open a little metal box on the floor and find some money—fifty dollars in fives and ones. There's a small popcorn bin next to the candy display with a switch on the back of it. I flip it up and a heat lamp comes on to give the leftover popcorn that just-popped appearance.

Aside from the projector and the cassette player, there's only a telephone, although why someone would call here is a mystery to me. What could they want to know? When the movie starts?

Whenever you want. A description of the storyline? Insert tab A into slot B.

As I sit in the chair, rolling it back and forth in the small booth, I see one other curiosity: a security camera. Odd that it's not pointed into the theater. It's aimed directly at me. I smile and wave at it. "Hi, Mister K."

The door opens and the psycho comes back in, holding the door open. He traces his index finger in a circle on the butcher's paper, as if drawing something only he can see. "So … you want to get coffee sometime?"

* * *

I unlocked the front door precisely at ten, as I'd been ordered to by the crazed FBI agent, and I've been sitting in my seat now for two hours … seventy-two hundred of the slowest seconds I've ever seen tick by. And, exactly at noon, a man walks in. He's about six-three with long hair and a neatly trimmed beard, wearing a *Midnight Cowboy* buckskin jacket with leather fringe on it. Over his shoulder is a leather bag. I don't really know what I expected my customers to look like, but he's definitely not it. The man walks up to the window in the booth, slaps a fiver on the counter and walks past me into the theater. He's done this before.

Okay, my first customer. The adrenaline is starting to pump. Let's see, first I press the button on the tape recorder...

...and suddenly that name will never be the same to me. Maria ...

Ah, Maria ... the most beautiful sound I ever heard accompanying anal sex. All right, that's done. Now the projector. I twist a knob and an image flickers to life on the screen, although it's so out of focus, I can't begin to identify what it is.

As I turn the focus ring on the projector's lens, one thing occurs to me: I'm thinking that, at four feet high and three feet wide, this has got to be the largest testicle I've ever seen. At least, that's what I think it is when it comes into focus. Yes, there's definitely some hairs on it. As I gawk at the screen, the camera pulls back to reveal a tubby older man giving a very spirited blowjob to a younger man.

I poke my head out and see the buckskin guy sitting directly under the opening of the booth, no more than three feet away from me. He reaches into the leather bag he's placed on the seat next to him and extracts something that fills his hand. It looks like a squat jar of some sort, but I can't be sure in the dark. He unscrews the jar's lid, unzips his fly and pulls out an already erect penis. The heavy lifting done, he scoops out about four ounces of gooey material from the jar, and immediately proceeds to masturbate vigorously. The light from the screen reflects onto the jar and I can now see that it's a tub of Vaseline. Man, this guy came prepared.

But he's wacking off in my theater! And the last thing I want to do is interrupt him by engaging him in a conversation about the rules of the theater as explained to me by a total loon. Oh god, I'm sorry I took this job. Make him go away!

The phone rings and I nearly jump out of the projection booth. I stare at the phone, hoping it's not Mister K, until, on the third ring, I pick it up. "Hello?" I say timidly, trying not to disturb the buckskin man.

"Hi, baby ... I want to stick my tongue up your ass."

This is probably not Mister K. But it is a man and I don't want to talk to him and I don't want to see what that guy's doing with the Vaseline and I don't want to see the film and I do want to be anywhere else but here. "I ... uh ... don't ..."

"I know you don't have time right now, baby. But how about tonight?" the man says hopefully.

"Who are you trying to reach?" I say.

"You, honey. I've got a long tongue."

"No, I mean who are you trying to call?"

"Barry?" he says, with a hint of alarm.

"No ... this isn't Barry."

The sound of a phone brushing against his chin. A paper being uncrinkled. "Is this Hollywood 1-5223?"

"Yes, that's the number, but there's no Barry here."

"He's the projectionist."

"Not any more. I'm the projectionist. This is my first day."

There's silence for several seconds until the man erupts into sobbing.

"Is there something else you want?" I say, not altogether compassionately.

He sniffles, then blows his nose. "Would ... would you take a message for Barry, please?"

"I'm not sure I'll see him."

"Please ... in case you do."

"Okay," I say, sighing. I grab a pen and a small pad of paper from a shelf underneath the projector. "Okay, shoot."

"Shoot?"

"What's the message?"

Silence while he considers what he wants to say. More sniffling. "Just tell him this: I can't believe you'd go away and not tell me when we can see each other next, and where—"

"Not so fast. I'm trying to write this down. Okay, ' … see each other next and where …'"

" … and where I can find you."

"Okay, got it."

"And write this down: sucking you is different than sucking any other guy and—"

Oh, jeez. "Are you sure you want to say that?"

"Yes, he's got a beautiful dick."

"No, I mean the grammar. The rule is *better than, different from*."

"I'm sorry?"

"What you want to say is that sucking you is different from sucking any other guy. Or you could say that sucking you is better than sucking any other guy. See what I mean about the grammar?"

"I guess. Thanks for catching that."

"It flows much more nicely now."

"One more thing I want to say to him: I feel real bad right now."

"Adverb."

"What?"

"Bad is an adjective. You need to modify it with an adverb."

"Where did I go wrong?"

"Real is another adjective. What you want to say there is really bad … not real bad."

"Thank you. You're really improving this note."

"It pays to be precise."
"Well, I don't want him to think I'm illiterate."

* * *

In my wildest dreams, I would never have predicted that this would turn out to be the best job I ever had. It's not that the work is interesting. It's not. In fact, it's numbingly dull. What makes it, well, stimulating is the fact that, for the first time in my life, I'm reading every day. This week alone I've plowed through the entire *Lord of the Rings* trilogy, tearing myself away from Frodo, Arwen, and Gollum just long enough to toss one or more people at a time out of the theater for assaulting the White Tower in a way Professor Tolkien never imagined. But those brief interruptions aside, I find that the time passes surprisingly quickly when I'm transported into the world constructed by a brilliant author.

Unfortunately, it's also the worst job I've ever had in the sense that I'm completely sedentary for enormous stretches at a time and I feel as if my muscles are in a constant state of atrophy.

The delusional FBI agent was right about one thing: the guys I throw out of the theater seem incapable of inflicting anything more lethal than a hurt expression. It's a very clean process. I tell them to leave, they get out of their seats, then slowly saunter out of the theater without a word. Truth is, I feel sorry for them because I get the sense they're humiliated. Being butt-fucked in a public place isn't what does it. It's being told to stop.

If there's such a thing as a gay look, these guys don't have it. For the most part, they come here wearing suits and ties, and I have the suspicion they lead straight lives, and come to the theater to realize their gay fantasies—which, I imagine, don't include being thrown out by a skinny kid who's not even old enough to attend the theater in which he's acting as bouncer.

I've been here now for one week and tossed out at least eight guys, and not one of them has said a word in protest. I'm happy they don't start an argument with me, or they'd find out how scared and easily intimidated I am.

The candy counter isn't exactly the profit center it is in most theaters. Over the course of an entire week, my total sales have included one box of Milk Duds which, it turns out, were then inserted, one by one, up a man's rectum. There's got to be an ad campaign in there somewhere.

I haven't seen Mister K the entire week, although I'm pretty sure he's seen me, courtesy of the security camera. It occurs to me that there's no certainty the thing is even hooked up, but just having it pointed in my direction is enough to discourage me from stealing. Not that I'd be tempted in its absence.

For twelve hours a day, I only see a friendly face when I pop in to the theater next door to use the bathroom, and then at the end of my shift when Rachel stops by to collect the cash I've taken in for the day. She's quite chatty and seems to want to engage me in protracted discussions every evening. It's a little surreal to carry on a conversation with an attractive woman—about mundane subjects like our favorite music, books, or food—while on the screen a man is unloading a jet stream of jism across another man's face. It makes me wonder if concentration camp guards were able to discuss their favorite films while going through the mundane task of gassing Jews. Hey, Klaus, did you see *Destry Rides Again*? Ach, that Marlene Dietrich ... what a dish! By the way, would you hand me that canister?

But there's no time to ruminate on Mister K, Milk Duds, Rachel, or anything else. I've got eleven guys in the theater, every seat filled but one, and I'm pretty sure I'm going to be kept busy removing some of the feistier lads. I guess I shouldn't be too surprised by the turnout, considering it's Saturday night.

A man in a hard hat, jeans and a white tank top enters the theater, walks up to the booth and plops a large, rectangular metal box onto the candy counter, then reaches into his pocket and pushes a five-dollar bill at me.

"What's that?" I say.

"Money," he says.

"No, I mean the box."

"It's a tool kit. I just got off work."

"You do construction?"

"No, I'm an accountant," he says, glancing at the screen. He yanks the tool kit from the counter and stomps into the theater.

From the opening in the front of the booth, I see him take a seat in the front row, next to a man who smiles and eyes him curiously.

Amazingly, the theater is full, and in the next half hour, I have to turn three guys away.

Now that I've put the hobbits behind me, I've started a book that Rachel recommended: *Narcissus and Goldmund*. I have to say, a little bit of Herman Hesse goes a long way, and I'm already bored with his assertion of the duality of nature. His characters feel shallow and unformed, his descriptions superficial. I can't figure out what all the fuss is about this guy. You'd think I would have learned my lesson from the other tome of his that I read: *Siddartha*, a book all my friends raved about but left me unsure whether I should pursue self-indulgence or self-denial. After a spirited discussion about the book with one of my friends, I had sex with her, so I guess that question's answered.

I can't imagine that I'll have the stamina to read yet another of his books, and I wonder if I'll even crawl all the way through this one. But it's the only thing I've got right now. I'm on page forty-six, and it's a toss-up as to whether I should congratulate myself for making it this far or ponder if I'd have better spent my time creating alternative lyrics for the music that accompanies the films I'm showing.

> *The most god-awful sound I've ever heard ...*
> *Maria, Maria, Maria, Maria.*
> *Maria,*
> *that transvestite slut named Maria.*
> *And suddenly that name,*
> *you screamed it while you came*
> *on her.*
> *Maria,*
> *in the air it's the name that is hanging,*
> *with your friends poor Maria's gang-banging.*

I find that I look up from my book about once every forty-five minutes, just often enough to witness the kind of behavior I could never have imagined just seven days ago. This week alone I've seen enough foreign objects being stuffed up men's butts to stock the tool section at Sears. Among the many delights inserted was a socket wrench (without the spark plug attachment), twelve-inch length of hose (male end), barbecue grill cleaning brush (presumably, not the end with the bristles, but you never know), oblong light bulb (without the pesky desk lamp attached), and a putty knife (perfect for scraping walls). If only the manufacturers could see how their products are being used. I'd love to attend the board meetings.

                    CEO
(reading from handsomely bound report)
Gentlemen, it says here that our Number 526 barbecue cleaning brush is being used for—and it pains me—the carnal pleasures of homosexuals.

                    Toady #1
It pains you, sir?

CEO
To read about it, you idiot.

Toady #2
Sir, perhaps there's a marketing opportunity here.

CEO
I'm not following you.

Toady #3
What I think Bob is saying is that the use of this product in such an unprescribed manner represents a brand extension that perhaps we can take advantage of. Is that where you were going with this, Bob?

Toady #2
Absolutely, Steve. You see, J.B., research shows—and I believe the report begins in the addendum on page 24-F—that there are approximately eight million practicing male homosexuals in this country, many of whom use their barbecues on a regular basis. It's quite possible that they experience a form of

carbon intoxication from the fumes of burning charcoal that produces a rather unpredictable symptom.

>   CEO

And that is ...?

>   Toady #4

The need to stuff something up your ass, sir.

>   CEO
>   (deep in thought)

Yes, I see.

>   Toady #3

We owe it to our shareholders to develop new uses for our products, J.B.—even beyond what we at this table might consider traditional uses.

>   CEO

Manufacturing cost?

>   Toady #5
>   (reading from leather folio)

Seventeen cents, J.B.

                    CEO
Price at retail?

                  Toady #5
Approximately eight-fifty, wherever
better barbecue accessories are sold, J.B.

                    CEO
           (tapping fingers on table)
Let's move on this. Have the boys in
R&D see what they can come up with.

                  Toady #4
Will do.

                  Toady #2
Good call, J.B.

                  Toady #3
I smell a winner, sir.

Oddly, many of the objects used to heighten arousal were of an edible nature—at least they were prior to use. Some of the more interesting things I found include hot dogs (Oh, I'm glad I'm not an Oscar Mayer wiener!), jumbo carrots (recommended by doctors everywhere to improve eyesight), and a smashed Twinkie (lacking the requisite tensile strength for optimum insertion).

And that's just the stuff I found. The list would have been longer if I had the stomach to glance into the theater more often.

Equally inventive is the use of restraining devices. It seems that rope is just passé. No, today's modern buggerer is using lamp cord, phone wires, and anchor chain.

Which brings me back to *Narcissus and Goldmund*, a book I find so stupefyingly boring that I'll take any opportunity to avert my eyes, even if it means looking into the theater. A quick check reveals the construction worker, still in his hard hat, kneeling in front of the man (no longer wearing pants) sitting next to him. The tool box is open and I can see by the light of the projector that he's wrapping a healthy length of duct tape around the man's ankles, having already taped his hands behind his back. When he's satisfied that enough tape has been applied, he cuts the end neatly with a pair of scissors and, curiously, hangs the roll of tape on the man's erect penis, as if returning a tool to the wall display at the local hardware store.

"Hey!" I shout, leaning into the theater. "You can't do that in here. You're going to have to leave. Now!"

Eight of the twelve patrons get up and amble wordlessly out of the theater, one of them hopping due to the fact that his legs are bound together. The roll of duct tape falls to the floor and skitters under a seat.

* * *

Week number two inches its way to its end in the manner I expected. I've tossed out fourteen patrons, an act that, on my first day, I regarded as bravery but now know that it could be completed every bit as successfully by a nine-year-old Campfire Girl. A syringe was left sitting on a seat, along with a length of rubber surgical tubing. I'm not exactly sure what I'd have done if I'd caught the person using it. *Narcissus and Goldmund* remained to the end as boring as I predicted it would be. I decide that I'd rather be locked in a room with Rudolf Hess than with Herman Hesse.

It's two-thirty on Sunday afternoon. I unlocked the front door at noon but have yet to see my first customer. Fine by me. You can only hear *Climb Every Mountain* so many times before you consider flinging yourself off the highest peak.

Coincidentally, the front door opens and I hear footsteps coming toward the projection booth. Over the two weeks, I've learned to affect a bored tone to my voice in order to begin the process of fending off the advances of randy patrons.

"Five dollars," I say, not looking up from *Portnoy's Complaint*.

"Can I blow you instead?"

It's Rachel, and she's laughing at what must surely be a stunned expression on my face.

"Sure, but don't expect that to get you any popcorn," I say, setting the book on the counter. "What brings you here in the middle of the day?"

"Congratulations. You're being promoted."

"To what? I mean, what higher calling is there in life but to show gay porn films?"

"Showing straight porn films. You're going next door."

"Really?" I say, feeling a rush of excitement. "What happened to the tight-ass FBI agent?"

"He was arrested for impersonating a federal officer."

"Wow!"

"Yeah. He apparently tried to pick up a hooker in Griffith Park who turned out to be a vice cop."

"No shit," I say, chuckling at the irony. "She busted him?"

"He."

"He ... who?"

"The hooker was a guy ... a male prostitute."

"Wow again."

"Anyway, let's lock up this dump and go next door."

* * *

As Rachel and I enter the projection booth, my first thought is how luxurious it is. Where the gay theater had a plywood box with a door and two openings cut out of it—one to take the patrons' money and one to project the film—the straight theater's booth is roughly ten by fifteen feet—a veritable ballroom, so to speak. I look through the window at the screen and see a close-up of a man's penis thrusting vigorously between a pair of large jiggling breasts. I notice that the movie has its own soundtrack which, at this particular moment, consists of a woman's breathless cries of ecstasy. As Rachel and I watch the film, two female hands on the screen reach up and press the breasts together creating, I presume, a more rugged flight path.

Yeah. That's more like it.

I look up and notice Rachel staring at me, and I instantly blush.

"You'll get used to it," she says.

There are so many ways to interpret that, none of which I care to pursue right now. Instead, I look out at the theater to see what appears to be eight or ten men, each sitting as far from one another as possible, in a theater that seats about a hundred and fifty people.

"See that Glade up there?" she says, pointing at a can of air freshener on a shelf. "After the movie's over, take that can and walk through the theater with it, spraying a little bit every so often."

"Seriously?"

"Think of this place as the Paramount, with tit fucking," she says.

"That'd make a nice slogan."

Rachel spends the next five minutes showing me around the booth, including the much larger projector, the amplifier for the audio track, and the motorized film rewind machine—everything I need to know to unleash pornography on the heterosexual citizenry of Los Angeles.

"Excuse me," a man says, poking his head through the doorway that leads from the lobby to the projection booth. "I'd like to buy some Red Vines."

"Enjoy your new job," she says to me, and disappears through the door, closing it behind her.

Some observations on how a straight porn theater is different from a gay porn theater: 1) I've gotten to know the captain of the local fire department very well, since he comes to the theater at least twice a week for surprise "fire inspections." Interestingly, he seems able to somehow divine the state of our fire exits, sprinkler system, and emergency lighting from his seat in the back row, a jumbo tub of popcorn on his lap. Several members of the Los Angeles Police Department apparently find the theater to be a logical hideout for ne'er-do-wells, judging by the frequency of visits our boys in blue make, often with elaborately dressed young ladies. Not once did any of these guys visit the gay theater. And not once did any of them pay to get in; 2) When I noticed that there's no easy access from the projection booth to the seating area of the theater, Rachel explained that I'm not required to throw out patrons who engage in sexual conduct. Why, I asked, if I was required to toss out gay patrons, am I not responsible for throwing out straight patrons? She rolled her eyes and said, "Isn't it obvious? They only bust us for the gay theater." Well, it didn't seem obvious to me. And it doesn't seem particularly fair; 3) Walking around a theater during intermission while spraying Glade is humiliating for both me and the patrons. What I'm telling them is that it smells bad in here, and they're responsible for it. To be perfectly honest, it smelled worse in the gay theater, but the admission fee didn't include air freshener; 4) A large number of single women come to the theater. I found this surprising until I was on a Glade-spraying mission one day and discovered a particularly attractive young lady administering mouth-to-genitalia resuscitation. Lesson learned: a single woman in a porn theater isn't here to expand her knowledge of the finer points of movie-making—although she's likely boning up on another subject; and 5) Rachel was wrong about me getting used to it. I find that I've got an almost permanent erection which, given the fact that there's a security camera mounted in the corner of the booth (not to mention Rachel's tendency to pop in whenever she gets bored), prevents me from even thinking about wacking off. I feel like a diabetic working in a Sees Candy store.

The door opens and Rachel comes in carrying a large, sealed manila envelope. "Would you mind doing me a favor?" she says.

"You have only to command, my princess."

"Do you know where the candy room is?"

"Yeah, I think I saw it the day I interviewed with your dad."

"Okay, great. Bring back a case of Junior Mints. And drop this on my dad's desk," she says, handing me the envelope.

"No problem," I say, turning the envelope over in my hands. "You mind if I ask a question about your dad?"

"Go right ahead."

"Does he ever comment to you on the dichotomy of being a member of the clergy while at the same time owning two theaters that feature pornography?"

I'm instantly sorry I asked the question, but Rachel appears to be giving it serious thought. "Well, he runs a reform congregation," she says, smiles, and heads out to the candy counter.

A glance over at the projector tells me that there's about twenty minutes left in the movie, plenty of time to run these errands and be back to turn up the house lights. I close the door to the booth behind me.

"Junior Mints, right?" I say.

She peers through the glass of the candy counter. "Oh, and some Sno-Caps, too."

"Got it." I swing open the door to the theater and stand in the back, letting my eyes get used to the darkness. On the screen a mailman is giving a "special delivery" to a woman and her sister.

Thoughtful of him to bring packages for both of them. In the far back corner of the theater, a young blond girl is sitting on a man's lap. Something tells me she's not his niece and he's not bouncing her on his knee. Oh well. Another day at the office.

My pupils sufficiently dilated, I trudge down the aisle and go through a door behind the screen. It's an odd place to be, knowing that a porn movie is lighting up the screen only inches away, only the audience can't see me on the other side of it. Another doorway leads to a hall. I tap on Mister K's door, wait a few seconds, then open it. There's no one home so I move to the desk and drop the envelope on it. As I turn to leave, I spot some light radiating from under the desk. I walk around it and stand next to Mister K's chair. There, on an aluminum stand, are three small monitors. On the left-most one is Carl, the new guy they hired in the gay theater. I smile when I recognize that he's reading the copy of *Narcissus and Goldmund* I left behind. I watch him for several moments and notice that he's glancing into the theater about every ten seconds. Yep, he's as bored as I was reading that stuff. I can see the inside of my new projection booth on the middle monitor. Good thing I don't jerk off in there. The third monitor is dark and I notice it's switched off. I'm curious where the third security camera is, and I consider turning on the monitor, but I don't want to be late getting back to the booth. I close Mister K's door behind me, move down the hall, open the door to the candy room, and switch on the light.

Odd, at times like these, the things that make an immediate impression. Mister K is leaning back against a wall, his hands behind his head—as if he's laying down, casually watching TV, except that right now he's standing up. It's also odd what you don't notice at first. Like the redhead in knee-socks and pigtails who's kneeling in front of Mister K. Holy Christ! The rabbi's not performing a bat mitzvah in there.

He's startled when the lights snap on and pushes the redhead away from him.

"Hey!" she says. "You didn't pay for any rough stuff."

He quickly pulls up his pants. "Get out!" he says, yelling at me.

I quickly shut the door, scramble up the hall, through the room behind the screen, up the aisle, past the candy counter, and into the booth—my pulse pounding in my head.

"Hey," I hear Rachel say, "where's the candy?"

But I close the door to the booth behind me and lock it. After a few moments, Rachel tries the door.

The movie ends and I turn up the dimmer for the house lights. I put the film on the rewind machine, thread it into an empty reel, flip the switch, then stand back and watch for three minutes as the film flies from one reel to the other, sweat pouring off of me, my breath coming out in rasps, the sound of roaring surf in my head. I put the film on the projector, thread it carefully, then plop down in the chair.

What in god's name do I do now? Twiddle my thumbs? Read *Portnoy's Complaint*? Casually chat with Rachel? Tell her why I didn't bring back any candy?

It's in the middle of this thought that the knob turns, the door opens, and I see Rachel, a key in her hand. She's glaring at me.

"You piece of shit," she says, irrationally angry about the candy. "My dad just called me from his office."

Oh, shit. But why the hell is she angry at me?

"And he's very disappointed in you." she says.

"Rachel, I'm so sorry. I didn't mean—"

"Didn't mean what? To take only a hundred dollars out of the envelope?"

Oh holy shit mother of god.

"My dad wants your ass out of here," she says, her lower lip trembling. "Now!"

So that's how her dad is playing this. What a weird way to—

Rachel leaps at me and begins pinwheeling her arms at my head. I instinctively bring my hands up to protect myself. "Jesus, Rachel ... what are you doing?"

But she's unconscious with fury right now, and acting it out in the most violent way I've ever seen. She's breathing heavily as she attempts to land blows on my face and head and emitting an animal scream. Worse, she's so enraged and adrenalized, she's not slowing down. I manage to grab her left wrist and hold it tightly, but that only seems to infuriate her more. She's punching at me even faster with her free hand, until I finally catch that one, too, and she immediately starts kicking at me.

"Rachel, you've got to stop and let me explain what happened."

But she doesn't stop, and somehow manages to kick me in the ribs, pain shooting through my body. "Stop it ... stop it!" I say, screaming at her. She aims a kick at my groin that I block with my knee, and I see pain on her face. I let go of a wrist and use my free hand to grab her throat and drive her back against the wall. Her eyes are starting to roll up and flutter, and I relax my grip only slightly, knowing I have to squeeze hard enough to keep this creature off of me.

Her breathing is coming out in husky gasps, mixed with fury and sobbing wails. Her face is wet with tears and snot, and I'm so conflicted by what I'm seeing in front of me. Mostly, I'm feeling pity for this woman, for the rage she's experiencing and for having a father who betrays her and her mother and then wickedly lies about it. At the same time, I need for her to like me, to not think badly of me, yet understand the truth of this awful situation.

We stare into each other's eyes for what feels like a full minute, our breathing slowing down slightly. I let go of her other wrist, testing her will to break free, but she remains still, pinned against the wall, my hand remaining on her throat.

I understand that whatever I say to her right now, if she hears it at all, will have consequences, and I'm doing the best I can to run each word through my head, playing them like little disjointed film strips until I find the one I can live with.

"Rachel ... your dad ... he's not telling you the truth."

Her eyes instantly narrow into slits and her jaw sets. "Then tell me," she says, looking as if she's about to spit at me.

"It was only fifty dollars."

* * *

My foot is quivering on the gas pedal and I need to quit thinking about this while I'm driving, so I flip on the radio. "Batten down the hatches, boys and girls," the caffeinated disc jockey says. "We're due for about three straight days of truly evil rain. The weather dude at our ABC sister station says that you may want to avoid driving for the next few days ... unless you don't mind floating down the street. Here's Albert Hammond with *It Never Rains in Southern California*."

Bachelor No. 3

My friend Nicole and I have just finished our bowls of Campbell's French Onion soup and, if tonight is like every other night that she comes over, we'll put on some Moody Blues or Iron Butterfly and have sex.

I take the bowls to the sink in my little kitchen as Nicole absent-mindedly flips through a copy of *TV Guide* that's on the card table in the corner of my living room.

"Hey, want to do some windowpane?" she says from the other room.

"What's that?" I say over the running tap water.

"You don't know what windowpane is?"

"Apparently not," I say, a little annoyed. "Is it some kind of clear drink?"

"How did you manage to be the only guy to grow up in L.A. who doesn't know what windowpane is?"

"I'm sure there are three or four other people who don't know what it is."

"Aren't you embarrassed to be so ignorant about a cultural reference?"

"I'm stunned. Mortified. Drained of all normal human emotion. I can get in touch with no feeling other than complete self-loathing. By the way, you want some cheesecake?"

"Yeah, cut me a slice."

I slide a Sara Lee cheesecake out of the fridge, cut a diminutive slice for Nicole, then bring the rest of it into the living room. "Dig in."

"Aren't you having any?" Nicole says.

"Yeah, this is my piece," I say, indicating the seven-eighths of the cheesecake still in the pie tin. "So, what's windowpane?"

"It's anything you want it to be."

"Really?" I say, cramming a forkful of cheesecake into my mouth. "If I want it to be a salad dressing, will it do that?"

Nicole, who tends to take bites no larger than she can fit underneath a fingernail, sets her fork down. "What are you talking about?"

"I thought we were talking about windowpane."

"We are. What's that got to do with salad dressing?"

"You said it's anything I want it to be. If you're going to talk in advertising jingles, you have to expect some confusion."

Nicole rolls her eyes up, a clear signal that she's exasperated because I'm not playing the game the right way. She wants me to be more curious and inquisitive, more fascinated by her circumspection. Finally, she pushes the cheesecake away, having consumed at least seventeen micrograms of it. "Maybe I should just go home."

"Don't do that," I say. "I really want to know what windowpane is."

Nicole opens her purse and pulls out her driver's license. "This … is windowpane," she says reverentially, offering the card to me as if presenting the Holy Grail.

I take it from her and stare at her little scowling photo. "Your driver's license is—"

"Turn it over," she says impatiently.

I do, and notice two tiny squares of what look like cellophane stuck to the back of it.

"These little guys are windowpanes?" I say.

"Windowpane," she says. "It's the best acid you can get."

She's presumably showing me her little windowpanes because she wants us to take it together, an idea that's not totally without some merit. Sure, I've had lots of opportunities in the past—hell, what twenty-year-old kid in L.A. hasn't? But I'd always heard it can get pretty freaky, and it's really important for your first time to take it with someone you have complete trust in. And I'm pretty sure Nicole's not—

"Okay, here's what I'm thinking," she says. "Right now it's six-forty-five. If we take the acid now, nothing's going to happen for at least an hour or so. So, let's take it, then go for a walk around the neighborhood until seven-thirty. That'll help speed things up. We'll come back to the apartment, put on some music, and I'll give you the best hummer of your life ... until eight o'clock. We'll probably just be coming on to the acid by then, so we'll go back outside and look at all the things in the neighborhood we saw earlier, except now we'll be on acid, and it'll be cool because it'll look so different. We'll get back here at about nine-thirty and then I'll leave, 'cause I'm meeting a guy tonight who's playing in a band. So you'll have a totally groovy time enjoying your first acid experience alone."

I didn't hear a word she said after hummer. "Okay. Let's do it."

She pries one of the little windowpanes up with her fingernail. Sitting on the tip of her finger like that, it looks so benign and fragile, but I imagine it's going to produce a wild ride for the next several hours. She transfers it to my finger, then pries up the other little square. We hook our arms, as if preparing to drink champagne.

"Down the hatch," she says, giggling, and we both touch our acid-laden fingertips to our tongues and swallow.

"Well, this ought to be interesting."

"Mind if I use the bathroom?" she says, already closing the bathroom door behind her.

As I move over to the couch, I hear her unzip in the bathroom, pee, and flush the toilet. She reappears with a piece of paper in her hand.

"What's that?" I say.

She reads it carefully. "It says Tuesday, September 28th, seven-thirty, *Dating Game*."

"Oh, yeah. I wondered where that went."

"I found it on the floor behind the toilet."

"I must have knocked it off the tank."

"You wrote yourself a note about watching something on TV?"

"No, it's an appointment to audition for *The Dating Game*."

"Seriously?" she says, smiling. "You actually want to be on that piece of shit?"

No, I don't actually want to be on that piece of shit. I applied for it because my brother Ken appeared on the show, and since my life never feels as interesting as his, I figure I can't go wrong overlaying his experiences on top of mine. But damned if I'm going to tell Nicole that. I'm also not going to tell her that the winner of the show he was on got an all-expenses-paid trip to Cancun along with the comely lass that chose him. Ken, usually glib and irresistible, suffered from an enormous case of performance anxiety that night and provided responses to the girl's questions that were totally incomprehensible. His consolation prize was a shoe shine kit, worth about nine dollars. Hey, who wouldn't want to be on a show like that?

"You never know, I could win a cool trip."

"Well, it says here," she says, running a finger (the one that had only moments before held a square of windowpane) along the note, "that the audition is on Tuesday, the twenty-eighth at seven-thirty."

"So?"

"That's today?"

A jolt of electricity surges through my body. "Oh, fuck."

"And it's a half hour from now."

* * *

We pull into the parking lot with exactly two minutes to spare, park the car, and run in to the building where the audition is to be held.

"There's the elevator," Nicole says, and we make a dash toward it but are intercepted by a uniformed guard, an enormous black man with a gold tooth.

"Where you two going?"

"I've got an audition for *The Dating Game*," I say, out of breath.

He seems to be spending an uncomfortably long time looking at my legs, then down and at my feet, and for the first time I notice what I'm wearing: running shorts, a tank top, and some tennis shoes.

"They slummin' now?" he says.

"Look, I'm gonna be late."

"Name?"

"Uh ..."

"Dennis Globus," Nicole says.

The guard tips his eyes down to a list on a clipboard. "Okay, sign in."

I quickly scrawl my signature next to my printed name, and Nicole and I dash for the elevator.

"Ninth floor," the guard says. "Don't forget to be effervescent. They like that."

"Thanks," I shout, and repeatedly jab at the elevator button. It arrives, and the two of us plunge in. As we blast off, I can hear the machinery of the elevator in motion: cables pulling, gears turning, hydraulics hissing. Odd, but I've never noticed that elevators make these noises. Each floor we pass produces a little ding, a musical note that changes at each floor. It's not until we arrive at the ninth floor that I realize we've just heard the intro to *Inna Gadda Da Vida*. As the elevator doors open, a cool rush of air hits my face. "Can we stay?" I say to Nicole. "I want to hear what else the elevator can play."

She smiles at me. "Wow, that didn't take long."

"Can I help you?" a self-consciously perky, middle-aged redhead at the reception desk says.

Nicole takes my hand and leads me to the woman. I start to answer her, but decide instead to touch her long flowing beard that's growing even as I watch it.

"It's very soft," I say.

"Good for you," the woman says. "Name?"

"Dennis Globus," Nicole says.

The woman looks on her list, finds my name, and puts a check mark next to it. "Have a seat in the waiting room. They'll bring you into the audition room in a few minutes."

"I go sit down now?"

"Yes."

I take a seat in a chair at the side of the reception desk.

"Sir, in there," she says, pointing to the waiting room.

"That's the waiting room," I say to Nicole.

"Yes, I know. That's where she wants us to wait." Nicole leads me into the next room and we take a couple of seats. The room's not particularly large, and there are a dozen or so folding chairs, their backs against the walls. Each of the chairs is occupied by young men and women all around my age who, I guess, are also trying out for a coveted spot on the show. The men are all wearing sports jackets and ties, and the women are each in sexy evening dresses. "Hi," I say to a woman sitting next to me, a thin blond with about seven inches of cleavage showing. "Hey, those are big!" I say.

She crosses her arms across her chest and begins a conversation with the woman sitting on the other side of her.

"I hope she's the bachelorette asking you questions," Nicole says. You're off to a great start."

"I'm going to be Bachelor Number One."

Covering the walls are large framed photos from *The Dating Game*. In every one, host Jim Lange shares a laugh with the contestants or joins them in blowing an exaggerated kiss to the studio audience. I find it somewhat unusual that in one photo, where his head would normally be, sits the head of an anteater. I'm wondering if maybe that was from a Halloween show, but then the tongue flicks out at me and I reflexively pull back in my chair. "Dennis," the anteater says, "I have one piece of advice for your audition tonight. Stay away from fire ants."

A door from an adjoining room opens and an extremely tall woman in a business suit steps in and the room falls silent. The faces of all the hopefuls look up expectantly. "Good evening, everyone," she says.

There's mumbling of hellos and good evenings from the group.

"Who are you?" I say.

She looks down at me for several moments, then grins broadly. "I'm Chessy Morgan, associate producer of ... *The Dating Game*," she says, putting a slight pause before the name of the show in order to underline its importance.

"Hi, Chesty."

"Yes," she says, and opens the black notebook she's carrying. "Tonight, we're going to have a lot of fun, because we'll be playing ... *The Dating Game.* You all know the rules."

"I do," I say enthusiastically.

"Well, that's fine. You look like you're eager to play."

"I think I'm hallucinating!"

"Isn't that nice! I hope everyone enjoys themselves as much as he is. In fact, the producers are looking for people who aren't shy about showing their enthusiasm." Chesty looks around the room at the hungry faces. "Well, you're all attractive people," she says, then stops momentarily to linger on me, apparently finding me especially appealing. "So now the producers want to see how well you play the game. And just like on the actual show, we'll have a lovely young bachelorette asking exciting questions of three charming bachelors. Are you ready to play ... *The Dating* Game?"

Another unintelligible group mumbling of false enthusiasm.

"Okay," the woman says, scanning a page in her notebook, "we'd like to see Megan Lowry, Paul Shorter, Michael Fletcher, and Dennis Globus. Follow me into the game room."

As I stand, Nicole takes my hand. "Dennis, you follow in the footsteps of Castañeda."

I'm about to ask her if she's referring to the left-fielder of the White Sox or that author guy—and what either of them might have to do with ... *The Dating Game*—but Chesty turns on her heels and I figure I better follow her and the other three contestants into the next room. She instructs the girl, Megan, to take a seat on one side of the room, then gestures for the guys to sit in the three chairs facing her. "Okay, guys, ready to impress a beautiful young lady?"

"You bet," Paul says.

"I'm ready," Michael says.

"Are there any fire ants in here?"

Before she can answer, two casually dressed men in their thirties enter the room and take a seat on a sofa that faces the playing field now occupied by the four contestants. Chesty smiles at them. "I think we're ready to play ... *The Dating Game*," she says.

"Thank you, Chessy," the more important of the two men says. "This is a great-looking group. I want you to relax, be quick on your feet and, above all, have fun. Now, Paul ... you'll be Bachelor Number One ..."

"I wanted to be Bachelor Number One," I say, not happy about the demotion.

The man smiles at me. "You'll be Bachelor Number Three tonight. But don't worry, statistics show that Bachelor Number Three is chosen every bit as often as Bachelor Number One."

I know the guy is speaking to me, but I find myself fascinated by the fact that his two eyes have moved inward and merged into one huge eye. Okay, that kind of shit just doesn't happen. That's the acid talking.

"Thanks, Mark," Chesty says, then turns to the lone female contestant. "Okay, Megan, it's time to get to know these handsome eligible bachelors."

It's Megan's cue to ask her first question, but she's paralyzed with fear and begins ripping little bits out of the folded piece of paper she's holding.

"Is there something you want to ask the bachelors, Megan?" Chesty says, prompting her.

Megan's now licking her lips as if she just finished eating dinner out of a dog dish.

"Megan?" Chesty says.

Megan manages to snap out of her coma long enough to unfold the paper, which now resembles a doily, and gawks at it for several seconds. "Bachelor Number Three," she begins tentatively, "how are you tonight?"

"Whoa, one question at a time!" I say.

"I'm sorry," she says to Chesty. "I'm a little nervous."

"You're doing fine, Megan. Go ahead and ask a question."

"Oh, okay. I'm sorry. Let me start over. Bachelor Number One ... if we were the only two people on a deserted tropical island, what would we do for entertainment?"

The two men on the sofa chuckle at what is presumably the provocative nature of the question.

Bachelor Number One, Paul, strikes an oversized grin, designed to communicate to the producers what a wonderful time he's having. "We'd spend our time working on my Porsche ... you know, listening to the engine rev, making little adjustments, polishing the chrome."

That's either the acid again or he just delivered what is quite possibly the stupidest answer I've ever heard.

Megan forces a nervous laugh. "Bachelor Number Two ... if we were the only two people on a deserted tropical island, what would we do for entertainment?"

Bachelor Number Two, Michael, picks out a spot on the ceiling, and stares at it dreamily, as if his mind is taking him to a faraway place. "I'd take out my guitar every evening and serenade you with a love song."

He's in for a surprise because I'm going to splinter that guitar against a palm tree. Which reminds me—I like palm trees. So smooth. Just yards of brown bark, and then cool fronds waving in the breeze. So calming. So peaceful.

"Bachelor Number Three ..." Megan says, looking at the paper yet again for prompting on a question she's already asked twice before, "if we were the only two people on a deserted—"

"I like coconut milk," I say.

Megan clearly likes my answer. So much so that her dress is changing colors—from electric blue to fluorescent orange to hot pink to radiant purple to lime green. Yeah, this lady digs me!

Chesty clears her throat. "Would you like to elaborate, Bachelor Number Three?"

"No, I like coconut milk just the way it is. I tried adding Nestle's Qwik to it once, but that just ruined it."

Chesty exchanges glances with the sofa guys, who smile. They obviously share my appreciation for palm trees.

"Okay, Megan ... another question," Chesty says.

"Can I go tinkle?" Megan says.

I begin braying with laughter, and accidentally fart.

"Can it wait, Megan?" the less important of the two men on the sofa says. "We'll only be a few minutes."

"I really have to make potty."

"We're almost done." Chesty makes a note in her book. "Your question, Megan?"

"Bachelor Number Two ... a year from now, when we're on *The Newlywed Game*, we'll probably win, 'cause you'll know so much about me. How did you learn so much?"

The two men on the sofa look at each other and burst out laughing. "That's a good question, Megan," the more important of the two says.

"First time I've heard that one," the lesser guy says.

Megan's beaming now, knowing she made a good impression.

Michael smiles and nods. "We'll take long walks on the beach at night, and we'll do nothing for hours but talk. I'm really looking forward to getting to know everything about you, Megan."

Maybe they'll talk about what I did to his guitar.

"Bachelor Number Three ..."

"Is it too late to be Bachelor Number One?"

"We've got a Bachelor Number One," Chesty says, and if I'm not wrong, she sounds a little cross. "Megan?"

"Bachelor Number Three ... a year from now—"

"Here's my plan," I say. "After we get back from Cancun, we'll do a couple of peyote buttons, and then walk to Denny's and sit in a booth all night. Man, that shit really opens your mind to the possibilities. Have you ever really thought about the Holocaust? God, the people who did that have got to be out of their fucking minds."

Good answer. It shows I care about my fellow man. And I can tell by the silence in the room that people are really thinking about it. It just proves you can never go wrong with the Holocaust. I only hope they heard the whole answer because the sound that Good Humor Ice Cream truck is making outside is driving me crazy. I can't believe how loud that music is.

Chesty whispers something in the ear of the more important man, and I see him look at me and nod. Yep, I'm totally in control now.

"Should I go on?" Megan says to Chesty.

"Continue, please."

"Bachelor Number One ... a year from now, when we're on *The Newlywed Game*, we'll probably win, 'cause you'll know so much about me. How did you learn so much?"

Paul seems momentarily stumped for an answer until struck by a lightening bolt of inspiration: "We'll take long drives together in my Porsche. And I guess we'll talk and stuff."

Christ.

"Really? Where will we drive to?" Megan says, enormously proud of her improvisational skills.

"Jeez, I don't know," Paul says. "Maybe to an auto parts store."

"Okay, final question," Chesty says.

"Okay, Bachelor Number One ... if I wore a dress that was a little too revealing, what would you do about it?"

"Ooh ... ooh ... can I answer that one?" I say, bouncing in my seat with my hand raised.

"Not yet, Bachelor Number Three," Chesty says.

This is boring. Worse, there's about five inches of water on the floor, but none of these dullards seems to realize it.

"There's no such thing as a dress that's too revealing," Paul says, laughing lasciviously. "I'd be happy to have you wear it when I see my friends at the Porsche Club of Southern California."

Hey, I'm starting to get the idea this guy has a Porsche.

"Bachelor Number Two ... if I wore a dress that was a little too revealing, what would you do about it?"

Michael's squirming in his seat and can't wait to answer. "I think a lady as lovely as you deserves to have a poem written especially for her. I'd call it The dress that revealed her inner soul."

"A poem ... for me?" Megan says, entranced. "How would it go?"

Yeah, you weren't ready for that, were you, Michael, you pandering simp!

Michael scrunches up his face, deep in thought. "It would go like this: 'Behold your nakedness in the night. This garment reveals a beauty that I might ... come to know. Lo, what is seen in all your nudity ... is to me not a crudity. It is your heart ... your soul ... your inner light."

Man, this guy's good. Who would have ever thought to rhyme nudity with crudity?

"That was just beautiful, Bachelor Number Two," Megan says to Michael, her hand over her heart, her eyelids fluttering. She looks up at Chesty. "Do I have to ask him this question?"

"Yes, and that'll wrap things up."

Megan mumbles something I can't hear. "Bachelor Number Three... if I wore a dress that—"

"Somebody wore a dress like that into the theater I used to work in and got a lot of attention. A guy sat down next to her and put his hand on her knee and they started making out. You know how those things go. It was getting hot and heavy, and pretty soon the guy was kneeling in front of her and sucking her dick."

The more important man leaps up off the sofa. "Okay, he says, excited, "I think we've heard just about—"

"Wait a minute. I'm not finished." But goddamn it, I've lost my train of thought, what with all the noise from that ice cream truck and the navies of Caesar Augustus and Marcus Antonius engaged in battle on the floor right in front of me. Hey, there's a little Porsche motoring through the water, but Augustus's navy just performed a flanking maneuver and have it hemmed in against the water cooler. My god, a hoard of ants is pouring over the side of one of the boats and they're dragging Paul out of the Porsche and eating his flesh!

Bummer.

Oh, yeah. "So, the sound track to the porn film I'm playing is the *Can-Can*—you know, that weird dance where all the ladies kick their legs up really high? And I'm thinking, this is really funny to see some transvestite getting a blowjob with his legs in the air while this music is playing, and—"

The security guard with the gold tooth puts a huge hand on my shoulder. "It's time to come with me," he says.

He leads me into the waiting room where I see Nicole sitting on the floor with about two hundred torn out magazine pages laid around her, the contestants watching her every move.

She looks up and smiles. "So, how did you do?"

"He was very effervescent," the guard says, and walks me to the elevator.

Sybil Servant

It's now what feels like the ninth hour of watching a numbingly depressing Ingmar Bergman film with Ed, a fellow Los Angeles City College film student. Seated in the back row of a Hollywood Boulevard theater that can comfortably seat approximately fifteen hundred patrons, but on this evening houses only a dozen or so, Ed and I pass back and forth the stubby remains of what was only minutes ago an obscenely bloated joint. My condition—not to mention the sheer incomprehensibility of the movie—allows me to follow the story for no more than twelve seconds at a time, which makes gleaning anything useful or enjoyable from the film impossible. The dialog, I learn from the few black-on-black subtitles I'm actually able to read, goes something like this:

> Depressed Man
> (gesturing at a row of rose bushes)
> The roses.
>
> Depressed Woman
> Yes. The roses.
>
> Depressed Man
> (in obvious emotional pain)
> They were …
>
> Depressed Woman
> Yes?
>
> Depressed Man
> They were on fire.
>
> Depressed Woman
> Yes, I remember … each rose … a pinwheel of agony.
>
> Depressed Man
> (sobbing)

> I found them beautiful as they were burning.

That's one of the brighter moments in a movie that is little more than an endless stream of morose observations. Although, I have to say, the director managed to coax his actors into exploring the entire range of possible emotions, from barely audible despondent whispers to terrifying shrieks of despair. This movie has it all.

As utterly horrible as I now feel about the human condition, the film has introduced me to an angel — the Depressed Woman. I'm thrilled to see her name in the movie credits, not just because I find her ravishing, but because the credits signal the end of The Longest Movie Ever Made. Her name, I discover, is Liv Ulmann, and sitting there in that dark theater, I know I'll never forget her.

"I've seen her before," Ed says, his voice booming about twenty decibels louder than what is necessary to communicate a thought to someone sitting eighteen inches away. "Norwegian, I think."

Yes, classic Norwegian — sharp cheekbones, Caribbean-blue eyes, and braided strawberry blond hair that makes her look like a descendent of Viking kings. I can't quite put my finger on it, but I'm unsettled by her — as if at any moment she might reach out from the screen, grab me by the wrist, then lead me into the flaming pits of Hell. And I decide then and there, through the depths of my pot-addled brain, if I ever get the chance, I will have this woman.

"God, she's gorgeous," I say, not really meaning to say it out loud.

"I'd do her," Ed offers charitably. "But she's not at the top of my list." And people sitting on the opposite side of the theater turn around to see who the loud voice belongs to.

"No? Who is?"

Ed is staring at something in between the fingers of his right hand, as if webbing had suddenly grown there. "Brigitte Bardot."

"She's French, I think."

Ed looks up at me, confused. "You think this film is bad? Last semester I had to see three Ingmar Bergman films in one night. That's when I started smoking pot. How else is a person supposed to get through this shit? What happened to that joint?"

I take a long pull on it, then hand it to him.

"So, who's at the top of your list?" he says.

"Are we supposed to have a list?"

"I'm not sure. Anyway, I know we have to see another movie tonight," he says, not altogether enthusiastically.

"Which one?"

"Brigitte Bardot."

"Is that the name of a movie?"

"No. She's at the top of my list?"

I'm confused. Ed isn't quite lining up his answers with my questions. "What list?"

"Didn't we already talk about that?"

"Not that I can recall. Anyway, what about Brigitte Bardot?"

"I thought we were talking about Liv Ullman."

"Yes, she was in tonight's movie."

"Well, I'd do her."

I open the box of candy I've been working on for the past ten minutes, knowing full well it's empty but hoping that a few new Milk Duds have risen Phoenix-like from the remains of the chocolate crumbs at the bottom of the container. No such luck. But I vow to check again in the near future.

"*Une Ravissante Idiote*," Ed bellows.

"Why are you speaking French at me?"

"Did you find any more Milk Duds? I'm fucking starving!"

"The box is empty," I say, whispering in a valiant attempt to get Ed to do likewise.

"I'll get some more candy," he says, and stomps up the aisle.

Considering how annoyingly loud Ed is, I'm glad to be sitting alone for awhile. I try to replay the movie I've just seen, but for some reason I can't remember a single thing about it. Oh, yeah ... there was some nonsense about burning roses, but that's the extent of what I can recall. Except for that woman who—

"You like Sno Caps?" Ed says, falling into his seat.

I take the box from him and discover that two-thirds of it is already missing. "Hungry little lad, aren't you?"

"We're seeing another movie tonight, you know."

"That would explain why we're still here. Got any idea which movie?"

Ed takes a small spiral-bound pad out of his jacket pocket and flips through the pages with a look of consternation, then finds what he's looking for. *"Une Ravissante Idiote."*

"That sounds familiar."

"Really?"

"Yeah, I get the feeling I've heard about it recently."

Ed turns a page in the little note pad and blinks at a handwritten entry. "Did you know we're supposed to see an Ingmar Bergman film?"

"You mean, aside from the one we just saw tonight?"

"Really? Was that tonight?"

"I'm pretty sure it was."

He brings the note pad up to his face in the darkened theater. "Is today the twenty-third?"

"I think so."

"Then we're definitely seeing an Ingmar Bergman film."

"I could be wrong, but I think we just saw it."

"Are they going to show it again?" he says, still locked on the note pad.

"I doubt it. I think we're about to see some French film."

"Ah, right. *Une Ravissante Idiote.*"

"What's that mean?"

Ed squints at the pad. "An adorable idiot."

"Is it a Jerry Lewis film?" I say, stuffing candy into my mouth.

"I don't think so. But I'm pretty sure Brigitte Bardot is in it," he says.

"Weird. I was just having a conversation about her with someone, but I can't remember the circumstance.

"She's at the top of my list, you know."

"You have a list?"

"Well, it's nothing I've ever written down," he says, flipping the little pad closed and returning it to his jacket pocket. "I just sort of think about it. You know, every now and then."

"And ...?"

"And what?"

"And who's at the top of the list?" I say, not altogether patiently.

"I just told you. Brigitte Bardot."

"She's in the movie tonight and she's at the top of your list?"

"That's right."

"I think this is all starting to come together for me."

Ed reaches across my lap and snatches the box of Sno Caps from the arm rest. He rips off the flap, and peers down into the box, disappointed. "Man, you're just inhaling this shit."

"Sorry, I meant to leave you some, but I got distracted. Want me to get some more?"

Ed tosses the empty box on the floor, then heads down the aisle again.

With him gone for who knows how long, I decide to take in the architecture of the theater. It's an old, ornate, '30s-era Hollywood-art deco theater, the screen covered by what looks to be thirty-foot tall red curtains that appear to be made from a single piece of velvet. I like velvet, and I imagine myself walking up to the front of the theater, climbing up on stage, and rubbing the soft material against my face. I wonder if anyone would—

Ed flops down in his seat, startling me. It seems like he's been gone about thirty seconds, but in my condition, I wouldn't want to bet on it. He sets a tub of popcorn on his lap and begins munching at it. I reach my hand in and discover that there's very little popcorn left in the tub.

"How long have you been gone?"

"I don't know. A while," he says, wiping butter on his jeans.

"Did you forget napkins?"

"Couldn't find any clean ones."

"How much do I owe you for the candy and popcorn?"

"It's on the house," he says, popcorn flying out of his mouth. "So who's at the top of your list?"

"I'm not sure I fully understand what exactly this is a list of."

"Women you wish you could sleep with, "he says, and a man about twenty rows in front of us turns around and scowls.

"I see." And for what seems like several minutes, I give the question serious consideration. "Janis Joplin," I finally say, proudly.

"Janis Joplin?"

"Yes. You know, she's the singer for Big Brother and—"

"Christ, is that the best you can do? As long as you're wishing, why don't you wish for someone who doesn't shoot heroin and isn't afflicted with syphilis?"

The remaining lights in the theater are suddenly extinguished and a scratchy black and white film starts up. And for the next ten or so minutes, I forget all about Vikings and Milk Duds and venereal diseases. Because I am introduced to a French goddess and I am in love. She is completely unlike what's-her-name from the first film. Her body is curvaceous rather than angular. Her lips are full and beckoning rather than pursed and anxious. And I realize that there is no one else on this Earth who matters more to me than Brigitte Bardot—until I see the girl on the cover of the magazine I see sticking out of Ed's military-green knapsack on the seat next to him.

Even from two seats away, even in the darkness of the theater, her beauty is radiant. Underneath the large red *Stern* lettering is a waterfall of wavy blonde hair that leads the viewer's eyes on a merry chase until arriving at her cheekbones, which appear to have been carved from a single, unblemished block of milky pink alabaster. I reach across Ed's lap and jerk the magazine out of the knapsack, bringing it close to my face. Yes. She is an ice water-eyed Teutonic amazon.

"I could go for a Coke," he says, using a fingernail to pry popcorn from between his teeth.

"Me, too." I start to get up, but Ed puts a hand on my shoulder.

"I'll get it," he says over his shoulder as he walks down the aisle.

I open the magazine and quickly scan the table of contents for her picture. There it is, above a caption in German that contains information about her I must know, along with a page number: 63. I flip through the pages, find 63, and there she is, every inch an adolescent boy's comic book fantasy, in a brown leather top, loosely laced across her ample breasts. I feel someone bump into the back of my seat and I turn around to give the person the frozen stare of death, but I can only see a large ass in jeans. It's Ed's ass and he's rooting around on the floor for something. Odd. He's prying the plastic lids from soft drink cups, looking at the contents, then replacing the lids.

"Ed, what the fuck are you doing?"

"Looking for a Coke."

"Why are you looking down there?"

"For the same reason Willy Sutton robs banks."

"I don't get the reference."

"Do you want a Coke or not?"

"Yeah, but—"

"Well, this is where most of the discarded cups are."

"Why don't you just fucking buy one?"

"You kidding? I don't have any money. I had to sneak through the exit door just to get in here tonight," he says, finding a cup with a suitable quantity of liquid in it. He climbs over the back of the seat and takes his place next to me. "I think it's Coke," he says, tipping the cup toward me. "Want some?"

"I'm glad I didn't ask you to get me some gum."

"Gum? You want some?" he says, running his hand along the underside of his seat cushion. He nods at the open magazine on my lap. "What did you find out about that blonde chick?"

"Not a clue. What's all this stuff mean?" I say, pushing the copy of *Stern* at him.

Ed squints at the page. "It's in German."

"Are you telling me you can't read it?"

"No, I'm just telling you it's in German," he says, sipping his drink through a straw whose tip is covered in red lipstick.

"I can see it's in German. Can you read it or not?"

"I'm not sure. I bought it because I'm taking a conversational German class and I thought it would help me with vocabulary and verb tenses. So far, it's been very useful. German is a very interesting language that—"

"Would you read the fucking thing already!"

"Okay. Hold your horses. This could take a while," he says, and brings the magazine closer to his face. His eyes dart across the column of words for what has to be a full minute.

"Well?"

"This isn't easy. This stuff goes way beyond what I learn in first-semester German."

"Do you understand anything about it?"

"Well, her name's Sybil Danning—"

"Sybil Danning," I say, entranced by its sheer Germanness.

"—and she's from Austria, although now she appears to be living in Munich. She must be an actress because it mentions something called *Gelobt Sei, was hart macht*."

"What's that? Is that a movie?" I say, trying to suppress a rush of excitement.

"I'm not really sure. Probably, though."

"Can we see it tonight?" I say, hopeful.

"I can't tell if she just made the movie, if it was just released, or if she just signed to do it. My German's not good enough to—"

I rip the magazine out of his hands and bring it to within millimeters of my face. There, staring me in the eyes, is Sybil Danning, at that particular instant the most powerfully nasty woman I've ever beheld. There's no confusing her with the two women from tonight's movies. No, this creature could have fallen off of an Aryan Dream Girls calendar. There is no coyness or pleading on her face—only the firm jaw set and mocking smirk of a woman who can dominate any man she chooses, at the precise moment of her fancy. What must it be like to know such a creature? What must it say about the man she makes herself available to? Why are such women so ridiculously out of my reach? Where did Ed find the gum he's chewing right now?

These questions stay with me as Ed and I trudge to the lobby and up to the snack stand, where we provision ourselves for a long siege.

* * *

I'm taking film classes at the city college because my brother Ken is in the film business. You'd be amazed how easy your life choices become when your sole ambition is simply to follow in someone else's footsteps. Besides, with the exciting time he seems to be having making movies in Europe, I could have worse ambitions.

You have to admire Ken's ability to identify what he wanted to do in life. Ever since we were kids, he wanted to be in show business. He aimed. He hit. Me? The only things I'm aiming at are the things Ken has already hit, a system the two participants have found enormously rewarding.

While he leads his fabulous life, the only thing I have to look forward to is hearing about it in his letters which, oddly, I always find simultaneously titillating and depressing. I imagine his adventures with actresses, makeup girls and costumers to be fascinating, but I'm miserable over the huge disparity between our lives that I never really thought much about until I started receiving his letters. Ken is a terrific writer, and he goes into great detail about the European women he dates, the stars he works with, the meals he enjoys, the sights he sees. I'd give anything to know them, meet them, eat them, see them.

Funny how life works. One minute you're a sappy film student at a dinky city college, the next minute you open a letter that changes your life—a thought that occurs to me after I read the part where Ken invites me to come to West Berlin to live with him and try my hand at writing.

The idea of living in a foreign country is insanely terrifying to me, considering that I've never travelled anywhere. And I know right where that fear comes from. My father drives the same route to work every day, changing lanes at the same precise moment as the day before, arriving at exactly the same time. My mother shops at the same supermarket, buying the same things, and paying at the same checkout counter. The family vacations at the same nearby lake year after year.

In my family, there is nothing safer than a routine. To have a routine is to be in control—the corollary of which is that in the absence of a routine, we are out of control. Which is why Ken's traveling has always struck me as concurrently exciting and repulsive.

What makes my going to Germany even remotely possible, in my mind, is that I'll be living with Ken in his apartment. He's cleverly anticipated all the reasons I could refuse his offer and undercut each argument in his letter. He'll order food for me at restaurants, buy my ticket at the movie theater, and guide me onto the right subway car when we need to go anywhere. Funny how he knew I'd raise those issues.

And when he's not showing me the ropes, I can try my hand at writing the television series he's been hired to write.

Writing? I've never written anything more substantial than a book report in high school. In fact, I've never given the craft even a passing thought. Yet Ken is telling me that, if I'm any good at it, I can make a living at it in Europe, just as he has.

How hard can writing be? You just slap a bunch of bullshit down on the page, imitate some other writer's highfalutin way of saying things, throw in some action, describe some pretty women, and there you have it. Writing. It's not like it's work or anything.

I'm going to Germany, I tell myself no fewer than seventy-two times per day. What strikes me the most about the knowledge that I'll soon be living in another country is my ambivalence about the whole thing. I'm tremendously excited, so much so that I bore my friends to death by reminding them hourly of my good fortune. But I'm also terrified to be going somewhere with a foreign language barrier, a different-looking set of people, in a country with a history of treating my ancestors like Pop 'n Fresh muffins.

Writing. I'm going to Germany. To write. I can only shake my head at the absurdity of it all.

How did I get so lucky? Why is Ken doing this to me?

* * *

I've just stepped out of a taxi onto Berlin's most famous street, the Kurfürstendamm, and I'm instantly struck by three things. The first is that, if not for the rather Germanic names on the storefronts and street signs, this could be any major U.S. city. The next thing I notice is how different I look here. I'm acutely aware that my somewhat Semitic looks are unique in this sea of thin lips, button noses, and pin-straight hair. And the third thing is that I've been disgorged from the taxi right next to a young nun who appears to be waiting for the light to change.

I nod at her and laugh to myself. Here I am, Jewish in Germany. Had I been standing at this exact location only three decades earlier, this nun might have sounded an alarm that would summon the SS to drag me off to the nearest concentration camp. But it's not three decades earlier. It's now and I'm standing next to this young nun, holding a piece of American Tourister luggage in my hand, and I'm not quite sure how to address a nun, let alone a German one. I smile at her. *"Guten Tag, Fräulein."*

I'm so proud of myself. I've made contact with an inhabitant of a non-English-speaking country. This is my first connection in a foreign language, and I know I'll always remember it and think of this nun fondly for her participation in the breaking down of cultural barriers.

She smiles at me. "It will cost thirty marks for a half hour, and you must use a rubber. I am—how you say?—menstruating right now, but you can fuck me in the ass, if that is your preference."

I'm fairly certain she's not a representative of the Catholic church, but I appreciate the warm welcome nonetheless.

I look around and notice I'm in front of a large building, the ground floor of which is devoted to a Mercedes Benz showroom. I feel lost already, and for several minutes I can only stand on the sidewalk and gape at the new cars through the window. The cab driver assured me this is the correct address, but I don't recall Ken telling me he lived in a car dealership. My confusion is bad enough, but now I'm getting the sense that people are staring at my suitcase as they hurry past, so I walk around the side of the building and find an entrance to the apartments above. Fortunately, there is a directory of the tenants. Unfortunately, there is no Globus listed. But I do find the word Manager, and I nervously press the button, wait several seconds, and hear a man, somewhat annoyed, say, "*Ja?*"

"Yes ... I'm looking for Ken Globus."

"*Herr* Globus?"

"Yes. I think Ken *Herr* Globus lives here."

"Who are you?"

I'm less disturbed by the impertinence of the question than I am relieved to find that the manager speaks English. "I'm his brother ... Dennis. From America. Well, Los Angeles, actually. It's a city in southern California about a hundred-fifty miles—"

"I know where Los Angeles is," he says.

"Sorry. I'm here to visit my brother but I don't see his name on the directory."

"Press the button for Herr Hartmann. Your brother lives in that apartment."

"Hartmann. Thank you very—"

Click. Apparently, the manager has had just about all the chit-chat he desires. I look at my watch and realize I've probably interrupted his dinner. The tenants are listed in alphabetical order on the directory, and I run my finger down the list until I find Hartmann, then press the little black button next to it. Another click.

"*Ja, kann ich Ihnen helfen?*"

It's Ken. And I'm immensely relieved to hear his voice and terribly impressed that he speaks German.

"It's me!" I say.

"Holy shit, you're here!"

I'm pleased Ken remembers I'm coming to live with him. You never know.

"Come up to the fifth floor."

I haul my suitcase up five flights of stairs and find Ken standing in front of his apartment door, grinning. We hug for a long time, and I'm so happy to see him.

He invites me in and shows me around the tiny apartment. I'm immediately struck by the fact that there is no bedroom. There is, however, blood stained into the grout between several bathroom tiles.

"That belongs to Herr Hartmann," Ken says casually. "The building manager told me that he picked up a male prostitute who killed him in the bathroom."

Good god! That's disturbing. Every time I take a whiz, I have to look at Herr Hartmann's Type O and think about his murder. I didn't know that kind of stuff happened in other countries.

"Did you have a nice flight? Are you tired? Want some food? Want to meet my girlfriend?"

"Well, I—"

"Let's go visit her. She's dying to meet you." Ken yanks the phone off the desk and dials quickly. He proceeds to have a brief conversation—mostly about me—that's half English and half German (sort of Germish), then hangs up.

"Okay, let's get going."

"Are we going out to eat?" I ask hopefully.

"We're going to my girlfriend's place. She's inviting a friend over in your honor, and we'll eat dinner there."

I can't imagine what sort of friend she's going to honor me with, but I'm hungry and curious about Ken's girlfriend. He leads me out of the apartment and out onto the Ku'damm, as he calls it. It's an absolutely breathtaking street that pulsates with activity from its clubs, restaurants, theaters, traffic, neon lights, and crowds—and Ken explains what he knows about each building as we pass it. He's an excellent tour guide, and I learn about the rather odd cultural and political history of the city. As he talks, it's easy to picture this throbbing metropolis encased in a bubble, hermetically sealed to prevent contamination by the godless Communists that completely surround the city. West Berlin, I learn, isn't so much a city as it is an oasis in the middle of a politically and socially inhospitable desert. Ken's excited to show me the city, and his explanations are coming as quickly as his walking. The Ku'damm is only one street in West Berlin, and yet I'm already dizzy with all the sensory input it offers. I try to relate it to a street in Los Angeles, but there really isn't anything in my experience on a level with what I'm seeing.

I follow Ken as he skips down a flight of stairs into a subway station, and we hop on the U-bahn. He smiles at me. "Well, what do you think?"

A good question. What do I think? I think I'm becoming nauseous by how different this place is from what I've come to know. I think I'm frightened by the prospect of having to learn a foreign language in order to get anything done when Ken's not standing right next to me. I think I'm anxious about the fact that I look so different to these people. I think I'm scared by what I can only guess to be weird food I'll find inedible, odd customs that are likely to offend people when I forget to observe them, and bizarre laws that I'm certain to inadvertently violate. What do they do with Jews who break the law these days? And I'm irrationally anxious about taking a stroll and finding myself in East Berlin, unable to explain to the secret police in trench coats that it's all been some horrible mistake.

I smile back. "I think I'm going to like it here."

"Isn't this place a trip?"

Indeed. A trip.

The subway car lurches forward and I hang on to the pole to keep myself from being flung into the guy standing next to me. He's wearing a small green knapsack and the kind of tiny granny glasses that were all the rage in my high school. There's some strange artwork on the cover of the paperback he's reading, and I instantly recognize it as the second book in the Lord of the Rings trilogy.

"Quite a book, isn't it?" I say to him.

He turns his head the minimal amount required to size me up and returns to his novel.

Ken giggles.

"I guess I need to learn some German," I say, whispering to Ken.

"He speaks English, doofus. He's reading a book in English."

"Then why didn't he talk to me?"

"Because you've got short hair and you speak English. He thinks you're in the army."

Great. Yet another thing to obsess about. Here it is 1971 and I've got short hair, thanks to my recent discharge from the Marine Reserves. Is this the way it's going to be? Am I going to be held personally responsible for Viet Nam and what the youth of

Germany apparently regards as an occupying army within their borders? Of course, when I think about it, the youth of Los Angeles isn't exactly enchanted by my short hair either. This is going to stink until my hair grows out.

As the subway car rumbles through the city, I'm struck by how serious and solitary the Germans are as they board, huddle in a corner, then hurriedly exit the train. I've never been to New York, but this is the way I imagine the riders there behaving— each person in his own world, refusing to make eye contact out of fear of provoking someone into some form of aberrant behavior.

It's my first day here, and already I'm feeling isolated and claustrophobic, and I'm thrilled when the doors slide open and Ken announces our stop. He pushes me out of the car and I follow him through a series of tunnels until we're squirted up to street level in a part of the city devoted entirely to post-war apartment buildings. I haven't got the vaguest idea where we are or where we're going and I keep bumping into Ken as he rounds corners. Finally, he stops in front of a building and punches a button on a directory.

"*Ja?*" a female voice says.

"It's Ken."

"Is your brother wiss you?"

"Yeah, he's right here." He pushes me up to the intercom. "Say something, Den."

Say something? "Well ... this is Dennis. You don't know me, but—"

The buzzer sounds and Ken pushes the door open and disappears into the hallway. I barely make it inside before the door shuts on me, and I follow Ken up several flights of stairs. Aren't there any elevators in this country?

On the seventh floor, Ken knocks on one of the doors, which opens wide enough to reveal an eyeball evaluating us. We apparently meet the eyeball's approval, and the door opens fully to reveal a very pretty young woman with long, dark hair. She smiles at us and invites us in. As if there were powerful magnets embedded in their faces, Ken and the young woman immediately lunge at each other and begin a very long kiss that involves tongues and produces a lot of slurping. I stare at a travel poster on the wall and try to imagine myself somewhere else. Anywhere else.

When the two lovers finally crowbar themselves away from each other, Ken introduces me to his girlfriend, whose name turns out to be Monika.

She's very sweet. And gorgeous. And sexy.

"Danneez," she says, "welcome to West Berlin. I have heard much about you."

"It's nice to meet you, Monika. Ken has told—"

A toilet flushes and another woman walks into the living room, and my jaw drops. She's tall and astonishingly beautiful, with long strawberry blonde hair, full lips, and perfect teeth.

"Danneez, Ken's girlfriend says, this is my friend Monika."

"I'm sorry. I thought *your* name is Monika."

"It is" she says, giggling. "And *her* name is Monika, also."

Considering what an awful memory I have for names, the fact that there are two Monikas in the room works in my favor. But I can see this is going to get confusing.

"We'll call you Monika *Eins*," Ken says to his girlfriend, "and we'll call you Monika *Zwei*."

"Ah, Monika *Zwei*," the strawberry blonde says. "*Ja, naturlich*."

"Monika *Zwei*?" I say meekly.

Monika *Zwei* smiles at me and I find myself wanting to grab her by the ears and lick her face.

"I am Monika *Zwei* ... Monika Number Two. And here is Monika *Eins*, which is Monika Number One." She puts her hand on my shoulder. "Do you speak any German, Danneez?"

I feel an itch that begins at the spot where her hand touches my shoulder, travels across my chest, meanders down my stomach, and radiates in my crotch. It's a good itch, except that it's hydraulically lifting my penis and I don't particularly want it hoisted right now. Not while I'm standing in a hallway. "No, I took Spanish in high school," I say.

"It is not a problem. Most people in West Berlin speak English. You will be understood."

Finally. I will be understood.

It's now ten at night, I haven't eaten since I landed five hours ago, and I'm hoping for some sort of meal. Something large, filling, and recognizable would be nice. As if reading my mind, Monika *Eins* disappears into the kitchen while the three of us make small talk at the door. I'm finding Monika *Zwei* to be incandescently alive, fascinating, and someone I'd like to use as a flotation device. Soon. And as I mull over that image, Monika *Eins* trots out of the kitchen with a platter of cheese slices on top of minuscule crackers. She takes them into the living room, sets the food on the floor on top of a large Oriental rug, and we sit in a solemn little circle around the platter, as if we're going to use the crackers as Ouiji pieces. I'm too hungry to be shy about being the first one to dig in, and I grab a cracker and whip it into my mouth. Not bad, but the cheese is a little stinky for my liking. But who am I to complain? I'm in Berlin, with my brother and two gorgeous women, with an interesting night ahead.

Ken seems to want to perform for them, and he snatches a guitar from against the wall and begins playing *If I Had My Way*, a rousing little number we've sung together for years. Since he obviously expects my participation, I feel compelled to leave the food alone, knowing how difficult it is to sing with a mouthful of crackers.

The two Monikas are suitably impressed by our ability to carry a tune, and they nod their heads in appreciation as we complete one tedious folk song after another. I can't tell if the women are bored with our singing, but I can tell I am, and all I really want is to lay these crackers between Monika *Zwei*'s breasts and develop an acquired taste for the cheese in my own special way.

A second food course would be nice, but it doesn't look promising. The women have probably already eaten dinner, given the late hour, and they likely expect that we have, too. So, it looks like I can't count on anything more than the cheese and crackers.

Not that it matters when Monika *Eins* announces that she has to work in the morning and that it's time for us to sleep. Suddenly, my hunger is being replaced by an anxiety about the sleeping arrangements. I expect Ken and Monika *Eins* to disappear into the bedroom, but that doesn't seem to be happening. Instead, she brings out two blankets and four pillows, then lays them out side by side on the living room floor. From the looks of things, we're supposed to form into couples and—

Wait … what the hell is going on here? Are we all sleeping together? This can't be happening.

But it is. Monika *Eins* is unbuttoning her shirt, and she's revealing two huge breasts that are doing their best to escape from an undersized white satin bra. As she begins to slide her jeans down, I'm vaguely aware that my mouth is open—wide—and I swallow hard. This can't be happening.

But it is. Ken casually takes his shirt off, then steps out of his pants. Oh, Jesus … he's wearing some sort of gold bikini shorts. What's come over him? This can't be happening.

But it is. Monika *Zwei* smiles at me and lifts the tank top over her head. While she is briefly blinded by the shirt, my eyes are filled with two gorgeous, milky-white breasts inside a tiny blue bra. Oh, god. She's undoing her skirt and letting it fall on the floor. This can't be—

But it is. At least, it's happening for them. I know I'm expected to strip down to my shorts, as everyone else has, but, Christ, this is my big brother in the room here. I can't possibly—

"Are you going to sit there looking like a goon?" Ken says.

That's the plan.

"I ... I ... "

"Take your pants off."

Only moments ago, my penis was an ornate tropical flower, rising to meet the morning sun. And now there's the sensation that it's retracting like a cheap car antenna. It's not that I'm shy around the women. It's Ken. I don't want to be here watching him do what he's very likely to be doing, and I sure as hell don't want him watching me doing what I'm expected to be doing and having him evaluate my performance. This is insane!

But it's happening. And it's coming at me like an enormous tidal wave that I'm helpless to run away from.

Monika *Zwei* giggles—at what, I'm not sure, and don't particularly want to venture a guess—and settles in under the second blanket. All three of them are now staring up at me, and my head is spinning. Let's see, what are my options here? I can run, screaming, out of the apartment, down seven flights of stairs. And then what? I'll find myself on some deserted German street, where it's pitch black. No, that's not a very good option. I could claim that I'm exhausted and that I'd just like to stay up and watch TV or something. But that's only slightly less antisocial than the first option. Or …

Despite my inclination to do anything else, I find myself slowly taking off my shirt, releasing each button as if I'm the world's slowest and stupidest stripper. I toss my shirt over the back of a wing chair, plop down on its cushion, then spend several seconds fussing with my shoe laces. God, this is torture. I kick the shoes off and slide my socks down, stuffing each sock into its appropriate shoe, an activity that's over all too soon. And it's come to this—my pants.

"Would you fucking hurry up, already!" Ken says.

However reluctant I was up till this moment, I now feel paralyzed.

"Are you not feeling well, Danneez?" Monika *Zwei* says.

Right. I've got a stomach full of writhing snakes that seem to get more venomous as I fast-forward the film of this evening. I can see myself taking my pants off and sliding under the blanket against Monika *Zwei*'s warm body. As the film progresses, I see her turn over and press her belly against mine, then run her hand down my back until finally her fingers find their way underneath the elastic of my underwear. She brings her face to mine and takes my earlobe in her mouth, running her tongue down my neck until it ends at a kiss on my shoulder. When she's finished, I kiss her mouth and, in one confident motion, unhook her bra from the front. It falls open and I stare down at ...

Jeez. This isn't making the removal of my pants any easier.

"Yes. I'm fine," I say, in a losing battle to look both confident and cheerful.

I've managed to consume a ridiculous amount of time fumbling with the clasp on my belt, and I finally get it open, then slide my pants down to the floor.

Ken giggles. "You're still wearing white Jockeys."

"I ... I ... "

Monika *Eins* puts a hand over Ken's mouth. "I think his underpanties look well."

With my pants still around my ankles, my hands covering my crotch, I once again long to be anywhere else.

"European guys wear bikini shorts, Den," Ken says.

Monika *Zwei* lifts a corner of the blanket, and I dive underneath, not so much because I've acquired courage, but because I want everyone to quit staring at me.

All four of us are now under the blankets, and for several painful seconds we all stare at the ceiling until Monika *Eins* slips out and lights several candles around the room. I'm transfixed by her breasts jiggling in her bra as she glides around the room turning off lamps. The desired ambiance now assured, she returns to her spot next to Ken.

I expect him to immediately tear off what little remaining clothing she's wearing, then mount her like a cape buffalo, but he's strangely inactive. Instead, he seems to be transfixed by something on the ceiling.

It's dark in the room and it's difficult to make out anything specific. There are a number of shadows against the walls, flickering from the candle flames. I can see the shadows of my feet that are uncovered by the too-short blanket. I discover I can do a little shadow dance against the wall by wiggling my toes. But it gets boring after about thirty seconds, and my thoughts return to the woman next to me. I want to touch her very much, and I'm sure I would if we were alone. I mean, it's not at all weird to by lying next to a woman. It's not even out of my frame of reference to have two women next to me. The weirdness in all of this is Ken, a guy who has spent a lifetime making me feel like there's nothing I could ever do to measure up to him, a guy whose approval I've never stopped seeking. So the idea of having sex in the same room with him just strikes me as a disaster in the making.

There is some rustling under the blanket next to me, and Monika *Zwei* pulls out her blue bra and tosses it on the floor behind her head.

Curious. It's hard to know if this is a green light or if she's simply trying to get more comfortable. But then, what is this night all about? Ken has taken me over to his girlfriend's house, a woman who has invited over a beautiful friend to keep me company. But what does keep me company mean in Germany? Is it a given that I'm supposed to have sex with her? She is, after all, one flimsy garment away from being completely nude. And the thing with the bra. I know there's not much illumination from the candles, but did she smile at me when she tossed it away?

Dammit, what does it all mean? Can't she just give me a clear signal? Was the bra intended to be a clear signal? Is it a form of non-verbal communication? Why can't she do something a little less ambiguous, like rolling over and sitting on my face. Now, that would be clear. And mostly non-verbal.

Let's revisit the evidence here. There was a gorgeous woman invited over for the express purpose of keeping me company. She is now lying about four inches away from me, and she's virtually nude. And I've got a throbbing erection that's sticking a few inches above the band of my goddamned white underpanties.

But the bra thing. That's disturbing. She clearly wore it until she got underneath the blanket, then removed it. Was I not supposed to see her breasts earlier? And if I wasn't supposed to see them then, why would she want me to see them now?

On the other hand, does a woman really need to take her bra off to get comfortable? I obviously don't know the language of bras, especially European ones, and I'd hate to misread this particular one. I may be over-analyzing this just a tad.

There's a noise coming from somewhere in the room and I can't identify its direction or origin. It brings to mind the flapping of fabric, like a bed sheet pinned to a clothesline in the wind. I consider sitting up and looking around the room, but I don't want Monika *Zwei* to think I'm attacking her. From my position on the floor, I can see the two windows, which are shut tight to keep out the late October chill. So that eliminates the curtains as the source of the noise, which seems to fall into a pattern of flapping for three seconds, disappearing for a moment, then reappearing.

I raise my head off the pillow slightly and see three faces pointed up toward the ceiling. Only Monika *Eins* has her eyes closed, and the strange sound returns every time she exhales. She's asleep. And she's snoring.

It's hard to see my watch in the dark, but I think ten minutes have elapsed from the time I got underneath the blanket. Jeez, this is going to be a long night.

My erection is rubbing against the scratchy wool blanket, and I think it's starting to chafe. I need to roll over on my side, but which direction? The obvious choice is away from Monika *Zwei*, but do I really want to make a statement like that? If the bra is some sort of unspoken communication, what would my presenting her with my back imply? Nothing good, that's for sure. Of course, turning toward her also says something. But what? First, it could say that I want some attention. Is that a good thing to say to a naked woman? Does she want to give me some attention? Would she think I'm being perversely needy? Second, she might infer from it that I want to give *her* some attention. And God only knows if she's ready to receive that. Third, she could just assume that I'm uncomfortable and changing positions. And then what? I'm left in the same agonizing situation I'm in now, lying next to a beauty, without a game plan. Fourth, it might be interpreted as my having fallen asleep. Yeah, that would be bad. On the remote possibility that she might actually initiate something, all hope is lost if she thinks I'm down for the count.

There is no good choice here. All I know is, the microscopic fibers of the wool blanket seem to be worming their way into my boner. That's it then. I've got to do something.

I can only think of the old tale about the mother who sees her child pinned underneath a car, and somehow gains the necessary superhuman strength to lift up the car and pull her child free. But who am I in this analogy? Am I the child? And is the blanket supposed to be the car? And who is Monika *Zwei*?

Yes, I understand now. I'm the mother. And rolling over toward Monika *Zwei* will require an act of herculean strength. And by facing her, I'm actually saving her. Hey, I'm on to something here! If I can just face her, I know I'll discover that she's a sexual gymnast who would like nothing more than to use me like a pommel horse.

As I slowly begin to roll over, I feel as if I can hear metal cables snapping and rusty gears turning. They don't want to release, but I'm far too strong to be stopped. Just as I complete the roll-over, I can imagine the sound of an ancient metal door creaking open. This is it. I have rolled. And the feeling is exhilarating.

My face is now just a few inches away from Monika *Zwei*'s left ear, and she does something totally unexpected. She turns her head toward me and smiles. Clearly, whatever I've communicated to her by rolling over hasn't upset her too much. But the smile? What does it mean?

No, it doesn't matter anymore. I have rolled. I am powerful. She must sense this. She surely must be in awe of my strength ... my certainty.

As if guided by divinity, my hand moves toward her, grazes her hip, barely skims across her belly, and settles on her left breast. Eureka! After a few moments, I can only deduce from her apparent lack of screaming or vomiting that my behavior is not unwelcome. I have arrived at the site of an unknown peak, and I've planted my flag. It's time to explore the territory.

If someone were to ask me, at this particular moment, what a perfect breast should feel like, I would have an answer. It is Monika *Zwei*'s left one—soft without being squishy, firm without feeling like a ripe casaba, large enough to fill the paw. This lovely mound of feminine flesh beneath my hand is flawless. And making it all the more interesting is the nipple which feels approximately the size of a silver dollar and slightly swollen away from the breast, leaving me with a clear impression of where the breast and nipple come together. I find the nipple's sheer puffiness fascinating.

I have discovered the first of what I hope to be many jewels. And before I do any further spelunking, I must know if her other breast is every bit as impeccable as the first. It's much easier now that I have some courage—plus a dim memory of the blanket fibers—and I slide my fingers in an arc down her stomach and back up to a point between her breasts.

Yes, my lady, I know what you want. But not so fast. I am only momentarily mapping the terrain.

I'm feeling a confidence now that I never could have imagined only moments before. This marvelous creature has accepted me. Me! But there is little time to ruminate on my good fortune. The journey continues with my hand sliding over to her right breast.

Odd. It doesn't feel a thing like her left breast. It's sort of knobby and fuzzy. No, beyond fuzzy. There are little, distinct course hairs.

I'm startled as Ken pops his head up and says, "What?" and as he does so, the blanket falls away from Monika *Zwei*, revealing Monika's right breast. But there's something terribly, horribly, incomprehensibly wrong. Ken's hand is on her breast, and my hand is on top of his.

We should be looking at each other and laughing at the absurdity of this situation, the confluence of events that have brought us to this point tonight, the shattering of old barriers that have ill-served both of us. I should assert myself, wink at him, and pull Monika *Zwei* to my body, leaving Ken to return to his snoring girlfriend.

But rolling over and going to sleep turns out to be easier.

* * *

I'm like a duckling behind Ken as he leads me around West Berlin, and I find myself astonished by what I'm seeing. On this corner is a huge cathedral, still bombed out from the war. On that corner is an outdoor cafe with dozens of patrons sipping coffee and smoking cigarettes. Over there is the dauntingly impenetrable Berlin Wall. And beyond that are gray tenement buildings whose occupants lead what I imagine to be the dreariest of lives.

I can't believe what I'm seeing. It's all so ... foreign. And except for the nun, very little of what I've seen so far reminds me of Los Angeles.

After three days in West Germany, I'm starting to recognize things on restaurant menus. Meat is *fleisch*. Pork is *schweinefleisch*. I find the literal translation—pig flesh—unnerving, so I order pizza at every meal. With my life in chaos, it's good to have a familiar routine. My parents would be proud.

Today's pizza is not unlike the previous five that I've eaten this week, the only difference being that there is a rather attractive, if bookish, blonde woman sitting at the next table. Ken has noticed her, too, and I find that I've lost my dinner companion for the night, so intent is he on meeting her. To my amazement, he does, and the next thing I know I'm walking back to our apartment alone.

Strolling down Kurfürstendamm—West Berlin's equivalent of both Fifth Avenue and Hollywood Boulevard— toward my apartment is like elbowing your way through a Mardi Gras parade. There is activity and noise everywhere I look. Since this is an upscale area of Berlin, the hookers, occupying every street corner and various points in between, are gorgeous. Music blares out of cafes. Drug purveyors openly sell *trips*, which I take to mean hallucinogens. It all makes me dizzy, and I duck in to what turns out to be a pharmacy. Except to escape the crowd, I have no business in here, but I walk up each aisle anyway, and I'm struck by the sheer number of items I've never seen before, and I have no idea which are meant to be ingested, applied, or inserted. What I do recognize, though, is a display filled with stationery supplies, and I decide to buy a little spiral-bound notepad like the one I saw Ed using in the movie theater. In it I will make note of all my Most Important Thoughts, a good idea, I decide, if I'm going to be a writer. I thumb through its blank pages, imagining them filled with snippets of stories, witty observations, and lines of dialog I want to remember for possible inclusion in some future masterpiece.

The notepad and pen I find aren't marked with a price, so it's anyone's guess what the things cost. I pull a twenty-mark note out of my pocket and nervously hand it to the cashier. She makes change—eighteen marks and five pfennigs—and asks me something in German. I haven't got a clue what she's saying, so I smile and say, *"Danke,"* which, I reason, is a sensibly noncommittal thing to say whenever anyone asks me something. In this case, it earns me a paper bag to put my items in.

Well, that wasn't so hard. My first cash transaction with a foreign currency, and I wasn't even humiliated.

I leave the pharmacy and once again take in the sights on Kurfürstendamm. There's so much about this I want to remember. I imagine myself writing about the incredible juxtaposition of antiquated and modern architecture, of the rapidity with which the Germans bulldozed the ruins of a war-torn city and replaced them with a metropolis, of the experience of an American Jew in what was, until not too long ago, a society that was encouraged to shun, then torment, then inflict violence, and finally eradicate my kind.

As I gawk at the scene in front of me, I decide that I will not move from this location until I've made note of everything I'm experiencing. I will root myself in this spot until the idea for a powerful story occurs to me, one that will move humanity with its insights. I vow that, even if it takes hours until the right idea comes to me, I won't take even one step until I make progress. I take out my little notepad, open it to the first page, and click the pen.

And I record, for all posterity, what this entire experience means to me.

Someone. Please. Help me.

* * *

It's been a week since Ken met Renate (the bookish blonde) at the cafe, and I haven't seen or heard from him since. Which means I've been too scared to leave the apartment. One of the few times I was willing to risk a solo trip outdoors, I stumbled into a book store that specializes in English-language novels. I didn't know such a thing existed, but I'm thrilled to find it, first because there's no TV in my apartment and I have nothing to do except to read, and second because it might be nice to actually read up on some of the material I'll be writing about. But mostly because the employees speak English.

The reason Ken is in Berlin in the first place is to write a weekly television series based on the stories of Jack London. So I buy *The Call of the Wild*, *White Fang* and a book of Mr. London's short stories, then spend the next week doing nothing but reading.

I've never been a huge Jack London fan, and reading his stories reminds me why they never resonated with me when I was forced to read a couple of them in junior high school. I find his basic philosophy to be annoyingly Darwinian, the locals extraordinarily rugged, and his characters overly simplistic. In virtually every story, the law of fang and club prevails—he who wields the sharpest fang or the mightiest club seems to win the day every time. There's little room for affection between man and beast or discussion between man and his fellow man. And women are pretty much nonexistent in his literary world. Too bad. A little sex would warm things up.

As I read them, I try to imagine how I'm going to turn this jumble of grunted dialog and icy terrain into a story I'll find interesting.

Of course, I don't even have the vaguest notion of how to write a script, so I search through Ken's book shelves until I come across a stack of written episodes of something called *The Frozen North*. Since they are each only about thirty pages long, they make for quick reading, and I recognize some of the characters from the Jack London books and discover that *The Frozen North* must be the name of the TV series. That's good to know, since I'll be writing it.

Ken has done a very nice job of telling a somewhat complex story in such a short format. He uses the first ten pages to introduce his characters and to establish some conflict. The next ten pages are devoted to putting the main character (Jack Kurz) in jeopardy. And the final ten pages are where the conflict is resolved and Kurz's life is miraculously saved. It's a formula I can understand, and one Ken seems to employ in each script.

There's something oddly familiar about Ken's stories, but I can't quite put my finger on what it is, until I get to the sixth script. In it Jack Kurz instructs Lo Ming, his Chinese hired hand, to gather some wood for the fireplace. While doing so, several bad guys sled up to Lo Ming and drag him away, presumably with the worst of intentions. Jack Kurz takes a sled team into town, kicks some bad-guy ass, and saves Lo Ming from the rope. It's a nice, familiar story that reminds me of ...

Holy Christ ... I'm pretty sure he swiped this story from *Bonanza*! Only now it's not Little Joe kicking ass, it's Jack Kurz. And instead of Hop Sing screaming in pidgin English, it's Lo Ming. And instead of horses running around, it's malemutes.

I scan the other scripts and discover that each one of them has been lifted, to one degree or another, from an American TV series. The one about a boy getting kidnapped is right out of *The Rifleman*. The episode where Kelly the barmaid tips off the lawman to a thieving rustler is a reconstituted

Gunsmoke episode. And there's even a script where Jack Kurz saves his rapscallion buddy from a bunch of guys who accuse him of cheating at cards. Yep. *Maverick*.

I'm shocked. Is that all there is to writing a television series? You just lift a story right out of your youth, change the names of the characters, add some snow, and you've got a script?

Hell, I can do that. In fact, I've got an episode of *Leave it to Beaver* that's going to work perfectly.

* * *

I've now been in West Berlin for almost three weeks. I've seen very little of the city. I've met no one. And I think I'm starting to develop an itchy hemorrhoid from sitting on my ass for roughly eighteen hours a day.

My meals have consisted of whatever Ken has on his shelves and in his refrigerator, which means the cuisine lately has been nothing but Kellogg's Corn Flakes and oatmeal. Being alone in a foreign country is my worst fear, and I find myself pissed off that Ken is spending all his time with Renate.

From out of nowhere, there's a burst of three high-pitched rings. It stops for a second or two, then resumes with another set of three rings. It's not immediately clear where the sound is coming from, but it seems to originate from the corner of the room. It's starting to grate on my nerves, and it must be stopped, whatever it is. As I explore the area around the single bed, it continues: *bdddding, bddding, bddding* ... and then it seems to rest up a bit, building strength for its next round of nerve-rattling jangling, until it finally stops. Thank god. I don't think I could have taken much more of that. I go back to the little desk and resume making notes about my story, when the fucking ringing starts up again. I'm going to find it this time, and I pull the bed away from the wall to discover an odd-looking device on the floor underneath it. It looks vaguely like a phone, except it's round and squat and doesn't sound like any telephone I've ever heard. As I stand over it, wondering exactly what to do, I'm unsure what the phone-answering protocol is in Germany. What do you say into a German phone you've just answered? Out on the street, people greet each other by saying *Tag*, which I take to be a shortened version of *Guten Tag* or Good Day. So, by saying *Tag*, what they're really saying is Day, which strikes me as bizarre. But it's eight in the evening now, and saying Day at night to someone on the phone seems kind of idiotic.

No matter. The phone has stopped ringing. Another problem solved through the power of inactivity. I go back to my work. I'm thinking of having Jack Kurz get in trouble when he saves an Indian woman from the overly amorous advances of a group of bad guys. I've abandoned the idea of borrowing from *Leave it to Beaver* and I've instead borrowed an old episode of *Wanted: Dead or Alive*. Who cares ... the Germans will never know the difference.

The great thing is that I can think of a whole library full of deceased American TV westerns I can swipe, and all I have to do is change a few characters here and there, drop the temperature about eighty degrees, and add a bunch of frisky dogs and rabid wolves. Man, writing a TV series is a lot easier than I thought, particularly when you don't have to come up with original ideas.

But that annoying phone thingy rings again, and I once more ponder what to do with it. On the fourth cluster of rings, I pick it up and say hello with some sort of grotesque German accent in the belief that I will be more easily understood.

"What the fuck are you doing?" Ken says.

"I'm answering the phone."

"I just called two minutes ago and it rang about fifteen times."

"Yeah, I heard it."

"Then why the fuck didn't you answer it?"

"I was trying to figure out what to say when you pick up a phone in Germany."

"How about hello?"

"Is hello German?"

"No," he says, sighing. "But even an imbecile will understand that you're answering the phone."

"Well, I—"

"And what's with that screwy accent? You sounded like you were doing an impression of Colonel Klink."

"Sorry, I was confused."

"Anyway, I spoke to Manfred Blau this morning."

"Who's that?"

"He owns the film studio I work for. I mentioned that you're in Germany and he offered to give you a job on a film that's starting tomorrow," Ken says, probably expecting me to be gleeful.

"Why?"

"What do you mean, why? Because it's a film studio, and working in the movie business is cool."

"What about writing the TV series?"

"What about it?"

"If I'm working at the studio during the day, when am I supposed to write?"

"I don't give a shit when you write. You can write while you're sitting on the toilet, for all I care."

"Are you going to be there with me?"

"No, I've got better things to do than to be a gopher on a movie set."

"What am I going to be doing on the film?"

"How the fuck should I know? Just be out in front of the apartment building at seven in the morning. You'll be picked up by a white van."

"Don't people in the movie business travel around in limos?"

"Not you, laddy. Just be glad they're not making you ride a donkey to work."

In the background, I hear a woman's voice, but can't make out what she's saying. Ken giggles.

"Am I going to get paid for—"

The phone goes dead, and I stare at the receiver for several moments. Well, I guess I'm going to be in the film business. Bright lights, catered lunches, gorgeous European starlets. This is the kind of opportunity the guys in my cinema classes dream about. I'll be around exciting people doing stimulating work. I'll have a chance to improve my German. I'll be out of the apartment every day. And I can't think of a situation more awful.

* * *

It's six in the morning. I'm an hour early for the van, but I reason that you can never be too early for Germans. It's snowing like crazy, and I jam my hands into the pockets of the long coat my mother gave me in anticipation of my needing it in Germany. She was right. Except that the coat seems to be insulated with a material the thickness of toilet paper, and I'm shivering uncontrollably and I've lost feeling in everything from the neck down. At this time of the morning, it's even too early for the hookers to be out, which means I'm the only one standing on what is normally Berlin's busiest street.

In the inside pocket of my coat, I can feel my pen pressing against my chest. I've brought along the notepad in case I'm called upon to write some zippy dialog or solve a nasty story problem. It would seem they'd want to take advantage of my writing ability.

No doubt about it, I'm starting to experience hypothermia. The numbness I felt in my lower extremities has now migrated upward and the only sensation is a pounding headache that's making me woozy.

"Ho, there. Are you Dennis?" the man standing in front of the white van says in lightly accented English.

I'm unable to say anything, I'm so cold, so I nod meekly. The man smiles and takes me by the arm and leads me toward the van.

"Please, get in. I'll turn the heater on."

It's a large van and there are several rows of bench seats. Barely able to lift my legs, I somehow manage to climb into the van and collapse onto the back seat next to a young woman. In fact, the van is filled with young women, and they're all staring at me.

"*Guten Tag*, Danneez," one of them says.

"*Guten Tag*," I somehow manage to mumble back through thick, purple lips.

"Dennis," the man says, slipping into the driver's seat. "I am Gerhard. I will be picking you up every morning at seven. I recommend that you don't wait on the street any longer than you have to. You will find that I pick up each of the women at their hotels first, and then I come for you exactly at seven.

There are so many people in the van that I'm unable to see the driver, except for his eyes in the rear-view mirror.

"These girls will warm you up with their beauty," he says, and all the girls giggle.

Now that he mentions it, these girls are pretty good-looking. No, they're astonishing, which is obvious even though each wears a long heavy coat and some sort of furry hat pulled down over her ears.

The van pulls away from the curb and I watch the buildings through the window. I'm too embarrassed to look at the women in case one of them turns around and catches me gawking. The last thing I want is for anyone to assume I'm leering on my first day of the film. Instead, I focus on the passing scenery and listen to four different incomprehensible conversations, Gerhard inserting himself in one after the other as he pleases. The women seem to enjoy his participation, and he seems surprisingly good at charming them.

As the city disappears behind us, we cross a bridge over a teeming river and finally pull into a parking lot next to what looks like a pile of rubble that was probably once a building prior to World War II.

The ladies seem to be waiting for something, but I have no idea what it might be, until Gerhard sweeps open the front passenger door and makes a deep bow in a show of mock gallantry. A woman chortles from inside the van, and I see her carefully place one knee-high black boot on the van's running board, then the other foot steps out onto the ground. She's wearing a long coat made from what is probably six or eight pelts from some endangered member of the African cat family, and she slings a large leather bag over her shoulder and removes a pair of delicate doe-skin gloves from inside, then puts them on as she walks. Her face is classic German with high, carved cheekbones, her complexion pink in the cold of the morning, and her eyes clear as ice cubes.

Led by Gerhard, the group of women enters the warehouse and I wait for the woman in the cat coat so that she doesn't have to walk alone. She smiles at me, revealing a set of perfect white teeth.

"You are a gentleman," she says in a low breathy voice, and I feel the blood pushing through my veins just a little bit harder. "Are you working on the film?"

I'm stunned that she's actually talking to me and I stammer for a few seconds until I'm able to spit out a coherent reply. "Yes, I think so." And I notice, despite the fact that she's covered from head to toe in winter clothing, how dizzyingly ravishing she is.

"How did you get the job?"

I decide to carefully consider this question, because I want to believe its answer will have some bearing on whether I see this woman again. "Manfred Blau asked me to work on the film."

She begins strolling toward the building and I walk beside her. "Ah, Manfred Blau," she says, seeming genuinely impressed. "What job did he ask you to do?"

Another red flag. I'd like to tell her I'm the producer, but that could get me in a lot of trouble. And I can't just invent a job, because I haven't got a clue what anyone does on a film set. I know there are people who do makeup and hair. And someone operates the camera. I'm pretty sure there are guys who set up lights and stuff like that. But there's no way I can bullshit some conversation about any of those jobs if she asks follow-up questions.

"I'm really not sure what I'll be doing."

She smiles again. "I'm certain that whatever it is will be an experience to remember," and she disappears through a door.

I follow her through and discover that I'm in a large studio in which some sort of magnificent ancient building stands. It's a huge, white structure with large Greek columns in front of it. As I walk around to the side, it becomes clear that this must be a fake building used in a movie, because there are no walls along the side where the rest of the building should be. Still, the front of it is an amazing architectural recreation of something I've only seen in pictures.

The gorgeous woman who was just talking to me is surveying the set, watching a few dozen people hurrying around, setting up props, sweeping, putting the finishing touches of paint on the building, and a multitude of other activities. She slowly takes her gloves off and puts them in her shoulder bag, then pulls off a hat that at one time was probably the conjugal mate to one of the pelts in her coat. She shakes a very long mane of wavy blonde hair free and it cascades down her back. Odd. There ... is ... something ... vaguely ...

Oh, my god in heaven ... it's Sybil Danning. She's here and she's standing right next to me and I just spoke to her moments before and I didn't even know it was her and she didn't even laugh at me and Ed will absolutely die when I tell him about this. I'm instantly terrified because I think I'm fighting a losing battle to avoid saying Duhhhh like Moose from those *Archie* comics when he sees a pretty girl. Anything I'm likely to say right now would make that guy seem positively articulate. She turns and looks at me and I don't care if she catches me staring at her. I *am* staring at her. Her eyes sparkle and she giggles.

"The beginning of a new film is always so exciting," she says. "You never know what's going to happen."

I'm too shell-shocked to answer.

"Did I hear Gerhard correctly? Is your name Dennis?"

"Yes ... yes, it is."

"My name is—"

"Sybil," I say.

She smiles. "Have you been reading fan magazines?"

"Just one."

"I'm very flattered that you remember my name," she says, waving goodbye.

I watch her slowly walk across the film set, all eyes looking up at her, all voices falling silent, all time standing still— until she disappears into a hallway. A dozen men glance at each other and smile, then resume working.

"*Wer sind Sie?*" a bearded man with a clipboard says.

"I'm sorry, I don't speak Dutch."

"Dutch?" the man says. He's repeatedly poking the side of his neck and I see that he's going at a series of pimples like a child gleefully popping bubble wrap.

"Sorry, I meant Deutsch."

"You are American?"

"Yes, from Los Angeles."

"What you doing here?"

"I'm in Berlin to visit my brother and maybe do a little writing," I say, thinking this just may impress him.

"I am asking what are you doing here on film set?" From his demeanor, he seems to be regarding me as an intruder.

"I was told that I would be working on a film here."

"What film?"

"I don't know."

"Are you actor?"

"No, I'm not really sure—"

"Then what job you are doing?"

"I don't know."

"Why you talk to that woman?"

"Because she was talking to me, that's why. Who are you?"

"I am assistant director."

"Congratulations."

"What you doing here?"

"You asked that already."

"How you get job here?"

This is starting to get annoyingly prosecutorial. "I was invited to work on the film."

"Who?"

"Who what?"

"Who invite you?" he says.

Poor schmuck. I didn't want to invoke the name of the film studio's owner, but this guy has it coming. "Manfred Blau gave me the job," I say, and I see the man's eyes widen and the color drain from his face.

He affects a huge smile, one he doesn't look particularly used to trying on, and claps me hard on the back. "Yes, yes. You work on my film. I give you best job."

Man, apparently Manfred Blau's name is pure alchemy around here. I mean, who would have thought this hostile, bearded dunce with a festering sore was capable of turning a one-eighty like that? What power it gives me.

"Here, you sit now. I find special job for you," the man says, guiding me to a folding chair next to the door.

As the man hurries away, I tell myself that I must use this power wisely, for the betterment of all. And then it hits me: this must be what Superman experienced when his rocket ship landed on Earth and he discovered he could toss Buicks, bend parking meters, and fly over the city and spit on picnic blankets. Of course, he was a baby when he landed on Earth, so he probably wasn't intellectually developed to the degree that he could compare his life after he landed to his life on Krypton. He probably just figured he was always able to turn every woman's shirt into a Saran Wrap blouse.

Would I get tired of that? I mean, as fascinating as breasts are, how many of them could I see before it started to be old hat? Do they all start to look alike after awhile? Does a guy ever get numbed to the infinite differences in shape, size, perkiness, and heft?

Yes, so much to consider about breasts, I tell myself, sitting heavily in the chair and leaning it back against the cement wall. There are a dozen different conversations going on, none of which I can understand, and after a short while they start to sound like the buzzing of bees ... the ... buzzing ... of ... bees.

There are probably better ways to wake up than to have the folding chair you're sitting in spontaneously collapse, pitch you backward, then trap your body in its frame so that you're unable to do anything but squirm like a hooked mackerel. Yet, I discover to my complete horror, this is exactly what has just happened to me, jarring me out of a sound sleep. I've somehow managed to jam both my ass and my arms through the metal bars of the chair, and no amount of flopping around on the floor will extract me. The assistant director rushes up to me and tries to pull me to my feet, but my ass is stuck in the chair's frame with the folded seat pressing behind my knees, preventing me from straightening my legs. Everyone on the set —and there are by now about fifty people, all of them in a state of confusion—stares at me and the assistant director, who valiantly dislodges me from the chair. A few people strike up conversations with each other, probably wondering who I am and how I got to be so stupid as to be pinned to the floor by an inanimate object; others just giggle and get on with their work.

"You okay now, American?" the assistant director says.

It's not so much a question as it is a statement with a question mark thrown up at the end as if he's using it as a grappling hook to help me to my feet and lift my spirits. Truth be told, no, I'm not okay. This couldn't be more embarrassing. Worse, I've pulled a groin muscle, but I don't know how to say it in German, and pantomiming it is likely to get me thrown off the set and possibly arrested. "I'm fine. Thanks for your help."

He smiles at me and shakes his head sympathetically. "I am Friedrich ... assistant director."

"I am Dennis." We shake hands. "Christ!" I say, looking at my watch. "I was asleep for thirty-five minutes."

"Yes, you make loud sleep noise."

Swell. "Did anyone hear me ... besides you?"

"No, no one hear, except people on film set."

Well, that's a relief. No one outside the building heard me. My first day in the studio and I've fallen asleep, snored like a pterodactyl, gotten twisted up in a folding chair and flopped around helplessly on the floor, and only about fifty people happened to notice. Whew! That's great news.

An older man with gray hair shouts something in German and everyone on the set gathers around him in a circle. Not knowing what else to do, I amble up behind a small woman with an eyebrow pencil behind her ear. The older man launches into what turns out to be a very long, unintelligible monolog. I really wish I had a sense of what he's saying because it sounds important, judging by the rapt attention he's commanding from everyone. Considering he's shouting in a foreign language, he's a lot less interesting than the reaction of the shoutees, who periodically nod appreciatively and occasionally chuckle in unison. My guess is that he's the film's director and he's giving them the Knute Rockne treatment before they shoot the first scene, but I can't be sure.

I tap the eyebrow pencil woman on the shoulder. "What's he saying?"

"*Ruhe, bitte.*"

I'm not sure what she just said, but she used the word *bitte* in the sentence, which I've learned means please. She must want me to repeat my question. "What's he saying," I say louder.

She turns and looks at me as if I've offered to stick my index finger in her nose up to the third knuckle. "Sssshhhh!"

The director shoots a burning stare at the woman, then continues talking, his voice rising in volume with each sentence. One by one, he points at various people, who respond by nodding solemnly, until finally his voice gets very quiet, and everyone leans in to hear what he's saying. It's an impressive display of leadership, each person hanging on every word. Finally, he waves a hand and everyone springs into action, going to his or her station. Everyone, that is, except me since I don't have a clue what I'm supposed to be doing here.

The director yells something and several lights come on, illuminating the front of the Greek building. From my earlier exploration, it's clear that the building is made of painted wood and styrofoam, and with the lights on it looks like it's carved out of one giant block of marble. The director issues a command, the man operating the camera says something back to him, the director yells again, and a young man in a toga exits the building and stands in front of it. He paces nervously for several seconds until the director yells something. The lights are immediately turned off and everyone mills around, tending to this or that. *"Noch mal,"* the director says, approaching the young man and explaining something to him quietly.

I'm watching a movie being made, and it's absolutely fascinating. There's so much excitement on the set, so much apparent anticipation about what's going to happen. I can't believe I'm actually here seeing this.

Friedrich waits for the director to finish chatting with the actor, then yells something through a bullhorn, and the young man in the toga disappears through the entry of the building, a large rectangular doorway. The lights come back on. The director issues his command —*Kamera!*—and the cinematographer responds that the camera's rolling. The director yells again—what must be the

German equivalent of Action!—and the actor in the toga strides importantly through the doorway, scans the horizon for a few seconds, then paces back and forth in front of the building.

I can't for the life of me see anything different between this take and the first one, but the director seems pleased with the improvements, yells, "*Ja, gut!*" and the lights are immediately doused.

Friedrich approaches me carrying a stack of folded white towels, divides the stack into two, then hands one of them to me. "These for you," he says.

"I don't understand. I'm not wet."

"These for ... how you say ... *mädchen*."

I have no idea what a *mädchen* is or why it would need so many towels, but I'm determined to get to the bottom of this. "Is the *mädchen* wet?"

Friedrich's eyes narrow. "No, no ... not wet ... *kalt*."

"The *mädchen* is cold?" I say proudly, feeling as if I've bridged another important cultural gap.

"Yes, *mädchen* cold."

"But not wet?"

"No, no ... "

"Just cold?"

I have a nagging feeling that if I only knew what a *mädchen* was, this would all make a lot more sense, so I pursue that direction. "What does the *mädchen* look like?"

There's a flicker of recognition in his eyes as he smiles and holds his hand up to my shoulder level.

"So, the *mädchen* is about this big?"

"Yes, yes," Friedrich says, grinning. "And like this," he says, moving his hand down a couple of inches.

"Does the *mädchen* shrink?" I say, feeling like I'm on a game show.

"No … there is many *mädchen*. We film them. Next scene."

"Are they some kind of animal?"

Despite a truly heroic effort on Friedrich's part, I get the sense he's losing patience with this conversation. Which is exactly when a door opens from an adjoining room, and about a dozen young women stroll onto the set.

There are three things remarkable about their entrance, aside from the fact that I'm twenty years old and the appearance of women is always a penultimate event. The first is that they are all approximately the same age, which I take to be about eighteen. The second is that they are all monumentally beautiful, although vastly different from each other in terms of hair color, height, and build. The third is that their breasts are all …

Their breasts? Oh, sweet Jesus, they're all naked! Completely ... except for sandals that crisscross up their legs and tie above their calves. And they've just ambled onto the set.

Friedrich nods. "Ja, they are come now. Here are the *mädchen*."

Yes, they are come now. The maidens ... none of whom appears to be either cold or wet, unfortunately.

Friedrich snatches a towel from the top of the stack and starts toward the women, who by this time are gathered around the Greek building and, apparently, discussing the architecture. He turns and sees that I haven't moved. "Please follow."

Which I do. Reluctantly. I walk behind him as he approaches one of the naked maidens, says, "*Entschuldigen Sie, Fräulein*," and, putting his cheek next to hers, wraps the towel around her shoulders.

I'm standing behind him, doing my best to keep my eyes riveted to the floor which, given the circumstances, isn't easy.

Friedrich puts a hand on my shoulder. "*Hier ist Danneez ... aus* Los Angeles," he says.

The maiden giggles at me. "Hallo, Danneez *aus* Los Angeles. We have previously met."

I'm doing my best not to stare at her neatly trimmed pubic hair, visible beneath the towel, and I lock my eyes onto hers. My head is spinning, but I know it's important to give the appearance that I'm actually paying attention to what she's saying. "We have? When?"

"This morning." She searches my face for some sign of human intelligence, finds none. "In the van," she offers.

Ah, yes.

Friedrich makes his way to each of the young naked maidens, says, *"Entschuldigen Sie, Fräulein,"* puts his cheek next to hers, and artfully wraps a large, white towel around her shoulders and torso. Clearly, he's done this before.

"You don't recognize me?" she says, slightly disappointed. And then it dawns on her. "Maybe I am now more naked."

Hmmm, yes. That's it. She is considerably more naked. It's always the subtleties that trip me up.

"Hello, Dennis," a female voice says.

I turn to see Sybil standing behind me, her long blond hair now in soft curls that cascade like a sun-drenched waterfall down her back, the apparent result of a dutiful hairdresser. She has on blue shadow and black liner that accentuate the iceberg color of her eyes. More importantly, she has her arms crossed under two large breasts made from delicate alabaster skin that reveals a translucent blue milk vein meandering to the center of an impossibly pink nipple slightly larger than a silver dollar. Not that I notice the details.

"Well ... ?" she says, allowing her eyes to shift to the stack of towels.

"Uh ... uh ... " I'm at a loss for what to do, so I hand her a towel.

"Thank you, Dennis. But you should watch how Friedrich does it. He's very suave, you know," she says, wrapping the towel around her shoulders.

"Yes, I guess he is. If you don't mind me asking, what is he saying when he whispers to the girls?"

"Well, I'm not sure what he's saying to all of them—because he might know some better than others—but I believe I heard him say to one of them, '*Entschuldigen Sie, Fräulein*'. It means Excuse me, miss." She smiles at me. "Can you say it?"

"Excuse me, miss."

She throws her head back and laughs. "No, I mean in German."

"I'm ... afraid ... not."

"Try this. Ent ... "

"Ent," I repeat.

"Shool ... "

"Shool"

"Dig ... "

"Dig."

"Enn ... "
"Enn."
"Zee ... "
"Zee."
"Froy ... "
"Froy."
"Line ... "
"Line," I say, relieved to be at the end of this ridiculously multisyllabic German phrase.

"Very good," she says, smiling broadly. "Now put it all together."

"Ent ... ghoul ... "

"Shool," she says, giggling.

"Ent ... shool ... "

"Good."

"Ent ... shool ... dig ... zee ... "

"Oops, you forgot part of it."

"Which part?"

"Ent ... shool ... dig ... enn ... "

"Ah, right. Ent ... shool ... dig ... enn ... zee," I say proudly.

"Now, don't forget to say 'miss' in German."

"Damn! I forgot," I say. "Fräulein."

"Excellent," she says, and seems genuinely pleased. "You'll find that *Entschuldigen Sie, Fräulein* is a very useful phrase in Germany, assuming you address it to a young woman.

"Enn ... shool ... dig ... enn ... zee ... froy ... line. Entschul ... digen ... *Sie, Fräulein. Entschuldigen Sie, Fräulein*," I say, very impressed with myself. I must remember only to call women *Fräulein*.

"I think you've got it now. Let me know if there's anything else you need to know," she says, then turns and joins the group of naked maidens. She instantly plunges in to their conversations, not one word of which I recognize.

I don't really understand why Sybil has shown me such kindness and courtesy, but it's amazing that she has. There are about forty strapping German lads working on this film, each of whom locked his eyes on Sybil when she strolled onto the set. And yet ... and yet ... she walked right up to me ... and spent five minutes giving me a language lesson. What exactly is wrong with her?

* * *

I find that I'm using my little notepad for everything except the one thing for which it was intended: writing down story ideas. I have no story ideas. Instead, I'm using the pages to keep me company in my downtime, which I have a lot of. One thing I never anticipated when I fantasized about being in the movie business is how much sitting around there is. My god, there is so much rumination, pondering the next shot, adjusting costumes (such as they are), reapplying makeup, giving instructions, moving the lights, and a hundred other things that add up to someone like me having absolutely nothing to do.

I'm finding that I crack open the notepad instead of having a cigarette, which I suppose is a good thing. Every time I experience any stress or anxiety, scribbling in the notebook seems to take my mind somewhere else. And, truthfully, my first week working on the film has been nerve-wracking, what with all the naked maidens, the short-tempered director, my sense that some people on the set resent me, and just the fact that I'm living in a very foreign country and don't have any friends. Except for the notepad, in which I write ...

My first week in show biz

1. I guess it's supposed to be a privilege to get a job in the movie business, and that might explain why so many people scowl at me. Maybe they're thinking, What is this pampered American doing collecting a paycheck that should go to a German. If they only knew. There is no paycheck.

2. Do a good job wrapping towels around naked maidens (which means, do it without grabbing their boobies), and you get a better job. They've promoted me from towel eunuch to boom man. I'm

the guy who holds the boom microphone. On my first day, I conked the same actor on the head three times with the boom mic to the point where I raised a welt. Toward the end of the day, he blew a take when he flinched as I brought the mic closer to him.

3. What the hell kind of film is this, anyway? The women seem to be naked all the time and, occasionally, even some of the men drop their togas. Jeez, foreskins are weird. God only knows what sort of bacteria and small animals are lurking in those things. I'm very worried that this is a porno film, but Friedrich assures me that it's a "normal German film." If he's right, I can only conclude that normal Germans have weird taste in cinema.

4. It occurred to me that I don't even know the name of the film I'm working on. That would be good to know. Friedrich told me the name is *Gelobt Sei, was hart macht*. I made him say it about 15 times before I was able to sound it out phonetically. Unfortunately, he didn't know how to translate it into English, so he huddled together with several members of the cast and crew. There was much discussion, a loss of patience, even a raised voice or two. But in the end, they agreed that the name of the film translates thusly: "Praise be what hardens you." It's an appropriate title, considering I've been walking around for a week with an erection.

5. I wear a long jacket on the set at all times, and keep it zipped up. I'm not sure if the *Guinness Book of World Records* lists the longest duration of a hard on, but I've got to be challenging the champion by now. Immortal fame appears to be a certainty.

6. Sybil told me that the West Germans are, apparently, a tad anxious about the upcoming Olympics in Munich. When I asked her why, she mentioned something about the inherent West German inferiority complex that stems from getting your ass kicked in sports events by the East Germans every four years. She also told me that this is what this film is about. Now, there's a shock. All this Greek architecture and these people running around in the nude has something to do with the modern Olympics? Sparta and Athens, she says, are metaphors for the two Germanys.

7. Sybil is quite an interesting person. Born in Austria, her family moved to Philadelphia when she was young, which would explain her perfect English that receives a mere dusting of an accent. Her family moved back to Austria a few years later. Maybe she likes to talk to me so that she can use her English. Or maybe she relates to the fact that I lived in so many cities as a kid. Maybe she's just mentally ill.

8. I'm not inclined to make generalizations about entire groups of people, but I'm comfortable saying this: Germans are fucking bizarre. Watching them walk down the street brings to mind the Arctic Circle where separate ice floes silently make their way to a destination determined by wind and current. (Note to self: figure out a way to shoehorn that last phrase into a story somewhere.) I've never seen so many people so unwilling to look each other in the eye.

9. The German language was invented by an ancient tribe that had nothing better to do than string together a dozen syllables to form a single word solely for the purpose of confounding future tourists. How else to explain nouns like *Gesundheits-wiederherstellungs-zusammenmischungsverhaeltniskundiger*? In English, we'll call someone a truck mechanic. In German, they take every known fact about the mechanic and throw it into a blender. Out comes a single word that it will translate into the German equivalent of a Truck Mechanic Who Charges Too Much And Picks His Nose While Wearing Absurdly Large Oil-Stained Overalls. Clearly, this language was created by sadists with a lot of patience.

10. Sybil acted as translator for a discussion I had with some old codger on the set who uttered the

words "international Jewish conspiracy." I told him he's absolutely right; there is an international Jewish conspiracy. And, if he'd like to attend, the delegates meet every month in a back booth at Canter's Deli over plates of kishke and rugelach. On the agenda for September was a spirited discussion of which national treasuries to plunder.

11. Every day at lunch I grab some food from the studio's cafeteria and sit outside by myself. There's a large building across the river and I never see any activity around it. Friedrich told me that the building is Spandau Prison and that the only prisoner it holds is Rudolf Hess, former deputy to the Fuehrer. I wonder if he's looking at me through a dusty pair of binoculars, wondering who this little Jew is who stares at him every day. I wonder what I'd do if I were in the same room with him. I wonder if he's lonely.

* * *

I haven't seen much of Ken in the last couple of weeks, and I'm not sure that's such a bad thing. Since he met Renate and dumped Monika *Eins*, he's changed into someone I don't recognize and isn't much fun to be around. Renate, I've come to understand, is studying psychology at the university, and Ken's internalizing her studies in the most negative and hostile way possible. He's yelling at waiters, refusing to give ground on Berlin's busy sidewalks, and applying Psych 101 analysis to everything around him. He seems to have entered some sort of fugue state where he's realizing his past was worthless and superficial. Mostly, he's become an angry guy, playing aggressive pseudo-intellectual word games with me, picking at everything I do and looking for The Deeper Meaning in everyone's behavior. It's as if, in this crank analysis, he's discovered a toxic pool he can't stop drinking from, one that has the unfortunate effect of poisoning everyone around him. Worse, he just doesn't seem happy. In fact, the closest he gets to it is the occasional moment when he experiences an absence of misery.

* * *

Sybil, who normally rides in the coveted shotgun seat every morning, has curiously begun to sit all the way in the back of the van. Since I'm the last person to be picked up, I take the only available seat, which happens to be right next to her.

"*Guten Morgen*, Sybil," I say.

She smiles broadly. "*Guten Morgen*, Dennis."

I clear my throat. "*Wie geht es Ihnen?*"

Another smile. I'm melting.

"Ich bin ganz gut, danke. Dennis, I'm very proud of you. You're becoming a master of German small-talk."

"Thanks. I've been practicing."

"You must be using one of those translation books for travelers."

"I am. How did you know?"

"Because they teach you to speak formally," she says, slipping off her gloves. "For example, you said *'Wie geht es Ihnen'* which is perfectly correct, technically. But it's something you would say to a superior or someone who's much older. I'm not that much older than you, Dennis." She giggles.

Funny, I never thought much about her age. Stunning women somehow always seem ageless and wiser. Thinking about her now—the smoothness of her skin, the firmness of her breasts, the perfection to be found everywhere I look—I guess her age to be about twenty-two.

I force a chuckle I hope indicates how absurd the notion is that she would be much older than I am. "So, what's the familiar way to say what I said?"

"Very simple. You just say *'Wie geht's.'*"

I roll the sound of the words around in my brain. Yes. *"Wie geht's."*

"It's always so much easier to be familiar rather than formal." She stuffs her gloves in her shoulder bag, then looks through the van's window at a Mercedes that has pulled up alongside a young woman at a corner. "Many of the men who work on the film speak to me as if I'm their superior, using formalities at every opportunity. That makes me uncomfortable."

The thought of anything making Sybil uncomfortable makes me uncomfortable.

As the young woman slides into the passenger seat of the Mercedes, Sybil looks back at me. "Please don't feel you have to be formal with me ... in German or English."

I'm at a loss for what to say, and I can only nod at her stupidly, hoping that she'll take it as some sort of agreement. She's right, though. The men on the film treat her as a goddess. And whether it's because of her looks, her fame in Europe or her star status in the movie, I'm not sure. But their behavior changes the moment she walks onto the set. They seem to straighten up, work harder, suppress their habit of making what I guess to be crude jokes—courtesies they reserve for no other woman in the film. And during every free moment, I notice them staring at Sybil. What they're thinking, I can't imagine. But I'm sure it's not too far from what I'm thinking.

"Do you like movies, Dennis?" she says, interrupting a burst of pointless lust.

"Do you mean working on them or going to see them in a theater?"

She tosses her head back and laughs. "Yes, I suppose those of us in the film business have to make that more clear."

Those of us in the film business ... God, I love the sound of that. Yep, we're just two movie folks chatting away, having a pleasant conversation while the rest of the world goes about their tedious jobs of dentistry, coat-hanger manufacturing, and rodent control. But we're in the film business, and at no time has that fact become more apparent than at this moment when Sybil conferred official film-business status on me.

"Yes," I say, "I really enjoy working on the film."

She smiles. "I'm sorry, I meant the other one."

"Oh. Sorry. Yes. I like to see films. I haven't seen any in Germany yet because they're, you know, in German."

"Would you like to go to a movie with me tonight? I can explain to you what's going on so you won't feel lost."

Hold your horses, missy! Did I hear right? Did Sybil just invite me to a movie? Me? The lowest nothing on the film? Surely she can do better than me. "A movie?" I say, my voice sounding whiny and unsure.

"Yes, you can pick me up in the lobby of the Berliner Hotel and we'll walk to the cinema. It's just down the street."

"I ... I ... "

"Ah, we're here," she says, as the van pulls into the studio's parking lot. "I'll see you at seven-thirty."

I'm dumbfounded and can only watch as the girls hop out of the van and toddle toward the studio. Sybil is the last one, and I take her by the elbow to help her out of the van, which she seems to appreciate.

Not nearly as appreciative as I am.

* * *

Sybil and I are walking down the Ku'damm side by side and I am completely disassociating, my body hovering above the two people walking down the street toward the theater. Some part of my brain knows that the sidewalks are molten with people hurriedly on their way to restaurants, department stores and discos, but right now I don't care. I'm vaguely aware that my thin jacket isn't beginning to insulate me from the chill that's bone-rattling at night in Berlin's winter. And I'm sure I'd normally find the lights and sounds of this amazing boulevard to be compelling and distracting. But right now, there's a guy down there next to what I can only regard as the world's most erotic creature, and nothing is penetrating my thoughts except for her voice as she tells me about her life in the film business. Actually, I'm not even sure I'm listening to her. What's important is that whatever she's saying, she's saying it to me.

As we make our way down the sidewalk—around high-class hookers and their potential johns; drug purveyors with their selection of acid, hash, and stuff I can't begin to recognize; and street musicians paying heartfelt homage to Neil Young and Paul Simon—I'm floating about thirty feet above us, watching us move through this carnival of activity. I look down and see this stunning woman, her blonde hair undulating as she walks, bringing to mind an endless wheat field in a soft breeze. She is talking sweetly to the young man next to her, he in an olive-drab Marine-issue field jacket. And, as I look down from above, I can't imagine what these two people are doing together on this improbable evening.

The young man gazes into her eyes and smiles with each thing she says. He laughs at appropriate times. Nods solemnly when seriousness is called for. Appears to pay close attention to her words, showing her complete deference. If, occasionally, she touches his elbow to emphasize some point in her story, he does his best not to jump out of his skin, and forces himself to maintain eye contact.

The couple arrives at the theater and the young man removes his wallet from the back pocket of his jeans, but the woman touches him on the elbow and removes some money from her shoulder bag. She buys the tickets and the two of them disappear inside the theater, and out of my view.

* * *

Sybil leads me to a seat almost exactly in the middle of the theater, sits, and removes her long coat and lays it across the seat next to her. Given that I'm enormously claustrophobic, I'd much prefer to sit on the aisle, but I'm not about to raise the issue now, so I sit down next to her, suddenly uncomfortable that I've forced her to carry the bulk of the conversation up till now.

"What movie are we seeing?" I say, hoping to fool her into thinking that I'm actually contributing something to the conversation.

"It's called *Anatevka*. Have you heard of it?"

"No, I'm afraid I haven't," I say, wondering why we're watching what sounds to be a Russian film in

Germany. But really, I couldn't care less what film we're seeing. It could be a three-hour epic on hog farming in Bavaria and I wouldn't give a shit, just as long as I get to sit next to this Amazon beauty and watch her face light up from the reflected glow of the screen.

Sybil once again valiantly tries to make conversation with me, but I'm too catatonic by my circumstances to pay attention to what she's saying. I can only focus on the fact that I'm in the seat next to her, our elbows touching on the arm rest, her body radiating a warmth and sweet scent of jasmine that is intoxicating. She's looking at me and saying something, but I'm disassociating again, hovering above us, once again looking down on these two people. As the woman speaks, she casually reaches into her shoulder bag, removes a tissue, then blows her nose in it. She apologizes and I know the young man wants to take the tissue from her, put it in his pocket, and store it in a scrapbook.

"Dennis?" the woman says.

The young man watches her return the wadded up tissue to her bag.

"Dennis?" she says again.

"Yes. What?"

"Are you all right?"

"I'm sorry. You were saying … "

"I was asking you what you do in Berlin when you're not working on the film."

A good question. And the only answer that comes to mind is, not much. "Well, I'm writing an episode of a TV series at night, but it's really hard for me because I'm so tired from working on the film during the day."

She looks at me and I can see concern on her face, and she slowly nods. "The van drops you home at about seven in the evening, then you write a TV series after that? And then you get picked up at seven in the morning? No wonder you're tired."

I nod. She understands.

"So what do you do from the time the van brings you to the studio until ten, when we start filming?"

"I usually sit on the set and read a book," I say, lying. The truth is, I find an empty office in the administrative part of the film studio, curl up on a sofa, and sleep. But, for some reason, I don't want to tell her that.

"Starting tomorrow, you can do your reading in my dressing room. Would you like that?"

Good god. No one is allowed anywhere near Sybil's dressing room. In fact, on the first day of shooting, one of the guys was canned when it was felt he was peeking inside her dressing room when the door opened.

"I'm in the makeup department in the morning and my dressing room is completely unused most of the time. I'm only in there for the last few minutes, putting on my costume. Please feel free to make yourself comfortable in there."

It's an astounding offer, and I can't imagine what people will think when they see me emerge from her dressing room every morning. They're already confused as to who I am and what I'm doing working on their film. Friedrich has told me that there is great speculation about me among the crew. He finds all the gossip and concern vastly amusing but doesn't feel inclined to set them straight. But they've got to find it odd that the guy who holds the boom mic—the person responsible for capturing every uttered sound on this film—doesn't speak a word of the local language. Jesus, I mean, these people already think I'm spying on them or something. What are they going to think when I start popping out of Sybil's dressing room?

"Dennis?"

"Yes?"

"Would you like to use it?"

"Use it?"

"My dressing room."

"Yes, I'd like that. Thank you very much." Wow, I get to be in Sybil's dressing room—a place no one is allowed to be. I'm not exactly sure what I'll do in there, considering I'll be by myself. But just to be allowed in there is beyond my imagination. I wonder if Sybil and I will ever—

The theater lights snap off and the movie starts up. I'm not really looking forward to this part of the evening, mainly because I won't understand the movie, but I can suffer it if it keeps me next to Sybil.

On the screen, an older man with some sort of cart that he pulls seems to be talking directly to the camera. The scene shifts to various people around his village, intercut with shots of the man explaining, I assume, the goings on in his little village.

Hey! This is *Fiddler on the Roof*! I never expected to be seeing this. What a crazy thing to be seeing in Germany. Ah, now I understand why they changed the title to *Anatevka*, the name of the village where the story takes place—*Fiddler on the Roof* was probably too dicey a translation that would have resulted in a single word a hundred-and-ninety-four letters long.

"He's a milk man," Sybil whispers close to my ear, "and he's telling us about his village of Anatevka." She watches the screen for a few moments, then nods. "He's saying that the most important thing in the village, the thing that holds everything together, is ..." Her nose scrunches up. "I can't think of the word in English. It's *überlieferung* in German."

"Tradition?" I say, not really intending it as a question.

Sybil grins. "Dennis, you surprise me. How would you happen to know an obscure word like that?"

I want to tell her that it's my fondest desire to learn every nuance of the German language, to study it day and night until I can spew out verb conjugations that address every conceivable tense, from simple past to future perfect continuous. But then she'd expect me to actually understand her when she speaks German—not that I'd respond any less articulately than when she speaks to me in English.

"I've seen the movie before," I say. "It's required viewing for ... "

She waits for me to finish, but I don't. "Required viewing for ... who?" she says. "Americans?"

"No, I'm sorry. Never mind." Uh oh, what did I just do? I just sat here and almost told this Aryan goddess that—

"Do you mean that it's required viewing for Jews?"

I search her face, looking for some sign of either disgust or approval, but Sybil has that maddening German icy inscrutability.

"Yes," I say.

"It makes perfect sense to me. If I were Jewish, I'd want to know everything about my history, including the kinds of things this film shows."

I want to kiss her on the mouth right now, but that would be preposterous, so I turn to the screen, where Tevye is kvetching to God about being so poor. He'd like a little money just to keep his family comfortable and always have food on the table. Shit, he thinks he has problems? He should try sitting next to Sybil Danning in a dark theater with his arm touching hers on the arm rest. And he should have to pay attention to a movie while sporting a raging hard on that threatens to poke out of the top of his pants.

Yeah, I've got your tradition right here.

Fiddler On The Roof, I suppose, is a great film—even when it's renamed *Anatevka* and dubbed into German. But I've got other things on my mind right at the moment, things like Sybil's bare knee and the part of her thigh that's exposed below her tiny skirt. Even in the darkened theater, the skin glistens and calls to me to touch it, something I desperately want to do yet can't imagine myself ever being bold enough to try. Monika *Zwei* was one thing. But Sybil's in a different universe.

I look up to see Sybil's face staring at me. Damn, she knows I've been looking at her legs and it's anybody's guess how she's going to react to my lechery. Inexplicably, she smiles, takes my hand in hers and draws it to the top of her knee and holds it there. Whatever gland it is that floods the body with adrenaline in moments like these is now behaving like the Hoover Dam with a seriously breached wall. My heart is racing and little beads of sweat are forming on my upper lip, and it's everything I can do to keep my hand from trembling on her knee. And then things get even more curious. Sybil leans her head against my shoulder and emits an almost imperceptible sigh. My brain tells me it's contentment; my gut insists it's something she ate.

Whatever, all this tension has created an excruciating cramp in my left calf. I can't sit still, so I stretch my legs out and push against the unoccupied seat in front of me, and all at once my world turns upside down—literally. The back of my seat breaks away and I'm pitched rearward into the row behind me. Somehow, I'm on my back on the floor with my seat back lying on top of me. Instantly, there is a commotion in the theater, people running at me from all directions, others shouting in German, and I feel a hand on mine pulling me to my feet.

"Dennis, are you all right?" Sybil says.

I'm stupendously embarrassed, but otherwise unharmed, and my first thought is to use the broken seat back to cover up my hard on.

"I think I'm okay," I say meekly.

"Stay there," she says, and climbs over my broken seat.

"Poor Dennis. You seem to have a problem with German chairs."

"A bit, yeah."

"Speaking for the entire country," she says, smiling, "I can assure you it's not a continuation of the Holocaust."

She read my mind.

* * *

It was an uncomfortable ride to the studio today because I assumed that no matter what Sybil and I talked about, somewhere in her mind would be the image of me doing a back flip in the movie theater. She's gamely making conversation with me, but my heart's not in it. I respond to her mostly with nods and grunts, knowing full well that the men she dates don't generally humiliate her in public.

We arrive at the studio and both of us make a beeline for her dressing room, where I immediately stretch out on her sofa and fall asleep. I wake up with a lurch several times as I dream about falling from great heights. And I don't need Freud here to tell me what my issues are.

I wake up for the final time when I realize I've shot my leg out and kicked over a small table at the foot of the sofa. It crashes to the floor and I'm startled into a sitting position. Sybil is standing naked in front of a full-length mirror, adjusting the leather thongs on one of her sandals.

"I would ask you what you were dreaming about, but I think I have a pretty good idea," she says, smiling.

A glance at my watch tells me it's nine-forty-five in the morning, time to head to the set and get my boom mic in position to record the first scene. I say goodbye to Sybil and close the dressing room door behind me. There are several members of the crew having cigarettes and conversations in the hallway outside her door. They get quiet as they see me emerge from the dressing room, some of them smiling at me, some of them scowling, all of them most assuredly wrong about what they imagine I might have been doing for the past couple of hours.

Sybil arrives on the set a few minutes after I do and I see her chatting with the director. He makes a last-minute adjustment to her toga, then calls everyone to their positions for the first shot of the day. It's a banquet scene, set in what's supposed to look like a large hall, with statues and columns along the one wall that's actually going to be filmed. There is also a ten-foot-long table densely covered with fruit. In the center is a huge platter on which is a giant roasted pig with an apple in its mouth. It's grotesque, really, but part of the culinary mayhem that was life in ancient Greece.

"Hello, Danneez," Eva, one of the other gorgeous female stars, says. "This looks like a good place for, how you say in English, an orgy," she says, pronouncing it like Porgy.

She's right. It does look like the kind of set where you'd want to film some type of sexual bacchanalia. I can only laugh at the thought of my friends in L.A. seeing what the hell it is I do here in Berlin. I wish I had a photo to send to them since it's not likely this film will ever be shown—

A photo! Hey, I should have the still photographer take a picture of me on this set. He's got nothing better to do, taking only the occasional picture which, I imagine, will be used for publicity purposes and maybe some posters that will get pasted on walls around the city.

As he carefully cleans one of his camera lenses, I approach him.

"Hi," I say. "My name is Dennis and I'm from Los Angeles."

"Yes."

That's sort of an odd, noncommittal thing to say. Yes hardly seems to be an appropriate response to someone who has just introduced himself. It wasn't said as a question, like I would do if an insurance agent rang me on the phone during dinner time and wanted to wax rhapsodic about actuarial tables while my Swanson's TV dinner got cold. No, it was said in that maddening way the Germans have of saying things without wanting to take actual responsibility for the content of what they say. Yes what? Yes, you heard me? Yes, you know my name is Dennis? Yes, you know I'm from Los Angeles? Yes, you know what I want even though I've yet to ask?

"I'd like to know if you would take my photograph."

"Why?"

"Well, I'd like to send it to my friends and relatives in Los Angeles."

"Why?"

Is this guy three years old, or what? "Because I'd like to let them know what I'm doing in Berlin."

"If I have time, I will take your photograph."

Man, this is like pulling teeth. "You seem to have time right now."

"What kind of photograph would you like?"

A good question. I look around the set, my mind racing. "Okay, what about this: I'll be sitting in front of that giant pig."

"This is what you want to tell people you are doing in Berlin?"

"Well ... "

"If that is what you want ... "

"Would you mind if Sybil is in the photograph?"

"I don't mind. Have you asked her?"

"Wait a second," I say, turning on my heals and rushing over to Sybil. "Sybil, would you mind posing with me in front of the banquet scene. I'd like to send a photo to my friends and relatives in Los Angeles."

Sybil looks at the huge fruit-laden table with the pig platter in the center and nods. "That will make quite an interesting photo. Have you asked the still photographer?"

"Yes, he agreed to do it."

"Okay. Do you want some of the other girls in the shot?"

I hadn't thought of that. This could turn into a very interesting photo after all. "Sure. Would you mind asking them?"

I watch Sybil approach a group of six young women. She's explaining to them what I want and, presumably, why I want it. The girls are smiling now and looking at me—a good sign. Sybil returns to me, grinning.

"The girls want to know if you want us all to be naked."

Hmmm, naked. There's a thought. "Well, that sort of thing isn't really important to me, but YES!!!" I say, and suddenly realize I might have blurted it out.

"Have you asked the director?" she says.

"No."

"You must get his permission."

"Are you sure? I mean, it doesn't really involve him."

"It's his film. It might appear discourteous if you involve some of his crew and cast members in something he doesn't approve of."

She's right, of course. It is his film. As I approach the director, he's engaged in a lengthy discussion with the cameraman as the two of them set up the next shot. I'm excited now, imagining what my photo will look like with all these stunning naked women ... and me. The boys back home are gonna shit! Finally, the cameraman moves away.

"Excuse me, Herr Schreiber."

A look of concern passes across the director's face. He's no doubt wondering what someone of my minuscule stature on the film might want badly enough to approach him about.

"Yes?" he says tentatively.

"I'd like to have a photo taken of me to send to my friends and relatives in Los Angeles."

"Why?"

Jeez. "Well, I, uh—"

"Have you talked to the still photographer?"

"Yes."

"What kind of photograph?"

"Nothing elaborate."

He looks concerned by my response, either because I was too vague or because he doesn't recognize the word elaborate.

In either case, I decide that more explanation will serve my case better. "I'd like to be in front of the banquet scene," I say, gesturing to it, "and maybe, you know, have some of the girls around me."

"Yes, I see." He stares at the banquet scene for what feels like an eternity. "We are about to start a shot, but when it is done, you may have your little picture taken."

Big exhale. "Thank you, Herr Schreiber. Thank you very much."

As I scoop up my boom mic, I'm picturing my friends in L.A. opening up envelopes and finding a picture of me with several naked girls, all of us in front of this enormous feast. It's got to make them incredibly envious. At least, I hope so.

Herr Schreiber calls action and two actors begin a conversation in front of the food-laden table. It's a long conversation, captured in one continuous, difficult shot, and there's a lot that can—and does—go wrong. The actors muff their lines. The lighting isn't quite right. The food needs to be adjusted. Makeup has to be reapplied. The girls walking by in the background are missing their cues. And then all the problems start over again. We've done about ten takes of this same shot, and I'm dying in anticipation of setting up my photograph. Finally, the planets align and the filming of this scene is completed.

Several crew members rush in to take away the banquet tables.

"Would you guys mind leaving the tables there for a few minutes?"

"Bitte?" one of them says.

Sybil explains to the guys what I'm planning, which they seem to find amusing, and I see them dispersing among the other crew members to let them know why the set isn't being struck.

"Okay," I say to Sybil, "are you ready for the photograph?"

"Yes. But let's do this quickly. The girls want to leave the set and go have a cigarette while they can."

I immediately jump into action. "Okay, Sybil, I'll sit here," I say, indicating a spot on the floor in front of the table. "You stand behind me."

"Okay," she says. "What about the rest of the girls?"

"Hmmm ... they can all kneel behind me, sort of holding the fruit in their hands, as if they're offering it to me."

Sybil wrinkles her nose, but directs the girls to their places. The entire crew—about fifty of them—stays on the set to watch, which I find curious, given that they normally leave the set between shots to indulge one addiction or another. But they seem fascinated and slightly confused by what's going on in front of them.

I take my seat on the floor, about five feet in front of the table, then spend about three minutes carefully arranging the women according to hair color, height, breast size, and the specific fruit they're holding. This is a real tour de force and I'm giddy with excitement. When I've got everything exactly the way I want it, I nod to the still photographer.

"Okay, I think we're ready," I say.

He lines up the shot in his viewfinder.

"Can you see the pig behind us?"

"No, Eva is blocking it," he says.

Eva moves a foot to the side, then looks at the photographer questioningly.

"Good," he says. "*Wunderbar.*"

"Okay, any time you're ready."

He looks up from the viewfinder and shakes his head. "No. Everything is too far away. I must change lenses." And with that he roots around in his camera bag, then takes his time carefully changing lenses.

"*Bist du betriebsbereit?*" he says.

I look back at Sybil.

"He wants to know if you're ready," she says.

"Yes, ready when you are."

He spends an agonizingly long time focusing and metering the camera, then looks up from the viewfinder.

"I'm sorry," he says, "I'm at the end of the roll. I need to change film."

Another delay, and a few members of the crew start to chuckle. The photographer spends another minute fishing around in the camera bag, inspecting each box of film for the appropriate one. He finds it, then opens the back of his camera. When he's finished, he nods at me.

"Sorry for the delay," he says. "I am ready."

This is going to be great. I've got girls. I've got a pig. I've got ... hey, I see something on the wall that could make this shot even better. It's a large phallus, hanging on a nail from a leather thong. I can't imagine what it's doing here, except that it will likely be used to decorate an upcoming scene. My god, did the ancient Greeks really have this kind of sex paraphernalia around? And wouldn't it be funny to hang it around my neck? Man, that's inspired!

"Excuse me," I say to one of the costume girls who has stayed in the studio to watch my scene unfold. "Could you please hand me that big, uh, dong over there?"

She speaks zero English and doesn't have a clue what I've just said, but gamely points in the direction of the dildo hanging on the wall.

"*Dieses?*" she says, surprised.

"Yes, that," I say.

She looks at the still photographer and points to the dildo. He shrugs his shoulders at her.

"Dong!," she says, not really sure, and removes the phallus from the wall. As she brings it to me, she holds it out away from her.

"Thank you so much," I say, hanging the object around my neck like an obscene cameo.

"Okay," I say to the photographer. "You can take the picture now."

"Are you sure?" he says, grinning.

"Yes, anytime you're ... "

As I turn around, I have a sick feeling in my stomach. All the girls have left the sound stage, apparently to go have a cigarette, tired of waiting around for the shot to be taken.

I hear the sound of fifty members of the crew, their talking muffled at first, then louder, and finally erupting into loud laughter. It being in German, I can't make out what they're saying— only "blah, blah, blah, blah, Los Angeles."

I'm alone in front of a table on which is a giant fruit cocktail and a six-foot-long roast pig with an apple in its mouth. There is large black dick hanging around my neck, swinging back and forth. The entire crew is pointing at me. There is laughter everywhere and the words "Los Angeles" echoing throughout the studio. I'm alone. And I'm cold. So very, very cold.

*   *   *

It's ten o'clock at night on the evening before the last day of filming, and I'm listening to Armed Forces Network, the only English-speaking rock station my pathetic little radio can pull in. I'm stunned by Emerson, Lake, and Palmer's new song *Lucky Man* because it features something I've never heard before. The DJ introduced the song by referring to a new musical instrument called a synthesizer. It's very, very exciting, but I can't imagine it's going to have widespread appeal beyond a song or two.

As I listen to the music, I'm a little down because the entire cast of the film is being flown to Spain tomorrow for exterior shots and, being a non-essential member of the crew, I don't get to go. I guess they can find someone there to hold the boom mic and wrap towels around naked maidens.

That's the problem with film shoots: you spend a couple of months getting to know people, building a surrogate family, and then you have to say goodbye to all of them, just when things are starting to get good. Come to think of it, it's pretty consistent with my life up till now. In twelve years of grade school, I was moved to eight different schools in four cities. Which means every time I started to feel comfortable, the rug was pulled out from under me. And now this.

I'm in the mood for a cigarette and I pull the pack out of my jacket. I flip open the box of Winstons and immediately notice something unexpected: a little wart-sized nodule of hashish and a tiny pipe made out of aluminum foil. Curious.

Ah, yes. During lunch today at the film studio, I was chatting with Klaus, one of the extras on the film, lamenting the fact that you can't get pot in Germany. I left my pack of cigs on the table when I went to take a whiz, and he must have given me a going-away gift. Thoughtful of him.

Since the film is ending production tomorrow, I decide to celebrate by getting ripped tonight. I drop the button of hash into the pipe bowl, hold a match to it, and take a huge lung full of smoke. Within five seconds, I'm almost incoherent. Man, I've never gotten a buzz like this from all those seeds and stems I've been sucking up in the States. No, this is something different. Whatever active ingredient hash has that produces a high is making my lips tingle and my hair follicles vibrate. This is terrific!

I shut off the desk lamp, the one light in the apartment that's on, and from the window of my dark room, I can see the cars whizzing past on the Ku'damm below, each one dragging what appears to be red fluorescent ribbons behind it.

When I glance down at my watch, I see that it's eleven-forty, which means I've been gawking out the window for over an hour and a half. Well, that was time spent usefully.

I'm absolutely starving and I head into the little kitchen to take a look at my provisions, and I'm disappointed to see that the only remaining edible item in the apartment is a box of soda crackers, which I decide is better than nothing. I take the box with me to my writing table and resume my observation of the street traffic while I munch on the dry crackers.

My mouth is starting to feel like I'm mixing cement in it, but I feel too stoned to get up to fetch a glass of water. Worse, I find I'm getting more and more depressed as I listen to the American announcer on the radio. He's stopped playing music and is instead yakking about life as a soldier in Germany and being so far away from his home in California. I wish he'd shut up and play some songs. There's a little voice in my brain telling me that I can turn the radio off, but my body doesn't seem to have the strength to get up and press the button. As a result of three hits from the hash pipe, I feel like I'm in some kind of alternate gravity where my body parts are ten times their normal weight and moving around is inconceivable. For all my ability to do even the most simple things—like flex my arms or wiggle my legs—I might as well be tied to the chair I'm sitting in. And as *Mother's Little Helper* comes on the radio, I tell myself it's okay that I'm paralyzed and my tongue has gone completely numb and feels swollen and shot with novocaine.

It is okay. Except that I hear the floorboards in the hall outside of my apartment squeak and it sounds like someone's standing in front of my door. Maybe it's someone looking for an apartment. Yes, that must be it. Except that I hear the knob turning slowly. Whoever is trying to get in keeps letting go of the doorknob, then trying it again, as if the person trying to open the door needs seven attempts in order to convince himself the door is really locked.

"Hebbo?" I say. "Who'th there?"

No answer. Only more fiddling with the knob. And from somewhere in the dark recesses of my mind, I remember Herr Hartmann, the previous tenant, who was brutally murdered right in this apartment. I've been unable to remove his blood from the grout between the bathroom tiles.

A key slides into the lock and I'm terrified to discover that I'm simultaneously leaden from the hash and infused with adrenaline. I want so much to be able to get up, to hide in the bathroom or under the bed. But I can't seem to issue the commands to my limbs.

Oh, holy Christ. The door is opening and the hinges are squealing. A couple of footsteps into my little entry hall. Shit, I wish I'd left the light on, but then do I really want to see who's killing me? A few more tentative steps and there's a person in the room with me. I can clearly feel his presence and even hear his breathing about five feet away from where I'm sitting. I get the sense that he's looking around the room, taking it all in, trying to get his bearings.

My fight-or-flight instincts are waging a war entirely without the benefit of my participation. Part of me wants to run away, and I try to gauge what I can reasonably expect in the way of cooperation from my paralyzed body, but I just don't think I can produce the strength to actually stand up, run to the door, flee down the hallway, then hurtle my body down five flights of stairs without killing myself. The other part wants to fight for my life. But with what weapons? A quick mental inventory tells me I have the following items within easy reach on my writing table: a pack of Winstons, a box of matches, and a small ceramic ashtray. I picture myself flicking lit matches at him, but even in my condition I can see it wouldn't be a particularly effective way to set him on fire. The box of Winstons? Useless. It would take years to foist lung cancer on him. Even the little china ashtray—at about two ounces, butts included—is too paltry to inflict any meaningful damage. If I threw it at him, it would probably just bounce off his chest and piss him off. Okay, there's a small box of paperclips, too. But how many paper clips would I have to fling at someone before I hit him in the eye? I'm fucking screwed.

There is the unmistakable sound of a hand rubbing against the wall, groping for something, and a jolt of electric current rips through my body. From somewhere, I summon up the energy to reach out my hand for the ashtray. But it's not the ashtray my hand touches. It's ... the ... typewriter. Yes, that's it! The typewriter. In one motion I grasp it on both sides, stand, and bring it over my head. As I move toward him, prepared to crush him with it, my mouth opens and a sound comes out that my body has never produced until this moment.

Eeeyahhhhhh!!!!

The room light comes on and a man is standing in front of me with his hand on the wall switch. When he sees the insane, shrieking bundle of raw energy coming at him, he shields his head with an arm and falls back against the wall.

"Jesus, god Jesus! What are you doing, Den?" Ken says.

Eeeyahhhhhh!!!!

My heart is thumping in my chest, my breath is coming out in tortured rasps, and my open mouth is still producing a high-pitched squeal.

"Jesus, Den!" Ken says, crouching against the wall, his hand still covering his head. "What's wrong?"

I can barely get the words out. "What … ? I can't … Herr Hartmann …"

Ken stands up, sniffs the air in the room, and giggles. "Have you been smoking hash?"

"Yeth."

"Are you okay?"

"I thought Herr Hartmann wuth in the room," I say, still holding the typewriter over my head.

"You shouldn't smoke that shit alone, you know. That stuff's a lot stronger than what you're used to." He looks at me for several moments. "Hey, would you mind putting down the typewriter?"

"I'm thorry. I wuth a little thcared," I say, returning the typewriter to the little writing table and falling into the chair. "What are you doing here?"

"I came by to pick up some of my clothes."

"Did it ever occur to you to call firtht?"

"Well, I didn't want to wake you up."

"I apprethiate your conthideration."

"What's with your tongue? Did you bite it or something?"

"It'th a little thick from the hath?"

"The hath?"

I pick up the pipe from the ashtray and hold it up.

"Oh. The hash." Ken opens the door to the closet and begins to remove some shirts and pants from hangers. "Anyway, I've got some good news for you."

"Really? What?"

"Manfred Blau likes your Jack London script. He's going to buy it."

"Oh, my god," I say, leaping up from the chair. "Ith he really going to pay me money for it?"

"Five hundred bucks," Ken says over his shoulder.

"Oh, my god!" I can't believe I'm getting so much money for so little work.

"He had an interesting thing to say about it. He called to ask me if I wrote it and then put your name on it."

"Why would he thay that?"

"Because he thinks our writing styles are so similar." Ken shakes his head and chuckles at the stupidity of it. "Weird, huh—him thinking you can write like me?"

"Yeth. Very weird."

"Anyway, I told him I had nothing to do with it, that you read all of my scripts and must have been influenced by my style."

I hadn't thought I was copying Ken's style as I was writing the script. But I'm incredibly flattered that Blau thought Ken actually wrote it.

Ken has all his remaining clothing draped over the arm he used to shield his head from me, and he closes the closet door.

"Well, I guess that's everything," he says. "See you later."

"Thankth."

"Yeah. Hey, is there any more of that hash left?"

"A little."

I hand him the pipe and he drops it in his pocket. He walks to the front door, opens it, then turns back to me.

"You don't have to be afraid of Herr Hartmann. He's dead. Now, the guy who killed him ... they still haven't found him."

Ken steps out into the hallway and closes the door. I lock it behind him.

* * *

I'm keeping my eyes closed because I'm afraid that if I open them, I'll discover that the lunatic dreams I've been having are real—that Herr Hartmann's killer really did cut off my penis and throw it out the window into the Kurfürstendamm traffic below. With my eyes still closed, I reach down and feel my groin. Everything is still connected.

I open my eyes and flinch at what I see. Instead of someone psychotic standing over me with a knife, there are two large breasts dangling only inches above my face and I let out an audible gasp and cover up my crotch.

"Oh, I'm sorry," Sybil says, holding a hanger with a tunic draped over it. "I hope I didn't startle you."

I swing my legs off the couch, rub my eyes, and remember where I am: in Sybil's dressing room.

"I was just having a bad dream," I say, for no apparent reason other than I feel obligated to say something.

"Poor Dennis," she says, and does something surprising. She picks up a large towel and holds it in front of her and sits on the sofa across from me. It's a baffling display of modesty, given that I've seen her stark naked every day for the past two months.

Why is she covering herself up? How can this beautiful woman who has engaged in numerous discussions with me about American politics, movies, rock and roll, and Nazi Germany—while completely naked—suddenly feel the urge to cover herself up? It took me a week to get comfortable talking to her while she was in that condition. Yeah, it sort of made me feel like a eunuch that she didn't regard me as a sexual being, but I could live with that for the opportunity to just be next to her, to have her choose to talk to me when there were so many other people on the set.

I consider all the reasons why she might be using the towel, and I start with the obvious one: she's cold. I suppose that's a possibility, but, Jesus ... it's her dressing room. She can set the thermostat to any temperature she wants. Besides, she didn't grab the towel until I woke up. Did she suddenly get cold at that precise moment? No, her nipples weren't hard and, from my vantage point, I had a pretty good look at them. Think, Dennis, think. Oh, god ... maybe she saw that I woke up with a boner. Would that freak her out? No, probably not, considering I had a continuous erection during my first week on the film until I got used to things. What then? Is there something about being alone with me in her dressing room that gives her the willies? That can't be it, because I've woken up every morning to find her nude. And she never grabbed a towel before.

Her behavior has thrown me off balance and I'm suddenly nervous. I reach into my jacket pocket and remove my little notepad and begin to make a show of capturing a thought for posterity. In truth, I'm doodling something asinine.

"Dennis," Sybil says, her voice low and husky. "You don't need to write about it. It's right here in front of you."

What on earth is she talking about. What's right here in front—

Oh ... the towel. That's what she's telling me. She's holding the towel in front of her for the most astounding and unpredictable reason of all. She wants me to take it away from her.

But why? Why me? Doesn't she know that in the entire universe of men she comes in contact with …? Can't she see she's scaring the hell out of me? Why now? Why on the last day I'll ever see her?

Yes, the last day. In just a few hours, she will be out of my life forever. I picture myself sitting in a dark theater with Ed and I'm explaining to him how the woman in his magazine covered up her nakedness and told me that it's right here in front of me. And that I was too filled with self-doubt to believe her. And I know I don't want to be telling him that. I want to be telling him—

I quickly move next to Sybil on the sofa and stare at her. There's something in her eyes that's telling me not to be afraid. And I start to detach from myself and hover above the scene. I see a scared little boy trembling next to a goddess. I see a child who is terrified of rejection from normal women, let alone this Aphrodite. And then I see the little boy morph into a young man, reach out his hand and slowly pull the towel away from the woman. She lets it slide through her fingers and looks into the young man's eyes as he drops it to the floor. And I feel myself drifting downward to rejoin him.

I lean close to Sybil and kiss her on the mouth, still afraid of how she's going to react, still expecting her to suddenly stand up, startled, mumbling something about this all being some sort of horrible misunderstanding. But she doesn't. She puts a hand behind my head a pulls me closer to her. And I reach up and cup one of her breasts, my heart pounding in my chest.

"Dennis," she says through our kiss. "You are so ... gentle."

I'm confused because, with her slight accent, it sounds as if she's just called me a gentile. But I don't care; I'm ready to accept Jesus if I get to continue what I'm doing.

I am kissing Sybil Danning. I'm touching her breast. And something tells me that I will never forget this moment.

Sybil slides her face next to mine and breathes into my ear. She whispers something about the set.

But I can't hear her. My fingers are tracing a line between her breasts, down to her stomach, and her breathing is coming in gasps.

"I have to go to the set."

"What?" I say, still kissing her.

"My scene starts in ten minutes."

"Your ... scene ... what?"

"I have to leave the dressing room. I'm sorry."

"Now?"

"Yes."

"But ... but ... but this is our last day," I say, almost whimpering.

"I know. I tried to wake you up earlier, but you were having ... *alpträume*."

"Nightmares," I say.

"Nightmares. Yes. I touched you on the shoulder, but you wouldn't wake up."

"What about tonight?" I say desperately.

"We're flying to Spain right after we finish shooting today."

"Then ..."

"Then I'll be gone." She touches my face, moves her cheek next to mine, perhaps sensing my crushing despondency. "But I would like to ask you something."

"Yes?" I say, sniffling.

"You know that I live in Munich, don't you?"

"Yes."

"This summer the Olympics will be in my city. Would you like to stay with me for a few weeks? We'll go to some of the events together," she says. And she actually sounds hopeful.

"I don't know."

"You don't know if you want to stay with me?"

I see another road in front of me, one that, far off in the distance, divides into two paths. In my mind, I watch myself take the path to Munich. It leads to a sunlit, tree-lined street that takes me to a fabulous penthouse apartment overlooking a huge park. The camera moves in through a window to reveal me in bed with Sybil. We've just made love in the morning and now we're drinking orange juice and laughing. I've got a German newspaper folded on my lap, and somehow I understand what it says. Sybil looks at the clock on her night stand and I'm startled when she jumps out of bed. The camera zooms in tight on my face to reveal my confusion. "Where are you going?" I say, but she has already closed the door to the bathroom. Now I remember. She's going to work as a model today. I'm sure it'll be a photo shoot where she's nude, because with her body she's nude in everything. The photographer will be tall and Germanic and into Nietzche and obscure modern composers. He'll invite her to lunch to discuss another photo shoot, and over plates of veal and glasses of vintage Riesling they'll laugh and make plans. While he's showing her what her future in modeling looks like, he'll occasionally reach across the table and touch her hand for emphasis. She'll smile and see international fame. And then she'll look at me one day and wonder what the hell she's doing with this jealous, unemployed little nebbish. She'll tell me it was fun. That the Olympics have been over for months. That she'll be doing a lot of traveling. That she'll have to give up the penthouse. That I must go now.

"Dennis," Sybil says, and I pop my head up and look her in the eyes. "Where are you right now?"

I swallow hard and look down at the floor. "In an apartment in Munich."

She puts her hands on mine. "Are you afraid to stay with me?"

I open my mouth to speak, but nothing comes out.

Sybil reaches into my jacket pocket and removes the notepad. She turns to the page on which I was doodling only minutes earlier and holds the pen over it. She's thoughtful for several moments, gazing up at the ceiling as if to find the proper words there, then lowers her head and writes.

I slowly stand and look at her for several moments, trying to memorize each feature, but knowing I won't. Finally, I close the dressing room door behind me, walk onto the set, and take up my boom mic. Friedrich smiles at me.

"You sick, Mister Los Angeles?" he says. "You fall out of chair again?"

"No, I—"

All eyes turn toward Sybil, wearing the white towel I dropped on the floor of her dressing room only moments ago. She walks up to me, smiles, opens my jacket, and slides the notebook and pen into my inside pocket. With the entire cast and crew staring at us, she leans into me and kisses me on the cheek, then moves away.

I make a show of inspecting my boom mic, unplugging it, dumbly staring at the end of the cable, then plugging it back in. I'm feigning indifference, and doing a horrible job pulling it off.

There's something irritating the skin on my chest above my heart, and I reach inside my jacket and run my fingers along the top edge of the notebook. The pointed end of the spiral binding is bent and is sticking me. But I'm going to leave it alone. Sybil put it there. And it's right where she wants it.

Mashed

EXTERIOR—MASH COMPOUND—DAY

From the yard we see Radar surrounded by a large group of soldiers.

> 1st Soldier
> I don't believe you, Radar. Where would you get syphilis?

> Radar
> Golly, if you don't believe me, you can ask Captain Pierce!

Hawkeye walks up to the outer edge of the group of men to listen to the conversation.

> 2nd Soldier
>
> Hey, here's Captain Pierce; let's ask him.

> 1st Soldier
>
> Captain, does Radar really have syphilis?

> Hawkeye
>
> You'll be happy to know that he really does.

Radar grins smugly.

> 2nd Soldier
>
> C'mon, Radar, tell us about it. What was she like?

> Radar
> (dreamy-eyed)
>
> I just can't find the right words to describe it.

> Hawkeye
>
> Excuse me, boys. You don't mind if I borrow your folk hero, do you?

Hawkeye leads Radar away from the group. When he sees that he's beyond earshot of the soldiers, Hawkeye stops walking.

>   Hawkeye
> Radar, why do you want people to believe you're something you're not?
>
>   Radar
> Sir, what do you mean?
>
>   Hawkeye
> I mean that you never had any kind of relations with Lt. Myers.
>
>   Radar
> Well, I've got syphilis, don't I? You even said so yourself.
>
>   Hawkeye
> Yes, Radar. I did say that. But you got it from sucking a snakebite.

There is a long pause while Radar thinks this over. He looks as if he could burst out in tears at any moment.

>   Radar
> You know, Hawkeye, I kind of enjoyed it when everyone thought that Lt. Myers gave me syphilis.
>
>   Hawkeye
> Radar, just between you and me, she did.

                              FADE OUT:

FADE IN TO:

INTERIOR—COLONEL BLAKE'S OFFICE—DAY

While Radar is busy at the file cabinet, Colonel Blake is sitting at his desk looking over some reports. He signs one of them.

>   Col. Blake
> Radar, where is today's list of incoming wounded?
>
>   Radar
> In your hand, sir.

Col. Blake
Just checking, Radar.
(pause)
By the way, are you going to the film tonight?

Radar
Sir, I think I'm gonna pass on this one.

Col. Blake
Why?

Radar
Well, sir, a couple of months ago we saw a film on obesity, and I started gaining weight. Then this last film was on venereal diseases, and I got one of those. So, I think I'll just skip tonight's film, sir.

Col. Blake
Why? What's tonight's film about?

Radar
Pregnancy, sir.

Radar goes back to his work as the colonel just stares at him. Theme music up.

THE END

* * *

Oh, man … this has got to be my ticket into the TV industry! I mean, it's pure genius. Radar takes a walk with a cute nurse who gets bitten by a snake. He's in a panic, but she calmly directs him to suck out the venom, which he reluctantly does—and then he gets syphilis. Radar being Radar, at first he's bummed out because he's got a serious disease, but when the other soldiers assume he got it from schtupping the nurse, Radar starts to enjoy the envious ribbing he's getting and "fails" to tell the other soldiers how it all happened. My god, the producers of *MASH* are going to love this!

My heart is racing and I couldn't be more excited. This is the first thing I've written since I got homesick and came back from …

Ah jeez. Germany. Does a day go by without me thinking of it? More accurately, of Sybil … of her gorgeous skin, her Arctic blue eyes, how she tossed her head back and flared her nostrils when she laughed at my silly jokes on the movie set? How she'd be there in her dressing room when I awoke from a nap? How she drew her lips close to my ear and asked me ... asked me if I was afraid?

Afraid?

Of what? Of being a little dark-haired, thick-lipped kid in a place where it felt like I was covered in pink day-glo paint? Of having people wonder What the hell's he doing with her every time we go somewhere? Of her proximity to powerful men who could give her so much? Of every man's desire to ravage her?

Scared? Of what? Of what might have happened if I'd gone to Munich? Of how my life would be different? That it might be better than it is now? That it might be worse? That she really just invited me there to watch the Olympics with her?

What's there to be afraid of? That an ugly kid barely two years out of high school will ultimately have his heart torn out of his chest by this anatomical miracle? That all the attention she showed me on the movie set, with all the hostile glares I got from the other crew members, was just part of an insanely elaborate cruel joke?

That I might one day open up the little note pad and finally learn what she wrote in it?

I want the memories of Sybil to be sweet. I want to be able to think of her and smile at how absolutely wonderful she was to me. I want to know why she found me, the lowest form of life on a film set, so fascinating. I'd love to tell my friends about my Berlin experiences without them calling me the world's biggest asshole for passing up such a glorious opportunity.

I have the sense that all the truth there is to know is on that note pad. Right in the inside chest pocket of the jacket hanging in my closet.

I say my goodbye to the specter of Sybil, knowing I'll be seeing it again very soon, and let out a deep, nervous breath and slide the thirty-page manuscript into a large envelope and address it to Larry Gelbart, the show's creator. In my opinion (and I think I'm pretty objective on this one), this script is so unique, so funny, and so …. well, *MASH*-like that I can't even imagine that the producers aren't going to just crap in their pants laughing and then fight each other off over trying to reach the telephone first in order to call me with the good news.

I spend the next several days trying on the Hollywood lifestyle, which includes buying a suit in preparation for the meeting with Larry Gelbart that's sure to come in the next few days, getting my teeth cleaned, and having a new muffler installed on my old VW so that it doesn't rumble and bleat like a dying water buffalo. Between the suit, teeth-cleaning and muffler, I've just spent almost a hundred dollars—way more than I can afford right now, but I have a sneaking suspicion that I'll be making a boatload of money pretty darn soon.

* * *

The phone rings, and I instantly experience a jolt of electricity crackling through my skeletal system. I take a deep breath and rip the phone off the hook. "Yeah?" I say, affecting the perfect amount of disinterest and a sprinkling of annoyance.

"Hi, this is Bill down the street. Listen, you borrowed my hedge clippers about a month—"

"Don't you know who's supposed to be calling me?" I say, screaming into the phone. I pound the receiver down. It's been two weeks since I sent the script out, and every time the phone rings my heart rate rockets up to about two-forty until I find out that it's my mother or my neighbor or an ex-girlfriend. I yell at them for tying up my phone line and then hang up, which strikes me as the only sensible thing to do in my situation. When I'm a writer for *MASH*, they'll understand.

When the phone rings during an oddly antiseptic doctor/nurse coupling on *General Hospital*, I nearly jump out of my skin. I've practiced the art of sounding aloof when I answer the phone, the better to convince the show's producers that I'm not desperate. "Yeah?" I say.

"Hi … uh … I'm looking for Dennis Globus," a woman's voice says, a little disarmed by my greeting.

Damn! I'm pretty sure Larry Gelbart's not a woman. "I'm a little busy right now," I say.

"Would you like me to tell Mr. Gelbart that you're too busy to talk to him?" she says casually, a hint of a smile in her voice.

"No!" I say, holding the phone about six inches away from my mouth and shouting into the receiver. "I'll talk to him now!"

"Okay," she says, chuckling. "I'll put him on the line."

O, great Greek gods in heaven … Zeus, Aphrodite, uh, D'Artagnon and Aragorn … I can't believe this is happening to me! This is it. This is what I've been waiting for. This is the moment Larry Gelbart is going to get on the phone and tell me that he loves the script and wants to buy it.

The wait for him is interminable, and I imagine his secretary and him having a great laugh over my feigned casualness. I glance down at my watch and scowl when I see that it's been a full seven seconds since she put me on hold. There is a click, and then finally The Voice.

"Hi. Is this Dennis?" the man's voice says cheerfully.

I know this is a point in most conversations where I'd be expected to say something. Anything. Instead, everything in front of my eyes goes white and I see little sparkles like shooting stars fly across my field of vision. Bile is beginning to bubble its way up my esophagus, and my rectum clenches like a terrified clam.

"Dennis," he says again. "This is Larry Gelbart. Are you there?"

Given that my body occupies space but that my consciousness is ping-ponging between a Maserati dealership, the Polo Lounge and the *Tonight Show*, that's a marvelous philosophical question.

"I ... am ... here." And just saying it begins to clear the fog from my eyes. "Yes, I am here. I am here," I say, hoping he doesn't think I've been drinking.

"Well, now that we've established that, I'd like to chat with you about your *MASH* script."

There is a pause, and I deduce that he must be waiting for some sort of response. "I am here!"

"I think that's terrific," he says, chuckling. "But what I'd like to know is if you can be *here*."

"Here?" I say.

"No. Here. Look, do you know where Twentieth Century Fox is?"

The Promised Land. "Yes." Gulp.

"Good. We're making progress then. Why don't you be here—where I am; not where you are—at ten on Friday morning. I'll leave your name with the guard.

"Yes," I say.

"Good," he says. "Well, I'll see you then. Bye now."

There's a long pause until I hear a click, and the line goes dead. I finally hang up the phone, look up at the ceiling, and scream at the top of my lungs: Wheeooooooo!!! Larry Gelbart wants to meet with meeeeeeooooooeeee!!! Me! Not my brother Ken. Me! And I laugh stupidly as I contemplate the two trillion people on Earth who are not meeting with Larry Gelbart, and the one who is. Me! Only me!

* * *

It's always amazed me how slowly time passes when you're compulsive about looking at the clock, whose sole purpose, it seems, is to measure the movement of glaciers. This is pretty much all I've done for the past three days—from the time I got the phone call on Tuesday afternoon to right now.

It's Friday morning. And except for a brief window between three-ten and three-thirty-five, I didn't sleep at all last night. I woke up to my neighbor's German shorthair pointer in bed with me, happily licking my thighs. That's not a wholly unpleasant experience, especially when you're asleep and dreaming of Sybil Danning, but I think the dog had been rolling around in something dead in the back yard and then decided to share it with me. By the time I shoved her out the back door, I was wide awake and once again obsessed with the clock.

My new light blue denim suit is hanging on a hook on the bathroom door, along with a white shirt I last wore about eight years ago to a cousin's bar mitzvah.

I've got two distinctly different ties lying on the bed, and I can see that it's going to be a tough choice. I don't know a thing about Larry Gelbart and his tie preferences. If he's on the conservative side, he'd probably appreciate the golf-motif tie I borrowed from my dad. If he's at all hip, he'd probably enjoy the one with all the lyrics to *Yummy Yummy Yummy (I've Got Love in My Tummy)* that I ordered from an ad in the back of *Rolling Stone* magazine a few years ago in the mistaken belief that my girlfriend at the time would enjoy its cryptic reference to fellatio. Too bad she dumped me before I could tell her what *Cat's in the Cradle* is all about.

The thorny decision made (not for the first time in the history of mankind has golf won out over blowjobs), I climb in my car and back out of the driveway directly into the extraordinarily tall curb on the other side of the street, ramming my new tailpipes through the muffler, which I realize when the sound of the car changes from a purr (pre-curb) to a guttural roar (post-curb).

That's nice. I've enjoyed my new muffler for a total of, oh, eight seconds. That turned out to be a real value-laden purchase.

As I pull away from the curb and head uphill toward Silverlake, the tailpipes fall out of the muffler and, as I look in the rear-view mirror, I see them rolling down the hill on Fargo Street.

No matter. I'm going to see Larry Gelbart. And it seems as if I'm about to have enough money to buy a gross of tailpipes and mufflers.

I wind my way through Hollywood, down Fairfax to Pico, until finally I'm staring at the giant 20th Century Fox sign. As long as I've lived in L.A., and as many times as I've seen this sign, my pulse never fails to quicken at its sight. I mean, this is the place where they filmed *The Grapes of Wrath*, *Miracle* on 34th Street, Cleopatra, The King and I, How to Marry a Millionaire, Patton, Butch Cassidy,* and about a thousand other historically significant films.

The guard at the gate eyes my car warily. I can tell he's wondering what business the driver of such a derelict car has on an important piece of property like this. He's saying something to me, but it's difficult to hear him over the rumbling the muffler's making. Finally, I just shout my name at him. He finds it on a clipboard, and begins pointing and holding up fingers in an attempt to pass along directions to Larry Gelbart's office.

I drive through the massive, block-long street scene that was the outdoor set of *Hello Dolly*, which the studio built over the backside of 20th's office buildings. When the movie was finished shooting—a time when film sets are typically broken down—20th left the set standing, and I get goose bumps driving down Main Street in turn-of-the-century Yonkers, New York.

As I make a left turn past a large sound stage, there's a small two-story building on my right. There's no address because —following Hollywood's amusingly syllogistic logic—if you don't know where a certain building is, you don't belong there. From the driver's seat, I squint at the building and see a tiny, copper *M*A*S*H* sign on the front door. I park, and as I step out of the car, there's a horrifying popping sound. The zipper on my tight, new suit pants has exploded. I fumble with it frantically, trying to force the two sides of the zipper to hold on to each other, but the damn thing is broken and, at this point, all I can do is cover it up with my briefcase which, at this particular moment, strikes me as an appropriately named object.

I push open the door to the building. Seated behind a large, moon-sliver-shaped desk is a cute redhead who looks like she might have just stepped off the boat from Dublin.

"Can I help you?" she says, and smiles.

I'm guessing that the people who usually come to this lobby are fairly important, and she's anointing me in that manner. She hasn't seen my muffler. Or my zipper.

I try to smile back at her, and realize that my teeth are chattering. "I'm here to see Mr. Gelbart."

"Do you have an appointment?"

"Yes."

"Good. At what time?"

"Ten o'clock."

"You must be Dennis Globus."

I nod exuberantly, which I can imagine from her perspective looks idiotic.

"Can I get you some coffee? We've got the good stuff—Yuban."

"No, thanks."

"Tea or a soft drink? We have Tab and 7-Up."

"Nothing, thanks."

"Why don't you take a seat over there," she says, gesturing at a small gray sofa against the far wall. "Mr. Gelbart will be out shortly. He's in a story meeting."

A story meeting. Those three little words thrill me because I'm going to be in story meetings with Mr Gelbart. I wonder if I should refer to him as Larry.

I take my seat, set the briefcase on the floor, then feel a rush of cool air streaming through my fly. I contemplate asking the receptionist for some safety pins, but I don't want to have Larry Gelbart stroll into the lobby and find me with my hands in my fly. So I follow Rule #14 in the "How to Be Dennis Globus" handbook: Instead of fixing a problem, cover it up. I return the briefcase to my lap.

There are large, framed poster-size photos of cast members on the lobby walls. There's Hawkeye, with that mischievous twinkle in his eye; a scowling Frank Burns; Trapper John; Radar, with his little round glasses; and Hotlips. What a fox! I'm going to meet these people soon. So exciting! And, for a moment, I can see my photo on the wall next to theirs.

Past the receptionist and down the hallway are the lesser *MASH* luminaries: Father Mulcahy, Corporal Klinger, Sergeant Zale, Nurse Kellye, and a bunch of others whose names escape me.

It's been about twenty minutes since I sat down, and if I were at any other kind of meeting, I'd be getting annoyed. But not now. Not today. The receptionist glances up from her paperwork, catches my eye, and gives me her best Sorry-he's-late-but-there's-nothing-I-can-do-about-it shrug combined with a Marcel Marceau frown.

"You sure I can't get you something to drink?" she says.

"I'm good, thanks." I smile at her, which has the immediate effect of causing her to return to her paperwork. Yeah, I'm that irresistible.

A door opens down the hall and two men stroll briskly toward me. As they reach the front door, only ten feet away from me, they look to be engaged in an important conversation, because they're keeping their voices low. After about a minute of this, one of the two men, the one with glasses and thinning reddish-blond hair, claps the other guy on the back.

"Let's talk about it again tomorrow," he says, and shakes hands with the other guy, who turns and leaves the building. The man with the glasses looks at me and smiles. "Are you my ten o'clock?"

"If you're Larry Gelbart, I am," I say, and instantly regret that I didn't come up with something funny, just to let him know that he's not making a mistake hiring me to write a comedy show.

"Well, thanks for coming in," he says breezily.

Thanks for coming in? Is he kidding? He's thanking me? I would have walked here on my ass, using only my butt cheeks for propulsion. "Yeah."

"I'm Larry Gelbart."

"Well, I'm certainly not," I say, trying to sound like Alan Alda doing Groucho Marx.

First … confusion, then … a weak smile crosses his face. "And you are…?"

"Dennis Globus," I say, standing. We move toward each other and shake hands. "But my mother calls me Den. I'm pretty sure I'm the only one I know who uses a reading room as a nickname. My mother says I was named after a Daniel. So, I asked her one time why she didn't just name me Daniel instead of Dennis, but she said that Jews don't name people for anyone who's still living. Daniel, I'm pretty sure, has some biblical—"

As I continue regaling him with the etymology of my name, a part of my brain detaches, listens intently, then whispers into my ear that I'm lapsing into some kind of demented, babbling hysteria. I don't have a clue what I'm saying right now, and I think I'm developing a facial tic. Mr. Gelbart's eyes are wide, and he has the kind of expression on his face you'd see on a guy trying to figure out if his puppy just pooped in the house.

He waits for me to take a breath. "Would you like some coffee? ... or maybe some tea? ... how about a nice soft drink? ... we've got Tab or 7-Up," he says, and I get the feeling he's trying to fill conversational space to keep me from coming unglued again.

"No, thanks," I say. "But I really have to pee." I hear giggling from the receptionist.

"Well, here," he says, and pushes me through the door to the men's room.

For several seconds I can only lean my head against the cool tile wall next to the sink. What the fuck am I doing? I keep serving him one heaping helping of stupidity after another. I don't have to pee. I just need a time out. And I've just left one of the most powerful men in television standing in the hallway. Jeez, I've got to relax ... have fun with it ... keep in mind that he must like my script or he wouldn't have invited me here ... realize that I've just got to let this thing play out without forcing it ... let him do all the talking.

I wash my hands. There's the muffled sound of two people talking in the lobby a few feet away from the restroom door. I'm guessing the receptionist is showing him some vexing paperwork when I hear her say, "My god, do you believe this?"

I push open the restroom door and I see Mr. Gelbart and the receptionist staring at me. "I'm sorry," I say. "I'm a little nervous. I don't really talk all that much except when I'm feeling anxious, and then there's no stopping me. I was thinking about it when I was in the bathroom, and I just wanted to say I'm sorry, and let you know that I normally don't talk this much except when I'm feeling anxious, and then—"

"That's all right. I understand," he says charitably. "Would you like to go in the conference room and we can relax and chat about your script?" he says, putting a hand on my shoulder and guiding me down the hall.

Yeah. We'll relax. And chat. Just me and ol' Larry. Talking about our vision for this episode of *MASH*. Who I'd like to see play the key role of the nurse. I could see Julie Christie doing it. Not because she'd be particularly appropriate for it, but because I'd like to have sex with her. I think I'll wait until the end of the meeting to suggest her. Yeah. I'm going to like this job.

He stops at a door, pushes it open, and gestures at one of the six seats that surround a small elliptical conference table. He sits next to me.

This is it. In only a short while—a few seconds, maybe—he's going to tell me how much he likes my script. And when he does, this is going to be the greatest day of my life. I'm beyond excited and my teeth are chattering again.

"You sent me a great little script with a very nice letter," he says slowly, "so I wanted to meet you personally."

Obligatory opening. About what I'd expect. He's negotiating.

"I found your script very interesting ..."

Yeah? Interesting, as in you were close to orgasm—or interesting, you wanted to wipe your butt with pages nine through twenty-six?

"... and you should know that I like it very much."

Oh ... oh, my god! Is he saying—

"I think your dialog is very true to the characters. And I have to tell you, I get scripts sent to me all the time from writers who don't have your ear for dialog."

More, Larry ... more! Do it to me, big boy!

"The idea for the story is completely unique. We've never done anything like it before, and I don't think I've seen it on any other show. That's a real accomplishment on your part."

Yes ... oh my god yes ... YES!!!

"And that's right where the problem is."

Yahooeeeee!!!

"We can't have Radar getting syphilis."

YESSSSSS!!! Huh? What the fuck? Problem?

"We're very careful how we handle Radar, and I just don't see him getting a venereal disease. But I want to thank you for giving me a chance to see the guy who wrote such a funny script."

I know he's saying something to me, because I can see his mouth moving. And I'm sure that what he's saying is meant to bolster my confidence and end this meeting, but I can't hear a single word through the crashing sound of angry waves against a rocky shore. He stands up. "Thanks for coming in. You can pick up your script from the receptionist." He takes my hand, pumps my limp arm.

"But ... I ..." It's too late. He's already gone.

I fly out of the building, gun the engine of my VW, then peel out of the visitor's lot. The crashing surf is still pounding in my head and now there's a swirling fog in front of my eyes. Something has gone terribly, shockingly, unpredictably wrong ... and I'm too stunned even to make sense of it.

What on earth just happened in there? Did I get invited to the Fox lot, only to have Larry Gelbart just tell me he's not going to buy my script? Am I going to wake up tomorrow to discover this has all been a horrible dream?

My eyes are wet and I'm finding it almost impossible to see. But I'm pretty sure that's Barbara Eden getting into a Jaguar convertible. I'd love to stop and talk to her. I'd tell her how much I admire her work and always look forward to seeing her on TV. I'd casually let her know that I've written a *MASH* script and I was just in conference with Larry Gelbart.

Part of me wants to stop and get out of the car and tell her all these things. I'd do that if I were in show business. But I'm not. And never will be.

O, Christmas Tree

When I got back from Berlin, I was full of excitement and anticipation for my career writing for television. Unfortunately, in the years since, I haven't sold a single script. In fact, I haven't worked in or out of television. Haven't even gotten the most menial job. I would say that the years have been a total bust if it weren't for the fact that I met and married Jamie, the single most energetic, kind, and supportive person ever. She's the one who encouraged me to write the *MASH* script, so it's her I blame for my current funk.

Well, it's not completely her fault. There's our pathetic financial situation, which would be absolutely horrible were it not for the fact that it takes my mind off the Larry Gelbart fiasco. I'm totally out of control with my new VISA card, having spent lavishly on presents for Jamie. It is our second Christmas holiday together, and it doesn't take a psychologist to tell me I'm overcompensating for last year, when I had no job and couldn't provide any presents. It felt awful. I have no job this year either. But I've provided presents. And the extent to which I've done it, that feels even worse than last year.

This isn't at all like *The Gift of the Magi*, where a loving husband pawns his watch in order to buy a set of combs for his wife, while the wife, unbeknownst to the husband, has just sold her scalp in order to raise money for a watch fob, whatever that is. That they have unwittingly torpedoed each other's gifts helps them to rediscover their love for each other.

Obviously, that couple never lived in a world of Sony, Air France, and Joan & David shoes. If they had, they'd be right where we are—which is cutting up my VISA card on top of the classified ads in the Sunday L.A. Times—instead of slobbering all over each other in love and gratitude.

I'm planning on spending the entire day dealing with my self-loathing in the same way a hog regards sewage, until this ad catches my eye.

> WANTED: ONE TAKE-CHARGE YOUNG MAN TO MANAGE CHRISTMAS TREE LOT. LARGE SALARY, BENEFITS, NICE CUSTOMERS. CALL 931-5223.

As I discover my first week on the job, there is nothing even remotely accurate about the ad, except that I am indeed working on a Christmas tree lot. But I'm not managing it. That's done by Maxine Lammers, the 48-year-old, chain-smoking, loogie-hocking, Harley-riding, braless, tank-top-in-November owner. She's a tyrant and orders me around endlessly, punctuating each demand by spitting at my feet, a habit that makes me queasy. It isn't until the second day that I get the courage to ask her to stop spitting at my shoes.

"Why?" she says. "Is it gonna burn your little feet?" And as she throws her head back and opens her mouth to laugh, I notice something that looks like a pre-cancerous sore on her tongue.

Regarding that little nugget in the ad that mentions a take-charge guy, I'm not being asked to take charge of anything. Except for cutting the strings that straightjacket the branches to the trunks of the Christmas trees. They arrive that way from the growers to make them easier to transport on large trucks. I also take charge of nailing a couple of wooden boards, crisscross, to the bottom of each tree so that they'll stand up in the lot. Finally, I take charge of hauling each tree to the customer's car after purchase. In all, it's repetitive, brainless, and deeply unsatisfying—just the kind of work I'm most suited for.

And the large salary, as Maxine explains it to me, takes into account the accumulation of all the hours I'll work from the end of November to December 24th. She's nice enough to promise me one large check, because she just doesn't have time to take care of payroll during the Christmas season. Knowing that I'll work ten hours a day, seven days a week for four weeks, and then get paid in one lump sum, provides the illusion that my sub-minimum-wage salary is truly large.

As for benefits, Maxine has no intention of giving me medical or a retirement plan, the job being one step up from selling Girl Scout cookies door to door. But she assures me that I'll have the pick of the lot; whichever Christmas tree tickles my Yule bone, she'll sell to me at half price. That is, any Christmas tree unsold as of closing time on December 24th.

I'm not, as I discover on the first day, even allowed to wait on customers. Whether it's because she doesn't trust me to handle money or because she values her sales skills so highly, Maxine alone accosts each customer the moment he swings a leg out of his car. She is aggressive, impatient and pugnacious with the customers, badgering them relentlessly to buy the trees she considers most appropriate for them. And she determines appropriateness by applying a formula that matches the value of the customer's car to a specific tree—the fancier the car, the bigger the tree foisted upon him.

In the process of leading her customer around the lot, she bounds from tree to tree, her breasts flying fully independently of each other, the front of her tank top looking as if Maxine is smuggling hyperactive schnauzers. She flings the stub of a still-burning Lucky Strike at the buyer's feet, a trail of spit meeting it there. Most of the customers, not anticipating being brow-beaten on a Christmas tree lot by a manic biker, leave in a state of exasperation and disgust. But none of them leaves without a tree.

Astute observation #1: I discover by the end of the first day that not one customer has thought for a second about how he's going to haul home a ten-foot tree. They don't bring pickup trucks. Or vans. Only Datsun 240Zs. What are they thinking? That the tree is going to sit in the ashtray on the way home? Maxine, thoughtful lass that she is, is kind enough to provide string with which I'm to secure the tree to the roof of the car.

Astute observation #2: This never occurred to me before I started working here, but there really is a difference between men and women. While many books have been written on the subject, I'm not sure any have been penned by a former Christmas tree lot employee. Too bad because from this perspective I've gained some valuable insight. It's not easy lifting up a large, unwieldy tree and placing it on the roof of a car. Noticing my struggle, each female customer, to her everlasting credit, says, "Don't hurt yourself." As it happens, men have a different take on my effort. They watch me carefully, head cocked to the side, eyes narrowed, and bark, "Don't scratch the paint!" Not that any man ever thought to bring a blanket or a beach towel to protect his car. While men typically buy larger trees than women, there is one area where I find the genders identical: neither has the slightest interest in helping me put the tree on the car.

* * *

It's the evening of December 23rd, and Casey's not wearing the red Christmas sweater I gave to him before I left for work, in the belief that he would appreciate a layer of wool on a blustery day like this. When I'd untied the ribbon and pulled the sweater out of the gift box, he didn't seem to know what it was, sniffing at it suspiciously. Even before I fastened the first button, Casey was so offended by the sweater, he tried to squirm out of it. And the moment I left for work, he apparently figured out a way to tear it from his body, then eat it whole.

I learn all this upon returning home from work this evening because, as Casey prances around the house, I see a corner of the red material hanging out of his butt. Casey is a Dalmation. And he's nine months old. And continuing his intellectual journey through the mysteries of cause and effect.

On any given day, a trip to the park yields a treasure trove of garbage for Casey to gnaw on, and, as a result, Jamie and I are very strict about his diet. While we'll give him huge amounts of kibble and Milk Bones, we never indulge him with table scraps. Jamie, in fact, is so intent on teaching Casey not to beg at the table that she doesn't allow him even to look at us while we're eating. Every now and then at dinner, I'll turn my head to see Casey lying near the little electric heater, watching me shovel a forkful of food into my mouth. When he realizes I'm watching him, he slowly turns his head and pretends to be staring out the window. I can't help thinking there's a scientific paper on animal behavior somewhere in Casey's actions.

As strict as we are, there is one little bit of human food we allow Casey to have. It's popcorn. And he's learned to distinguish the Jiffy Pop from all the other packages I occasionally take out of the pantry. Once he spots the bright colors on the lid (and they say dogs are color-blind!), he leaps away from his precious heater, slides across the kitchen floor, and sits in rapt attention as I go through the procedure of putting the Jiffy Pop on the burner. Casey's black ears twitch as the first kernels begin popping. His nostrils dilate as the scent of butter belly dances through the kitchen. As he observes that the kernels are popping less often now, it becomes almost unbearable for him, and he begins salivating and moaning, finally breaking out in a full-throated howl. It's unclear if he's experiencing the pleasure of high expectations or the pain of delay.

My turning off the burner is Casey's signal to leap up off his butt and begin doing a sort of four-legged Irish jig around me. I stop to pour a glass of water for myself, and Casey, clearly frustrated and ravenous beyond my comprehension, narrows his eyes and growls. Frankly, he's making quite a racket over a few pieces of greasy popcorn. Finally, I cut open the foil, further releasing a bouquet whose effect on Casey is unmatched by any vintage of Chateau Margaux on the most stuffy wine connoisseur. Casey is now spastic from a combination of anticipation and ecstasy. And I can torture him no longer. I grab a handful of popcorn and throw it across the linoleum. Remarkably, Casey manages to catch a couple of the popped kernels before they hit the ground. He pounces on the rest, using his tongue like a powerful magnet sweeping through paper clips. It's quite a sight. And it's all over in about four seconds.

As insane with desire as Casey has been, once he's done, he pays absolutely no attention to me slowly eating the entire bowl of popcorn. Instead, he curls up in front of his little heater, lying so close to it I sometimes think his head is glowing red. Jamie is convinced that his continual close proximity to the heater is responsible for what looks like a combination of canine hyperactivity and Attention Deficit Disorder. I cheerfully offer that Dalmations are often skittish and high-strung, which is, historically speaking, why they've been used as fire dogs. Jamie notes that observation with skepticism, and even I can't get enthused about supporting it as an argument.

Whatever, virtually nothing can rouse Casey to move away from the source of warmth and comfort.

In the summertime when the weather's warm, a knock on the door will usually produce in Casey an aggressive hysteria that makes him practically want to tear off the doorknob to get at the intruder. But in the winter, a knock on the door generates in him a half-hearted growl. He might be concerned for our safety, but damned if he's going to get cold protecting us.

* * *

This evening, despite my gloom about finances, Jamie and I inexplicably find ourselves in the Christmas spirit. And it's her idea to make tree ornaments from bread dough. While not resistant to the idea, the possibility that anything useful can come from a gooey mixture of flour, water, and salt strikes me as alchemy. I watch in total fascination as she combines the ingredients, then grabs a little blob of the resulting paste.

"My god!"

"What?" she says, alarmed.

"You've made a perfect little house ... with a chimney."

She smiles. "Do you like it?"

"I think it needs landscaping Maybe some ferns under that picture window there."

Yeah, we're having a good time now. She laughs, then becomes distracted by the ornament I'm working on. "Hey, that's nice. Is it a cannon?"

Hardly. The only ornaments I can think to make are of a pornographic nature.

I'm not sure why, but right at this particular moment, I'm aware of feeling intense love for Jamie. Maybe it's the fact that we're doing a fun project together. Maybe it's the Christmas season. Or her beautiful gray-green eyes as she studies her ornaments. Or her black hair in corkscrew ringlets across her shoulders. Or the possibility that I'm delirious from inhaling airborne flour.

In about half an hour, we have a neat tray of about twenty-five ornaments, separated into two groups: the good ones, and the ones I've made. Of course, mine are not all meant to be erotic, but they all have something in common: each is completely unrecognizable. Still, she insists they all belong on the tree I'm to bring home the next day, and she begins jabbing little wire hanger thingies through them. She suggests we allow them to dry for awhile.

Well, that was fun. But we're hungry, and we leave the house to get some food. On the way out of our low-rent Hollywood Hills duplex, I look up to see our upstairs neighbor through her large picture window. Paula is an actress and stupefyingly gorgeous. And, at this particular moment, she's stark naked, doing some kind of interpretive dance around her Christmas tree, flinging tinsel at it.

Three hours later, Jamie and I stumble through the front door giggling, tipsy from two wicker bottles of Chianti, only to discover no fewer than six piles of vomit, resembling in size the great termite mounds of Africa. Casey is now in the corner by the TV, yorking up pile number seven. I check the rest of the house. There are no more mounds, but Casey, having consumed a half-pound of salt, has completely drained the toilet bowl of all available water.

We shovel out the mess. Amazingly, we're still in the Christmas spirit, and we laugh at this evening's events as I spray carpet cleaner on the last stain. We vow to move forward and try again. Although not with bread dough.

* * *

This has been the longest four weeks of my life. I'm on the lot ten hours a day, and the time absolutely crawls by. I don't do well in jobs where I have no intellectual stimulation, and almost nothing is less stimulating than nailing wooden crosses onto

IF I ONLY HAD A BRAIN

Christmas trees. I'm pretty sure I'm not the first Jewish boy to have a noteworthy relationship with a cross.

It's December 24th. Since Casey had such a rough time of things last night, I bring him to work with me, and he has spent the day sleeping in Maxine's little trailer while I attend to my final day on the job. Per Maxine's instructions, I wait until the last customer leaves, then scour the lot for a tree of my own. I discover that she's been selling them off at fire-sale prices, given that the demand for them is about to evaporate. What remains of the trees is ridiculously scraggly. Maxine watches me deliberate, grabs a scrawny six-footer that looks like it has Dutch elm disease, and shoves it at me.

"Fuckin perfect," she says, and disappears into her trailer. She's in there maybe three seconds before she yells, "Shit!"

I run into the trailer to see her with one foot in the air, scraping the bottom of her combat boot across the back edge of her desk. Casey, who was sleeping in the corner, is now startled awake and trembling in fear.

"Sorry, Maxine. My dog hasn't been feeling well."

"Then why the fuck don't you leave him at home?" she says, not altogether wrong.

"Well, it's my last day—"

"And you wanted to show your dog around the old workplace? Aw, that's sweet," she says, wiping off the bottom of her boot with a McDonald's bag she's fished out of the trash can. "You're gonna pay for this."

"Pay ... for what?" I say.

"I'm gonna have to have this carpet shampooed, and it's coming right out of your paycheck."

"Speaking of that, if you don't mind me asking, when am I getting paid?"

"Well, I was gonna give you your check today, till this happened. Now I'll have to have my CPA cut another one, minus this," she says, pointing at the squashed pile on the trailer floor, "and also that nice Christmas tree you're taking home."

"I guess that's fair. When can I pick up the check?"

"Well, leave me your address and I'll—"

The phone rings. Maxine smiles and winks at me conspiratorially. "Hey, time for you to take off. I've been waiting for this call."

* * *

I'm finishing wrapping our single strand of lights around the new Christmas tree, and I see Casey coming in through the doggy door. He stops and sits down in front of me, and I pat his head and scratch behind his ears. He likes that, and he cranes his neck to force his head into my fingers. I'm mindful that all of the ralphing on my carpet and crapping on Maxine's has been stressful for Casey. So I decide to treat him to some more popcorn. He seems to have forgotten about last night, and he's elated as the Jiffy Pop slides out of the pantry.

But what to do with the leftover popcorn? Since I'm not in the mood to eat it, Jamie suggests we get needle and thread, then string the popcorn up like ancient 20th century families used to do. Seems like a great idea to me, except for one thing: if Casey is willing to risk turning inside-out over some bread dough ornaments, what's he going to do when we make his favorite food available to him? But Jamie reasons that Casey only eats the popcorn we toss on the kitchen floor. He shows no apparent interest in it otherwise. Which sounds mostly logical to me.

A note about crafts: if your entire frame of reference consists of old Spencer Tracy movies, stringing popcorn looks like a fun, family kind of thing to do. But in real life, the popcorn crumbles the moment you try to pass a needle through it. All Jamie and I have to show for two hours of work is a single three-foot strand, stiff backs, and crippled hands. Still, we're proud. And we attach the strand to the upper part of the tree, above the single strand of lights, well out of Casey's reach.

We clean up, give Casey a can of Alpo as a preventive measure, and go to a friend's house for Christmas Eve dinner where we enjoy a spectacular roast duck in a port and cherry sauce. But on the drive home, we're filled with a sense of foreboding. How could we have been so stupid as to expect that Casey would leave the tree alone, when a choir of little buttery angels is calling him to it?

I put the key in the lock, turn the knob, push the door open about two inches, and look in. Casey's nose is about a millimeter away from the heater. Everything seems okay. I push the door open and see … a Christmas tree, upright, with a strand of popcorn around the top. Just the way we left it. Is it possible that Casey's miserable retching has taught him something about cause and effect? Was Jamie right about him only eating popcorn from the kitchen floor? Could it be that he simply didn't notice the popcorn on the tree? Did the Alpo work its mojo?

Whatever, it is truly a Christmas miracle. Jamie and I embrace, then shower Casey with affection, merely for doing nothing but planting his ass in front of the heater. If he's confused by this outpouring of late-night love, he doesn't seem to mind me scratching his stomach.

Well, that's enough adoration for one night, and Jamie and I head off for bed. We fall asleep as the last article of clothing flutters to the floor.

* * *

What do you know ... it's Christmas morning! But it's not seven or eight o'clock, which is when normal people wake up to open presents. It's exactly two-thirty in the morning. And what wakes me up is not Southern California's winter sun streaming through the window, not due for another few hours, but a persistent and annoying knocking sound coming from somewhere in the house.

I slide on my underwear, and nothing more, since it's a widely accepted cinematic convention that underwear provides all the protection from danger you'll ever need. Well, that and a golf club I keep propped up next to the closet. (Parenthetically, I believe it's a Spalding Sure-Shot 7-iron, my only accurate club.)

I listen carefully for the knocking, trying to pinpoint its location in the house. Yes, it's a loud rapping noise. And it seems to come in pairs: clunk, clunk! It sounds as if it's coming from the bathroom. Well, now, that presents a problem. Our bathroom is so small, I'll never be able to swing the club at an intruder. So I hold it like a billiard cue, fully intending to do some major corneal damage. I move toward the bathroom, leap inside, and turn on the light. But there's no one here.

Clunk, clunk! The sound is at once rhythmic and menacing. In fact, it sounds as if someone's inside the refrigerator, trying to kick his way out. But as I fly into the kitchen and yank the fridge open, the light comes on, and of course there's no one in there. What the hell was I thinking?

Clunk, clunk! Yes, it's definitely in the living room. But where is Casey? He should be barking. Is he okay? In a flash, I'm insane with panic and fury. If he's been hurt, I imagine myself saying to a robber, I'll crush your fucking...

But I can't see Casey in the living room. What I can see is our Christmas tree. Well, actually, I can't see the whole tree. I can only see the wooden cross that the tree sits on, and right now that cross is all that's preventing the entire tree from being pulled through the doggy door. I stand there slack-jawed as the cross goes clunk, clunk against the sides of the doggy door, unable to go through, despite Casey's repeated attempts at yanking it.

Watching all this, I make an observation: while Casey seems to exhibit a somewhat agnostic demeanor towards the Christmas season, he really didn't intend to destroy our tree. He simply wanted the popcorn, and to get it, he had to bring it down to his level. From all the forensic evidence I could gather, it's likely that, while attacking the popcorn, the string of flashing lights somehow got caught on his collar, scaring him half to death. And when he gets scared, he heads out through the doggy door, whether he has a Christmas tree attached to him or not.

After giving the matter of cause and effect a great deal of consideration, Jamie and I have arrived at a solution that should forever fix this problem. From now on, we'll be celebrating Chanukah. Casey doesn't care much for candles.

The Magic Kingdom

Maybe it's the fact that I washed out as a student at the Columbia School of Broadcasting. Or that I'm now on the dark side of my twenties. Or that Jamie has been persistently wondering what my plans are for the future. Whatever the reason, I've found myself using this year to engage in a recreational sport that is entirely unfamiliar to me: introspection. And what I'm realizing is that I'm sick of meandering in and out of meaningless, unfulfilling, short-term jobs that offer minimal satisfaction and microscopic paychecks.

Not that this year has been a total bust. My final assignment at disc-jockey school was to put together a one-hour radio show that features me introducing songs, interviewing a celebrity, and reading ads I wrote for local businesses. My instructor observed that my voice is thin and monotone and wholly unsuitable for a career in broadcasting. He did, however, think my advertising copywriting was excellent, and suggested I pursue that as a career instead. The instructor would have saved me over a thousand dollars in tuition fees had he mentioned my lousy voice at the beginning of the school term instead of at the end. But maybe it's worth a grand to find out I'm good at something, even if that something is something other than what I dreamed it would be.

Chasing a career in the ad biz isn't an entirely awful idea, I guess. As disappointing as my nipped-in-the-bud radio career is, at least writing advertising would offer me a job that's sort of creative while I earn a respectable living, although it's debatable if being in advertising can be considered respectable.

When I relayed my instructor's line of thinking to Jamie, she did what she always does, which is to switch into combat mode and try to figure out how to knock down each obstacle to success that I might erect. When I lamented that I have no idea how to get started, she remembered that she knows a guy who's an art director at J. Walter Thompson, one of the largest ad agencies in the country. Maybe, she said, he can help me put together a few ads that can serve to show people I can write. When I sadly observed that I don't know anything about the ad industry, she waved that off and said that I can check out some library books on the subject. And when I whined about not having any idea how to contact potential employers, she recalled once having seen a copy of *AdWeek*, a magazine for the ad industry in which, among other things, people offer their copywriting services in the want-ads section.

If there's anything Jamie excels at, it's arming the troops, raising their morale, and clearing the land mines so that they can charge at the enemy, bayonets mounted, unhindered, the rebel yell bursting from their cracked lips.

That's exactly what ticks me off about her. When a tough decision needs to be made, I prefer to dither, agonize and wallow, and her incessant problem-solving makes that impossible. Jamie's persistent optimism and energy deny me the opportunity to stay in my dark place, an inky gloom my eyes have had well over two decades to become accustomed to. Sometimes I wish she could just join me in celebrating the joylessness of life, but she's just too busy getting things done and excitedly anticipating what's around every corner. Given my family experience, I consider her mindset freakish, but it seems to work for her. And now she's determined to make it work for me.

I'm considering all this as I drive toward Anaheim, my knees knocking at the prospect of being interviewed by my first real, live advertising client. Having no actual ideas of my own, I followed Jamie's advice and met with her art director friend, put together five sample magazine ads, and ran an ad for myself in the back of AdWeek. Miraculously, someone saw it and offered to interview me for a small freelance job, which is why I find myself scared shitless as I pull into Disneyland's employee parking lot.

"I've got a ten o'clock meeting with Tricia Concannon. I'm Dennis Globus," I say, as if urging the uniformed guard to consider mine a name he'll be hearing a lot more of in the future.

He checks his watch. "You're forty-five minutes early," he says.

I have no idea where he's going with this. It's not clear if he's criticizing me or merely making an astute observation. In any event, I don't want to offend him. "Yeah, I'm sort of punctual," I say, smiling.

He mumbles something under his breath that sounds alarmingly like *You're sort of a pussy*.

Well, this is a development I didn't anticipate. The first person I meet at Disneyland is calling me a pussy. That's a song the Mickey Mouse Club never prepared me for. "Who's the leader of the club that's made for wimps and freaks? D-E-N-N-I-S P-U-S-S-Y."

He shrugs and searches for my name on his clipboard. "Never show up early for an interview. Makes 'em think you're desperate, not punctual. Employers respect self-confidence, not desperation. Show up when you're told to show up."

This is sage career advice coming from a middle-aged gate guard at an amusement park. I'm relieved when his finger comes to a stop next to my name.

"Go up Tomorrowland Way," he says, indicating a narrow street directly in front of us, "turn left at the Mad Tea Party, go past Pinocchio's Daring Journey, make a right at the Fantasyland Fruit Cart, and it's the third building on the left." He's reciting these names as if they're all perfectly normal.

I nod at him, mumble something outrageously clever, dangerously hostile and completely unintelligible, and slowly head down the narrow street. On my left, between a couple of buildings, two guys are chatting. What makes this scene unusual is that one of them is wearing a Goofy costume and the other is dressed as Bashful.

"You've got to tell her sooner or later," Goofy says. Bashful leans his giant head back against the side of the building, and lets out a long tortured moan.

I'd love to hang around to see what's eating Bashful, but I've got a meeting to be forty-five minutes early to, and I continue up the street. I reach the intersection and glance to the left. There it is—the inside of the park, and I see a half-dozen excitedly yapping children around Snow White who, even from this distance, is strikingly beautiful. She laughs and gives each child her undivided attention as if the kid's babbling is the single most precious thing in her life. I don't really understand how some human beings can dispense unconditional love. And not just all day long like her—at all. As I watch her, my cogitation on the nature of selflessness turns into a fantasy about taking her by the hand, leading her to a place between two buildings, lifting her skirt, and showing her who's the fairest one of all.

The building I'm looking for is surprisingly nondescript, given the overwhelming grandness of the theme park. It's a squat, two-story beige structure with no identification on it except for a small decal that says Marketing. I push open the door and see dozens of ads, blown up to poster-size, lining the walls. There's Huey, Dewey and Louie wearing leis and doing the hula while a comically befuddled Donald, playing a ukulele, is beaned by a coconut that's just fallen from a palm tree. The headline says *Have a Spectacular Hawaiian Vacation ... at Disneyland.* On another one Chip and Dale are wearing weird Bavarian costumes and doing some kind of beer hall dance I can never remember the name of. The headline reads *Have a Spectacular German Vacation ... at Disneyland.* And over there is the famous scene from *Lady and the Tramp*, with the two dogs sucking opposite ends of a spaghetti strand. The headline says *Have a Spectacular Italian Vacation ... at Disneyland.*

I suppose the images are colorful and fun, but then they ought to be—they're yanked right out of Disney movies. You can hardly laud the marketing department for that. And those headlines. Limp and uninspired. But I suppose that's why I'm here. I'm Dennis Globus, copywriter. I come up with copy, and then I, uh, write it.

The receptionist, who apparently notices that I'm very early, has me take a seat on a small blue sofa in the lobby. There's something oddly familiar with this whole setup—the couch, the lobby, the posters. And as I'm leafing through a Disney comic book, it dawns on me that this is eerily similar to my appointment with Larry Gelbart. I hope the wheels don't fall off this meeting, or my advertising career could be as short as my TV career.

After about forty-five minutes, the elevator doors snap open and a chipper blond in a Farrah Fawcett 'do emerges. She smiles at me, and I notice two rows of gleaming-white teeth that look like they were fabricated at a Chiclets factory. "Are you Tricia's ten o'clock?"

"Yes, I am," I say, mumbling.

"I'm Paula, Tricia's assistant," she says, extending her hand. "I'll take you up to her office." I follow her into the elevator. As the doors close, I'm instantly uncomfortable, and I don't know where to look. I could gawk at her breasts but, historically speaking, that's never eased anyone's elevator tension. I could make small-talk with her, but that would involve, you know, actual talking. In the end, I decide to become fascinated with the elevator's lighted floor indicators, not a particularly satisfying diversion in a building with only two floors. I'm relieved when the doors open, and I follow her through a large room in which dozens of people are hunched over drawing boards and typewriters, presumably creating the kind of pulse-quickening advertising I saw on the posters downstairs.

Paula leads me into a room in which an attractive woman in a crisp gray business suit reviews some papers on her desk. Her dark brown hair is cut into a kind of Jane Fonda *Klute* thing. When she sees me, she stands, and we shake hands. "Hi, I'm Tricia Concannon. You must be Dennis. Have a seat," she says, gesturing to a small leather chair opposite her desk."

There's a photo on the wall of her lying on a sofa. A man sits next to her in an upholstered chair, and he's making an exaggerated show of writing on a note pad. In the photo, Tricia is laughing, although it's not apparent what she finds so funny. "Is that you in the picture?" I say, asking the obvious.

"Yeah, that's me and my husband. It's from about ten years ago when he just got licensed in California to be a psychologist, and I was pretending like I was his patient. If you look closely at my left hand," she says, rolling her chair near to the photo, "you can see that I'm holding a cigar."

"Uh huh."

She looks disappointed. "It's a Freudian allusion, and we were just having a laugh about it."

Yep. There's nothing like proxy-penis references to remind mental health professionals that they live their lives out there on the edge.

"I got my license, too ..." she says, lost in the photo, until she snaps her head back to me and rolls her chair behind her desk. "Do you have some work I can look at?"

"I do," I say, already feeling defensive about my lack of professional experience. "It's all spec stuff. This will ... would be my first real job."

"Isn't that nice!" she says. "I get your cherry ... assuming I like your work, of course."

I open my briefcase and hand her a few boards. She looks at each visual on the front, scans the headline, then turns the boards over to read the copy on the back.

She hands the boards back to me. "Good. This ought to be a breeze for you."

"You ... you mean ... you're hiring me?"

"Yep."

Wow. Just like that. My first advertising job. If only the TV industry had been this easy to break in to.

"Here's what you need to know. Once a year Disneyland decorates the park to look like a festival in a foreign country. We've done Italy, France, West Germany, and Hawaii."

"Is Hawaii a foreign country now?" I say, and I instantly regret it.

Her lips purse momentarily. "No, but its ancient customs are pretty foreign to most of us mainlanders. Anyway, this year the park will have a Mexico theme. We'll have Mexican food at several of the food stands around the park, and we'll feature mariachi music and dancers."

"Nice!" I say, far too enthusiastically to be credible.

"We've got a visual of Mickey and Minnie dancing around a sombrero. All we need is for you to come up with a catchy headline."

"I think I can do that," I say, snapping the briefcase shut. "What day do you want to see me again?"

"What day?" she says, squinting slightly at the stupidity of the question. "How about yesterday? We've got a screaming deadline with the *L.A. Times*. I want you to go into the next office and spend some time on this. Take an hour, come back, and we'll pick the best headline."

I'd sure rather go away for a few days and torment myself over the importance of my first advertising job, but she's denying me that pleasure. "Right now?" I say stupidly.

"Yes."

"Next office?"

"Right there," she says, pointing at the wall on which her photo sits. "Oh, one more thing. We tend to overuse the word spectacular around here. Ever since Mister Disney built this place, everything's been *spectaaaaacular*, and to tell you the truth, we're absolutely sick of it. So do us all a favor and whip out your thesaurus. No spectacular. Got it?"

"No problem," I say, and head out of the door, then turn back to her. "If you don't mind me asking ... I don't know exactly how everything gets done, but I just wanted to know ... well, you know ..."

"Seventy-five bucks," she says. "You'll have a check within a week."

"Good. Thanks." Wow! Seventy-five dollars, for an hour of daydreaming. This could turn out to be a fun profession. Hi ho, hi ho ... it's off to work I go!

Except for a small metal desk and a chair, the office is completely bare, but it somehow feels like the Magic Kingdom in miniature to me, considering it's the site of my first advertising job and it's at Disneyland. I set my brand-new Samsonite briefcase (a gift from Jamie) on the desk, unsnap it, and pull out a large pad and a new Cross pen (another gift). I look at my watch. It's ten-fifteen, and I'm excited and anxious to get to work on this project.

I put my feet up on the desk, the pad in my lap, and imagine that this is the way most big-time copywriters work. Okay, let's see ... mariachis ... burritos ... Mickey and Minnie ... a Mexican fiesta ... bright gowns ... piñatas. Dancing around a sombrero. Cinco de Mayo. Aztecs. Pancho Villa. Remember the Alamo. Cesar Chavez. Corporate farmers exploiting migrant workers.

Hmmm. I could be heading into the weeds here. Stay with what's important about this event. Forget eight thousand years of irrelevant Mexican history. Okay, I'm on the right track. Making progress now. Feeling good. Mind clear. Brain focussed like a laser. God, that Snow White was luscious! What an ass! And Tinkerbell—there's an erotic little flying nymph. Oops, mind wandering. Becoming weak. Must ... stick ... to ... subject ... at ... hand.

I put my pen to the pad and write *Festival Mexico:*

The colon following Festival Mexico is important because it indicates there's more to come. That's crucial for me to remember with images of Snow White so intrusive.

Okay, *Festival Mexico: the biggest block party of the year.*

Hey, that's not bad! Maybe I'll use the remaining fifty-plus minutes for some half-hearted diddling with other headlines or daydreaming about myself as the Eighth Dwarf: Horny. On second thought, maybe that's not such a smart idea. Tricia mentioned that at the end of the hour, we'd pick the best headline. That would imply that she's expecting more than one. Dammit.

Okay, *Festival Mexico: all the fun of a south-of-the-border vacation, minus the gut-wrenching diarrhea.*

Am I good at this, or what! Someone must have drained the ink out of my pen and refilled it with liquid gold. Every word I'm writing is priceless!

Now that I read it again, it occurs to me that the allusion to wet, runny shit might suppress food sales at the Festival. I should probably tone it down a notch. Let's try this: *Festival Mexico: you'll never have so much fun getting Montezuma's Revenge.*

Too bad. The wet shit's still there—just different words. Think, Dennis, think! Lose the feces. You can do it! Let's give this one a shot: *Festival Mexico: all the fun of a vacation, without the Kaopectate.* Yeah, by god, that's it! I'm done! She's going to love this.

Maybe I should do one more, then call it a day. I'll write a piece of garbage just so I can say I gave it my all, then I'll shift her attention back to the

Kaopectate line. Let's see ... *Festival Mexico: a mammoth explosion of sight, sound, color, and culture.*

Damn. That may be a little too good. She might like that one instead. No sweat. She'll like Kaopectate even more. Oh well, back to my three-way with Snow and Tink.

I take a seat in the guest chair opposite Tricia, excited because I'm pretty sure she's going to love my Festival Mexico stuff. But you never know. From what I've read about creative directors, they can be enormously finicky, making so many picky-ass little changes, they might as well have written the damn ads in the first place. Tricia's frowning as her eyes scan a piece of paper she's holding, not noticing me fidgeting in the chair.

"I'm reading your résumé," she says, not looking up. "You've had quite an action-packed job history."

"I ... What?"

She finally looks up at me. "You've done a lot of different things. It's not every kid who begins working at the age of ... how old were you here ..." She holds up the résumé and points to a line of typewritten text. "... working on a golf course?"

"I was five when I picked up balls on the driving range. And then six, I think, when I started shining shoes."

"Just a baby."

"My mom liked to be alone with her thoughts, and she'd do pretty much anything to get the kids out of the house—including getting us jobs."

"Yeah, but at five." She studies the page again. "I hope you at least made some money."

"Well, enough to buy a golf bag."

"Uh huh," she says, urging me on.

"And then I had a creative disagreement with one of my customers over my post-modern interpretation of the color palette."

"And that means … "

I'm starting to notice that she's able to ask questions without the back-breaking labor associated with affixing interrogative punctuation at the end of her sentences. "I screwed up his expensive golf shoes. I thought they came out great at the time. But now that I think about it, I can sort of see why someone wouldn't necessarily want black and brown saddle shoes."

Paula enters and slides an art board in front of Tricia, who studies it, then turns it over and signs the back. Paula flashes her Chiclets smile at me and whisks the board away.

"I took up golf about two years ago, and I love it," Tricia says. "You must have been good, starting so young."

"Didn't play."

She gives her head a quick shake, as if clearing the cobwebs. "Did I miss something? You saved up to buy a golf bag."

Yeah, I suppose it could sound pretty loopy from her perspective. "I decided to quit before it got too frustrating. Would you like to see the headlines?" I say.

"Okay," she says, giving me the distinct impression that she'd rather dissect my employment history. "Read one out loud."

Right, enough about golf, lady. This is my moment to dazzle. I take a deep breath, part of me ruminating on the importance of what the other part of me is about to recite. I open with my weakest headline. "Festival Mexico …" I say nervously. "… the biggest block party of the year."

"Uh huh," she says dismissively, then picks up my résumé. "You sang for Judy Garland."

I sigh impatiently, then immediately hope she didn't see it. "I did. My brother was the Tin Man and I was the Scarecrow."

"You gave it up."

"It was a one-night gig," I say, trying not to sound incredulous.

"I mean singing. You gave it up even though you got paid for it at fourteen years old. Seems like if you were good enough to do it for Judy Garland, you were probably good enough to do it for other people."

I don't really have an answer for this, but I sure wish she'd show a little more interest in this project. This is my first advertising job, and I want to remember it as fondly as I do my first sexual encounter, although I'm hoping this involves fewer tissues. I'm thinking of a way to steer the conversation back to my headlines without offending her, but she seems obsessed with my résumé.

"And you were a movie-theater projectionist," she says. "Was it one of those classic-movie art houses?"

I'm really not anxious to tell her it was a porn theater. "I suppose ... if you consider *Rear Window* a classic. Anyway, I really think you're going to like the other two headlines."

She drops the paper. "Right. Read another one."

I stare at the pad. Which one should I read first? Kaopectate or mammoth explosion? I really want her to buy the Kaopectate line, but if I read it now, she may infer that I'm saving the best for last. On the other hand, her attention to this project is so fleeting, she just may zone out completely by the time I get to the third headline. Jeez, which to choose ... which to choose? "Festival Mexico," I say, still not committing to either one. I look up to see her gawking at the goddamn resumé again. That settles it. "... a mammoth explosion of sight, sound, color, and culture."

"Huh?" she says, dropping the resumé on her desk. "Read that again."

"Festival Mexico: a mammoth explosion of sight, sound, color, and culture."

"That's incredibly good," she says, nodding thoughtfully.

"I don't know what to say," which is absolutely true because I really don't know what to say, considering that isn't even the headline I want her to buy. "I could dink around with it." Maybe just enough to shoehorn in Kaopectate.

"No, it's perfect just the way it is. It captures the excitement of the event and really gives the reader a sense of what the Festival experience will be like."

Dammit. I gave this headline about three seconds worth of thought, and she's becoming fixated on it before she hears the other one. "You know, I worked in Germany," I say, pointing at the resumé on her desk.

She picks it up. "Right. You wrote a TV series or something."

This always impresses people. "Yeah, it was based on the stories of Jack London."

"And it was on TV."

"I don't know. I left after writing an episode or two."

'Really."

"Yes."

"And the laundry ... "

How do I tell her nicely to climb out of my butt? "Yes ... what about it?"

"You quit."

"Not exactly. That one sort of ended on a disastrous note."

"You worked in the movie business in ..." she says, searching for the appropriate line on the résumé. " ... West Berlin."

I give her a sanitized version of the Sybil Danning experience, about how scary it was living in Berlin, about how I relied on Ken for things and how lost and lonely I felt when he moved in with his new girlfriend.

"Any other jobs I should know about?" she says, smiling.

Hell, I'm pretty sure she didn't need to know about any of them. But what do I say to her? "I once tried out for *The Dating Game*," I say, fumbling for a topic that will distract her from my failures.

"Really." she says, folding the résumé in half, then half again. "Tried out as opposed to appeared on."

"My mind was on something else that night."

"And the longest you've ever been employed is … "

Hmmm. Never thought of that. "Probably Berlin. I worked on the film for about six weeks."

"Not very long."

Yeah. I suppose it's not. "If you don't mind me saying, you seem pretty interested in my job history."

She smiles. "Tell me about the script you wrote for *MASH*. It's at the top of your résumé, so I assume it's the first thing you want me to know about you."

"Well, not everyone's written a script for *MASH*."

"Very true. But since you're here today, and not at Twentieth Century Fox, I assume you didn't sell it."

Ouch. *That dream died along with the script, lady.* "I went to Larry Gelbart's office to meet with him about the script."

"He was there … with you."

What an odd question … or statement, whatever it is. "He invited me to the studio to have a meeting with him. After a couple of minutes, he told me the script wasn't right for him."

"And you said ... "

"To him?"

"To him."

I wonder if all my advertising jobs will be like this. "I didn't have much to say."

"He liked your script."

"Said he loved it."

"Invited you to his office."

"Made an appointment and everything. Even offered me a beverage."

"Just to tell you he wasn't going to buy your script."

Now that I hear someone else saying it, it does sound peculiar. "Right."

"And now you're in advertising."

Huh? I'm not sure I like the sound of that. "Yep, haha. Here I am." Thank god I don't have to live with these relentlessly oblique questions. "You know, I'm just trying to be sensitive to your time and—"

"Let me worry about how I use my time." She leans back in her chair. "You're a mystery to me, Dennis. I'm thinking to myself, Here's a budding young creative talent sitting in front of me. I'd like to forge a long-term freelance relationship with him. But his past worries me."

"My past? Why? Why should that worry you?"

"Because, from what you've told me, you've screwed up just about every opportunity you've had. I'm thinking your copywriting career will probably be another lark," she says, opening her desk drawer, and dropping in the résumé, "until you get bored, frustrated, or frightened ... if you don't mind me making that observation."

"No, heck, why would I mind that?"

She chuckles. "Okay, the sarcasm was deserved." She sighs as if the act of talking to me requires a supreme effort of concentration on her part, one she's only just now resigning herself to. "You read *Call of the Wild*."

"The first Jack London book I read."

"You liked it."

"Lots of dogs. Lots of snow. That pretty much sums up my reading experience."

There's a trace of disgust as she shakes her head. "You miss a lot in life."

"I'm not follow—"

"You read *Call of the Wild* while you're in Germany, and all you see are the animals and the weather."

"Well, there was lots of snow."

"Yep. So much snow that people sometimes completely lose their sense of direction. Look, the story's about what happens when a domesticated dog finds itself alone in the wilderness." For the first time today, she gives me a warm smile. "That remind you of anything?"

I give it some thought, but I can't think of another book with a similar story.

"The dog is domesticated and happily living with someone it loves and trusts. Then one day it finds itself torn away from its friend, and all alone in the wilderness. And ... ?"

Is she expecting some sort of response here? "I'm not really under—"

"It's you, Dennis. You're the dog."

"The dog?" I say, forcing a chuckle. But I'm feeling a tightness in my throat that I've felt a thousand times before.

"You had a great job in Germany, and you ran away from it, all because you were afraid of something." She taps a pencil on her desk. "It's scary being a domesticated dog in the wild."

"Yes. It is." My chest hurts now, and I make a meaningless doodle on my note pad.

"It must have been so scary for you that it was easier to leave the excitement of being in Europe, Sybil, and a terrific job just so that you could be comfortable at home in Los Angeles." She briefly glances at herself and her husband in the photo. "And the Larry Gelbart misadventure. No successful producer invites you to his office for the sole purpose of rejecting you. He could have had his secretary do that over the phone. Hell, that's the way I'd do it. These guys don't have the time to waste. And no producer is sadistic enough to get your hopes up by inviting you to meet with him, only to reject you."

A fat, salty tear skates past my nose, stops momentarily on my upper lip, then does a cannonball onto my note pad. Little veins of ink emanate from Kaopectate.

"Larry Gelbart invited you to his office because he was going to offer you a writing job of some kind, and he wanted to meet you first." Paula enters the room again, grins at me and shoves some papers in front of Tricia, who begins signing them. "But he must have seen something in you that gave him the impression that you weren't ready to work in TV."

I feel something coming up from my stomach, and I want to push it back down. I've got to distract myself. Yeah, that's it. Sybil Danning. Larry Gelbart. Monika *Zwei*. Wendell, the blind guy.

Rachel and the rabbi. Oh jeez, this isn't helping at all.

"Shit, Dennis, if it were me at that meeting—and I can only dream about being lucky enough to be there—I would have come prepared with a dozen other ideas to sell him. I would have had a synopsis prepared for each one of them, and I can guarantee that at the end of that meeting he would have seen me as some sort of creative fountain that he needs to drink from on a regular basis. That's what he was looking for from you. He liked your script enough to invite you to a meeting. He wanted to be dazzled by a guy with more ideas—usable ideas— and he wanted to see a guy with confidence ... someone who can stand up in a meeting with a group of highly paid TV writers and producers and make them laugh their asses off. Somehow, you convinced him you couldn't do that."

More drops on the note pad. I want to tune her out like I've done with a thousand other people and just hear blah blah blah, but every word she says feels piercingly loud and echoes through the room and caroms around inside my skull.

"You're a hard guy to figure. Every time you get close to a goal—whether it's a golf bag, Sybil, or a TV career—you throw away the prize because you're too naive or unprepared or you get pissed off or tongue-tied." She finishes signing the papers, raps them on their edges to align them, and hands them to Paula who, thankfully, isn't paying the least bit of attention to this conversation. "Even when I told you that I was hiring you for this job, you made a snotty comment about Hawaii being a foreign country. I surprised myself by not throwing your wise little ass out of the office. So, aside from *MASH*, the Jack London TV series, *The Dating Game* and some of the other things on your résumé, how many opportunities have you torpedoed because you've got a shitty self-image?"

Oh, my god. She's telling me she's not going to work with me again. The tears are coming faster now, obliterating almost the entire block party headline. Tricia pushes a box of Kleenex to me. I grab one, two, wipe my eyes, blow snot. And I say the only words that want to escape my lips. "I feel ... I feel ... like such a failure," I say, and begin sobbing.

And then she does an odd thing. She reaches across the desk and puts her hand on mine, and smiles maternally. "You've got to be kidding," she says. "Everything you've ever done has led you right to this place ... on this day. Here. Now. Failure? Please! You're a huge success on your first advertising job. Your headline is perfect. In fact, it blew me away. And I can see that if you actually give it some effort, you've got a long, happy career in advertising ahead of you."

"Why are you telling me all this?"

"Because I may want to hire you again in three weeks, and I don't want to find out you bailed on advertising. Besides, you're fun to dissect. Your mess is just right out there."

My sobbing is turning into something like hysterical giggling now, and I feel simultaneously silly and proud that she likes my first copywriting effort so much. As I'm deliberating whether or not to read the Kaopectate line, I see something grotesque in my peripheral vision. The guy in the Goofy suit shuffles into Tricia's office, flops down on the couch, and yanks his head off to reveal a man sweating profusely.

"Christ, it's hot out there," he says to Tricia.

"Brad," Tricia says, "this is Dennis. He's a freelance copywriter."

Hey! Regardless of what's happened in this office today, at least now she's conferring professional status upon me.

"Right," Brad says, extending a flaccid white-gloved hand at me.

Ah, the guy in the photo. "Nice to meet you, Brad. I think I saw you outside chatting with one of the Seven Dwarfs."

"Yeah ... Bashful. He's coming out of the closet and dealing with how to tell his wife."

"I've always thought Bashful was gay," I say.

He squints at me. "You do realize he's just a cartoon character, don't you?"

There's an oddly uncomfortable silence until Tricia chuckles. "Dennis wrote a TV series in Germany."

"Great," Brad says, and it's difficult to tell if his lack of enthusiasm is due to the fact that he's genuinely unimpressed or because he has to wear a heavy costume in ninety-degree weather. Hey, talk about torpedoing a career! What's a shrink doing dressed as Goofy?

"He's done some really interesting things in his life," Tricia says.

"Like ... ?" Brad says, challenging me to amuse him.

It's not the weather. He really is unimpressed and barely civil. Ordinarily, I'd find that lack of validation crippling, were it not for the fact that, since that picture on the wall was taken, he's banged his chin on every rung while sliding down the ladder of success.

"I'm surprised you haven't written a book about all this stuff -- not that I want you to abandon your advertising career. But this stuff's hilarious—in a, you know, therapeutic sort of way," Tricia says.

"A book?" I say incredulously. "You mean about all the weird jobs I've had?"

"Sure."

"You mean, like, about Sybil Danning and *The Dating Game* and stuff like that?"

"Sybil Danning?" Brad says, suddenly interested. "You know her?"

Brad, I decide, is a dick, worthy of ignoring. I focus on Tricia. "Anyway, I think I'll stick to advertising. I seem to be marginally competent at it."

"Marginally competent?" she says, chuckling. "Read that second headline to Brad."

Brad's posture has changed since he heard the magic words *Sybil* and *Danning*. If he knows anything about her, he's picturing two perfectly orbital Austrian breasts right about now. "Yeah, tell me about Sybil," he says.

"The headline, honey," Tricia says firmly to her husband.

Brad looks disappointed. "Yeah, first the headline."

"Uh ... okay." I notice the pad is damp and streaked with ink. "Festival Mexico: a mammoth explosion of sight, sound, color, and culture."

He's nodding his head. That's a good sign. "Helluva headline. Much better than those fortune-cookie slogans we've been using."

Hey, he likes me! Maybe he's not such a dick after all.

"Let me see it," Tricia says. I slide the pad over to her. She looks at it thoughtfully, then giggles. "I love that line about Kaopectate. That's a riot! There's something about diarrhea that just cracks me up." She studies the page for what seems forever. Finally, she picks up a red pen. I see her write something next to the second headline. "Brilliant!" She slides the pad back to me. "Here's our headline."

She's written one word on the page. And in that one word is an image in a crystal ball that provides a revealing look at my future in advertising. She's crossed out the word *mammoth* and above it written a single word.

Spectacular.

Reading Group Guide

1. We can all agree that getting hit in the testicles is one of life's greatest pains, akin to giving birth to a table saw. Discuss the first time you can recall getting hit in the nuts or, if you're woman and therefore unlikely to have nuts, recount the first time you took a ball-peen hammer to a male's crotch. Was it your prom date? By the way, the author knows you're a woman; you are, after all, in a book club.

2. In the chapter *Out of Diapers, Into the Labor Pool*, the 5-year-old protagonist's mother insists he get a job on the weekends. Do you think it's a crime to force such a young child into the labor pool? If you

do, should my mother have been executed for it? If you don't think it's a crime, isn't it about time you put your own children to work?

3. It's clear from *The Cotton Candy Machine* chapter that family outings are rife with disaster and should never be attempted. Discuss why, on your next vacation, you plan to dump your children on the couple who just moved into the neighborhood only two weeks before. Does the fact that there's an odor of chemicals wafting out of their kitchen window influence your thinking?

4. Discuss the worst presents you ever received for Christmas or Chanukah. Have you forgiven your first husband yet?

5. Blue jays are loud, messy, and mean. Would the world be a better place if we eradicated this particular species? All types of birds? Just the ones not found in the meat counter at your local supermarket?

6. In the chapter *If I Only Had a Brain*, the protagonist mentions that he has the hots for his typing teacher, Miss Lefkowitz. Discuss the first teacher you ever thought of in a sexual context and

try to recall the precise date that a restraining order was issued.

7. Discuss the impact Judy Garland had on the entertainment industry. What do you think her lasting legacy is? Is the reason that so many gay men adore Liza Minnelli because she looks like a gay man herself? Would you prefer to be a gay man or Liza Minnelli? What good is sitting alone in a room?

8. Do you think rabbis—or any member of the clergy, for that matter—should be permitted to own businesses that deal in pornography? Have you ever met a rabbi? Have you ever met a Jew?

9. The chapter titled *The Secret Life of Duct Tape* describes gay sex in alarming detail. As a woman, does the thought of two men engaging in sexual acts sicken you? Is it true that all women are only one drink away from having lesbian sex? If you should happen to meet the author, would you mind if he buys you a drink?

10. At the end of the chapter, the protagonist decides to accept blame for stealing the money, rather than tell Rachel he caught her father

schtuping a hooker in the candy storage room. Do you think the protagonist made the right choice? Don't you wish they still made Sno Caps?

11. The protagonist was under the influence of LSD when he auditioned for ... *The Dating Game*. From a contemporary perspective, how might his experience have been different had he taken ecstasy instead? Crystal meth? By the way, would you happen to know where the author can score some good pot?

12. Would Paul (bachelor no. 1) have been less repulsive if the object of his obsession were an Alfa Romeo instead of a Porsche? Do you think Italian cars are sexier than German cars? Which of the three bachelors did you find most appealing? Do you mind if the author gives Paul your phone number?

13. In *Sybil Servant*, the author recounts the time he saw a photo of a beautiful European movie star who he actually meets not long afterward. Have you ever had sexual fantasies about a celebrity and then met him later? Please tell me it wasn't Randy Quaid.

14. More than once, the author recalls that he had little ambition in life other than to emulate the things his brother Ken had already done. Do you have a sibling who's more successful than you? Have you always wanted to follow in his or her footsteps? Well, you should have. Look at the mess you've made of your life.

15. At the end of the story, Sybil invites the protagonist to stay with her in Munich for a few weeks during the Olympic games. Implied in the invitation is that she would be having sex with him. Why do you think he turned her down? Is it because the author looks like Liza Minnelli?

16. Do you think Radar O'Reilly contracting syphilis as a result of being a good samaritan was too "racy" for television? Did you ever contract a venereal disease in your "experimental phase?" Did we ever date?

17. In a later chapter, the protagonist gets a job on a Christmas tree lot. Explore your own feelings on this matter. Don't you think Chanukah is spelled funny? Can you think of any other words that begin with C-H where the C is silent? The author

can't, and he's given up trying. Frankly, you should too.

18. The author fondly remembers the time his Dalmation ate an entire sweater. What's the oddest thing you ever pulled out of a dog's butt?

19. I'll say it right here: there's something about Tinkerbell that's highly erotic. Have you ever thought about having sex with a Disney character? I'm betting it was Captain Hook. You seem like the type.

20. In *The Magic Kingdom*, the protagonist gets his first paying advertising job, at Disneyland. Did you know that during the early '70s, Disneyland banned gays and hippies from the park? Discuss how they figured out who was gay and who wasn't. That must have taken some sleuthing.

21. In considering the totality of this remarkably entertaining book, do you think the author rags on his mother too much? Do you continue to have "issues" with your mother? Write your own damn book.

22. Do you think this book was worth the price you paid for it? Looking back, do you wish you had stolen it?

23. Disregard question #11. The author remembers a good source. Now, where did he put his editor's phone number?

Thank You

A lot of people read all or parts of this book, and I'd never forgive myself if I failed to acknowledge that their input guided me (to one degree or another) on my path. They include ...

The various critique group members who saw in these stories something unusual, funny, and compelling. There are dozens of you I'd like to personally thank, and I feel rotten having forgotten so many of your names. To all the writers who gave me thoughtful and useful input, thank you so much for taking the time and expending the energy. It was a pleasure to incorporate your ideas. And to those folks whose comments I chose to ignore, I only have this to say: I heard you. I honestly thought about it. I just disagree.

Suzan Globus, my cousin in New Jersey, who read many of the chapters and always made them better. She is, without a doubt, the single busiest person I know, and it's a miracle that she actually found the time to help me. I'm eternally grateful.

Claudia Kawczynska, Editor-in-Chief of *Bark* magazine, who printed an excerpt of *O, Christmas Tree*. It was my first publishing experience, and my mother kvelled when she showed the magazine to all of her friends. She died soon after, but I'm pretty sure my writing had nothing to do with that.

The Pacific Northwest Writers Association, whose yearly conferences gave me the tools and the enthusiasm to begin this book. Whether you've attended a writers' conference or not, you'd do well to attend theirs. Special thanks to Al Sampson (past president of PNWA) for encouraging me to read the chapter *If I Only Had a Brain* at open-mic readings. As a humor writer, you learn a lot by listening to an audience's reaction to your stories.

Philinda Robinson, my neighbor, who kept my mind fresh and alive by engaging me in numerous philosophical discussions about such topics as religion and politics while I was writing this book. She did everything you'd want a good neighbor to do: got my mail when I was out of town (no easy feat, considering my mailbox is about two hundred yards up a steep hill), looked after my dog Wally a couple times a week, and provided a quiet atmosphere.

Phil Herring, my former boss at the Herring/Newman ad agency and best friend, read every word of this book. While not particularly interested in the piddling stuff, like commas and adjectives, his criticism was always spot on and delivered with a broad brush that covered a lot of wall space. That's the great thing about having plenty of people reading your manuscript. There's always folks who fixate on the little things, and other people, like Phil, who tackle the big issues. It's good to have both kinds of people on your team. It was especially good to have Phil. This book would be a lot longer (and infinitely more tedious) without his input.

Matt Smith is going to be shocked when he reads this section of the book and discovers he did anything at all to inspire me. But he did. Around the same time I played the memory game with Jamie that led to the idea for this book, I saw Matt in one of his legendary one-man shows. It was called *Helium*, and it actually floored me, it was so funny. But what was really important about it is that it showed me how it's possible to write about yourself without seeming repetitive, self-serving, or narcissistic. Matt made it all look easy. Since *Helium*, I've seen two other of Matt's one-man shows: *My Last Year with the Nuns* and *Beyond Kindness*. Matt is also a successful actor (*Sleepless in Seattle*; *Spiderman*), improv teacher, corporate trainer, and auctioneer. You can see what makes him tick at www.Matt-Smith.net. Surprised, Matt?

David Sedaris, a guy I've always admired. He's an absolutely sublime writer, and I'm hoping you've read some or all of his work. Before I even had an inkling that I'd be writing a book, I read every one of his stories. Through studying his work, I got a sense of how a master uses humor to surprise his readers. No one, in my estimation, even comes close to him. That some people choose to compare my writing to his—for whatever reason—makes me dizzy with glee. Thanks for the inspiration, David. It's likely that if you didn't exist as a writer, neither would I.

Sybil Danning, a one-woman support group for me when I lived in Germany. She translated for me, showed me incredible kindness, and made me the single most confusing offer I've ever received. To this day, I still can't figure out why she did all this for the least significant person in her life. But I'm glad she did.

Ken Globus, my brother, and the only person I could talk to who was actually present at some of the events recounted in this book. We chatted a lot about what it was like the night we sang for Judy Garland and how awful it was to work in our dad's linen rental supply warehouse and what our experiences of living in Germany were like. Ken also performed one other service: he provided the sharpest criticism I received from anyone. The smartest thing I ever did was to put aside our old sibling mishegas and just appreciate the excellence of his input, comments that I executed on nearly every page of this book. I can tell you that *If I Only Had a Brain* wouldn't be nearly as funny or unique if Ken hadn't been involved. You should also know that Ken was one of the world's foremost bird trainers and could take someone's vicious and psychotic parrot and hand-tame it in minutes. He was The Bird Whisperer (meet him at www.TheBirdWhisperer.com). Fortunately for me, he was also a terrific writer and a sweetheart of a brother. Ken passed away not long ago, a loss I still haven't completely recovered from.

My wife Jamie Stone. As I mentioned in the Preface, she gave me the two most important things that allowed this book to be written: the opportunity and the encouragement. Jamie has given me totally unqualified support from the very beginning, most of which took the shape of reminding me that this stuff is actually funny, when all I wanted to do was erase it and start over. On the occasions when even that kind of support didn't get me to the keyboard, she was versatile enough to change direction and put a boot up my ass when I felt so paralyzed by fear that I'd allow myself to be distracted by other things for weeks at a time. She wouldn't let me quit, no matter how many times I tried. One more thing: you have no idea how wonderful it is to be watching the Mariners on TV (that's not the wonderful part, believe me) while Jamie's in another room laughing so hard from reading one of my stories that she develops an attack of asthma. The asthma's a drag, but what brings it on is pretty sweet. As I recall, the section of the book that required the most puffs on her inhaler was the sequence where I took LSD and auditioned for ... *The Dating Game*. Jamie, thank you for your love and encouragement.

DennisGlobus.com

Made in the USA
San Bernardino, CA
07 April 2016